T0198619

Children Have Abilities, Now Go Educate

J. Patrick Carriere

iUniverse, Inc.
New York   Bloomington

Children Have Abilities, Now Go Educate

iUniverse books may be ordered through booksellers or by contacting:

iUniverse
1663 Liberty Drive
Bloomington, IN 47403
www.iuniverse.com
1-800-Authors (1-800-288-4677)

ISBN: 978-1-4401-6621-1 (pbk)
ISBN: 978-1-4401-6622-8 (ebook)

Printed in the United States of America

iUniverse rev. date: 2/23/2010

Dedicated to:

My mom
The men who lost their lives in the blowout in Syria
    Carlos Yap
    Danny Strong
    Martin Kelly
    Joe Carpenter.
    The Unknown Arab Man

We will never forget.

Also to all the stewards of this land, the good people who are oppressed by the governments of the world, those who have died of stress-related disease, war, hunger, and famine, inflicted by people in leadership roles.

Many governments and businesspeople will deny the truth. They know the greed societies live in and do nothing to correct it. When we have no air, water, and food, we will realize the blindness we have accustomed ourselves to through needless regulation. When we are out in the cold, frozen to the core, with no shelter, digging in garbage cans, we will remember God and how we have failed. Whose fault? Many will not know until they die.

Preface

My name is John Patrick Carriere. I was born in Roblin, Manitoba, Canada, on January 15, 1954, the ninth child and last son of a large country family of fifteen children. I grew up on a farm twenty-three miles north of Roblin in the hamlet of San Clara.

I have traveled extensively with my work in the oilfield to different areas of the globe, and have found it quite fascinating. Throughout my travels, I tried to make sense of the things I had seen and done. I was confused and depressed and didn't understand. I was having problems with work and found myself becoming withdrawn from society. I was a mess, angry most of the time, feeling sorry for mankind. I was becoming political and had many thoughts running through my mind. I was opinionated and adamant about how I felt about our society. Around May 15, 2004, I read a book written by Og Mandino, *The Greatest Miracle in the World*, which has changed my life, inspiring me to tell my story. On that day, I found myself trying to make sense of all that had been going on in the world since 9/11.

Fighting depression for many different reasons, recollecting all that I had seen and talked about with different people and cultures around the world, I found myself trying to remember as far back as I could, back to my early childhood.

As I read on, I kept hearing a soft yet convincing and humble voice pushing me to remember further. With head in hand, I began to think, searching my mind. This voice was saying, "Come on, you can do it." My mind began to work. I started to shake and sweat, realizing that I had continued to remember a lot more than humanly, worldly things. I remembered conception, swimming through a sea of sperm and egg, being picked as the match rather than a million others, then separating from the egg and going it alone. I was remembering from the Wild West back to the Ice Age and beyond. I reached a large gate that was locked. I knocked for a short time, and the gate opened. This soft, humble, and convincing voice greeted me and asked me to sit down.

"How are you?" the voice asked.

I replied with anxiety, "Not real well."

I felt sick. My rib cage was sore. I was short of breath, and my mind was racing. I had a million questions to ask, but every time I opened my mouth to speak, I was a babbling, confessing idiot of all the negativity as I was accustomed to.

This voice would say, "Tut, tut, tut, tell me something good. I know everything, so all I want to hear are good things. What good have you done?"

Again, I started thinking and found it difficult to remember the good things but managed to get a few out. I realized that this meeting was very important for both of us.

He was interested in what I had to say, and I began to relax. During this time of relaxation and comfort, I realized the Holy Spirit within me. Time seemed to pass quickly between us, and soon, I was back in my chair. Before I could speak, this voice said very clearly, "Tell your story. You have a story to tell, but remember, it must have a positive outcome." How vivid in my mind is that voice!

A Child was born in the image God had created for man over two thousand years ago. With him, he brought a message of hope, peace, love, charity, happiness, and forgiveness. Through his teachings, we learned,

> If we lived by the sword, we would die by the
> sword
> To love thy neighbor
> About the den of thieves
> How to live life
> How to save ourselves
> How to pass on the Word
> How to educate
> About our powers, to name a few, and much more

Chapter One

My father was a poor farmer with a quarter section of land north of Roblin in the hamlet of San Clara. He worked away from home logging for a time then was hired on with the forestry department, working long hours on a tower, watching the Duck Mountains for fire. When the forestry department cut back, he was out of a job for a brief time. He sold the farm and bought Carriere's General Store when his father retired. Until then, we raised a few head of cattle and some pigs, chickens, geese, and turkeys and had a large garden. We would plant one acre of vegetables and another acre of potatoes, all of it worked by hand. With wood to fetch, weeds to pick in the garden, water to haul (as we didn't have the luxury of running water), cows to feed and milk, pigs to slop, and chickens to feed, everyone had chores to do. When the potatoes grew, we would pick the potato grubs and beetles by hand, placing them in tin cans, and destroy them. We hilled potatoes by hand; then when harvest came, we dug and bagged our potatoes for the winter months. In the fall, we butchered chickens and turkeys and plucked and cleaned them. We had pork to butcher for the winter and sometimes a deer if Dad had time to hunt. Harvesting grain was done with horses and hayracks, hauling sheaves to the threshing machine. The neighbors would pitch in and help each other until the farm work was done. At times, the pressure was so great Dad would turn to alcohol for a couple of days at a time.

Mother!!! What a pillar of strength, hope, and inspiration! When I hear people complain about work, it nearly drives me mad, but "Tut, tut, tut." Tolerance … Remember?

She would milk cows, sew clothing for us all, make mattresses out of hay and flour sacks, and make blankets, pillows, and coats. At times, we would see her cry while making a blanket or a coat of many colors from patches she cut from worn clothing. We would ask if she was okay, concerned for her. She always answered she was, but we knew she was thinking about something, worrying about how we were going to make it perhaps. At times, I'm sure she would think of her family. She didn't have the opportunity to see them very often; sometimes as many as fifteen years would pass between visits. She would cry from time to time, I'm sure in loneliness. She would pick up her composure, continuing on for hours on end, many nights past midnight. She had bread to make (about sixty loaves a week), as well as cakes and cookies for lunches, clothes to wash, cows to milk, and children hanging off her constantly, demanding attention, food, bandaging, often with some squabbling, all the things kids do. The poor woman had no time or space for herself as we lived in a two-room shack, about six hundred square feet, with beds in every corner and a dirt cellar for storing food. Never did she give up hope. She leaned on her beliefs in the church and God, always finding a way. As I begin this story, she is still alive, and though her strength is down, her spirit is high. God surely knows he created a perfect miracle in her.

The six-hundred-square-foot house we lived in had a dirt cellar, tentest (a type of panel board used at the time) walls, no insulation, and yellow stucco on the outside surface, which was deteriorating and cracked. There were four beds, with Mom-made mattresses, blankets, and pillows, one in each corner of the bedroom. The girls slept in three of the beds; Mom and Dad slept in the other, while the three boys slept on a couch in the kitchen that folded down into a bed. As a source of heat and means of cooking, there was a wood space heater in the bedroom and a wood cook-stove in the kitchen.

Many winter mornings, we would wake up with our blankets frozen to a wall. We lived well below the comforts of today. A small cupboard with a tin counter held our mixed set of dishes, cutlery, medicines, and food. A small basin with a water pail and dipper sat in a smaller nook in another corner, while the washing machine was pushed in beside it. When it wasn't used for washing clothes, Mom stored bread inside the machine tub. A large table with five legs, which were four inches around, stood against the north wall of the house over the cellar hatch with a few beat-up chairs. Every time we moved the table for a meal, the legs would fall off; sometimes, the dishes would hit the floor and break. We ran short of dishes, and due to the size of the family, we had to eat in shifts. Sometimes the last ones to eat did not get the benefits of the whole meal, and the pouting, crying, and squabbling would drive poor Mother to take action, restoring order and control. She was gentle but tough and firm in her decisions, so most of us knew not to get under her skin too deep; however, some of us would push the buttons a little too far, and disciplinary action (quite uncommon by today's standards) was taken and the household restored to order, once the crying stopped. Thanks, Mom and Dad, for the discipline. It shaped us into who we are, without resentment.

Mother would say, "Boys, I'm baking bread tomorrow, and I'm going to need a good pile of wood." Hitching the horse to a stone-boat, taking the ax and swede saw with us, out we would go to the pasture to fetch wood. The girls would do dishes and clean up the house while Mom milked the cows.

The barn was a small, old, rickety building that would hold about six milk cows. It had a dirt floor, which was hollowed out in the center from use. Numerous times when it rained, the center of the barn would become a cesspool of manure, which had to be cleaned when it dried. A small coal-oil lantern in the center of the barn was all the light we had when milking the cows. While milking, we would sing, *"Ky yet ky yet ma vache."* A cat would wander in meowing for food and Mother or my oldest brother, whoever was milking, would squeeze the cow's teat in the direction of the cat, and it lapped the milk out of midair. A small pen in one corner kept the newborn calves from falling into the cesspool.

The chicken coop was an old log structure with a roof that slanted from front to back. It had chinking of mud, straw, and horse hair between the logs and two makeshift windows on the front, which were covered with chicken wire, not glass, and a homemade door of planks, braced at the bottom and top with two-by-fours along with one running diagonally for support. Inside were boxes about eighteen inches square, the bottoms of which were covered with straw for the chickens to lay their eggs in. The floor was dirt, with straw placed inside to help keep the place clean. The chickens were allowed to run loose along with the turkeys, free range during the day, coming in to roost at night in the old slanted log shed. Every day, we collected the eggs, afraid sometimes, because an ornery chicken would peck at our hands—the cluckers, as mom called them.

An old wooden granary stood about forty feet to the east, between the chicken coop and the barn. It had a manual cream separator inside. After we milked the cows, the milk was separated and the cream canned, in preparation to be sold at the local creamery in Roblin. It was a source of income for the family and religiously done every day.

One day, while I was separating milk with mother, an electrical storm was brewing. Lightning was flashing all around us, and then we heard a sizzle followed by a loud clap of thunder. Sparks jumped rapidly from nail to nail in the granary, so Mother decided to shut down until the storm passed, telling me we were pretty close to being hit.

We stopped keeping chickens. The log shed coop was now home to the pigs, complete with corral, slop trough, and wire mesh. We had about five sows with litters and three boars. The cows were sold and the barn used to house the brood sows and their litters. Most table scraps were saved and fed to the pigs. Sometimes, if we had enough grain, we would heat up a pail with grain and water on the stove in the house and then feed it to them, especially in winter.

Being the ninth child in the family, I had no shortage of playmates and workmates. The older ones would do all the work, while the younger ones played, and when the work was done, everyone would play tin can, fox in the goose, or hide-and-seek for hours. When not playing games, sometimes we would try to build things.

One day, when I was around five years old, my brother Emile and I were building an airplane. We had the propeller, fuselage, and wings built, but we needed a spacer to put between the propeller and fuselage. I went into the house and sneakily took the butcher knife from the cupboard and then went out to make the spacer. Being a kid and not realizing the dangers of using this huge knife, I proceeded to make the spacer. Taking a piece of a small poplar branch, about three quarters of an inch round, an inch and a half long, holding one end carefully so as not to chop my fingers, I raised the knife. Bang. I hollered blue murder. Blood was pouring from my finger. I had chopped my finger. My brother came rushing to me. Seeing the blood, he immediately started to calm me down. "You can't tell Mom," he told me. Although my finger was cut pretty badly, we decided not to say anything and bandaged the cut ourselves with some gauze and electrical tape Dad had.

We must have done all right because when we went into the house, immediately, Mom asked, "What happened?" Of course, I told the truth—when I told her I caught it in the door. She looked at it, put peroxide and iodine on the wound, and then reassuringly told me I would live.

Oh, what fun it was being a kid! All the memories! School! We had two small schools in the hamlet of San Clara, in which a hundred-plus children from grade one to grade eight were taught. Every morning, we would get up and get ready for school, squabbling for clothing and boots. What a job it was for poor mother sending ten kids off to school. We were poor, and with the family so large, we would have a lot of hand-me-down clothing.

The boys did not want to wear the girls' boots to school because of the ridicule they would face. Everyone made fun of what we wore, even though they were not well off either, but they were blessed with a little more than we.

Mom would put her foot down and say, "Never mind about how you look and what the kids at school say. You need to go to school and get an education. Put them boots on and get going." We obeyed. Disgruntled as kids get, we walked the mile from our house to school, lunch kit in hand, filled with jam or peanut butter sandwiches, cocoa, an apple or an orange if times were good, and cookies when Mom had time to bake. Sometimes, we had mashed Velveeta cheese and tomato soup mixed together as a treat.

When berry-picking time came along, we would pick saskatoons, pin cherries, chokecherries, raspberries, and blueberries. The family would climb into the old rainbow truck, a fifty-five Chevy short box, and off we would go for the day. Everyone had a pail; the copper boiler and washtub had to be full. The whole day was spent picking berries.

When we arrived back home, we cleaned the berries in preparation for canning. The next morning, Mom would be hard at it canning and making jam. We were thankful to have wild berry jams and syrups for our lunches. Although poor, we always had enough to eat because of our faith in God to provide for his children.

It was fun to be at school learning to play with other children and how to read and write. We enjoyed recess and lunchtime activities, like playing football, soccer, baseball, running ball, and crack the whip. Mrs. Lachance (bless her soul) taught my dad and all of us children. We would play little tricks on her thinking she wouldn't know only to find ourselves being disciplined. She drew a circle on the blackboard, just high enough out of reach of our noses; then we had to stand on tiptoes and put our noses in the circle for ten minutes or so. The whole class would get a good laugh at us standing there, trying to keep our noses in the circle. Most of us had fun with it, as she was such a kind, gentle teacher. How horrid this type of discipline is today! She meant no harm and gave us a big hug when it was over, which today, is not allowed. We wonder why there is no respect for the teachers. They can't show affection to their students as most probably would like to, because of sexual harassment charges caused by a few deadbeats. I can still hear those little high-heel shoes clicking on the floor from the teacher's quarters to the classroom and then her entering with "Holy teapot!" when she caught us doing something we shouldn't have been doing.

Winter or summer, we walked to school, but at times, we were allowed to take the horses when the older kids were able to control them. After hooking up the horses to the sleigh or wagon, we would pile into the hay to keep warm, and off we would go. After school, the wagon box would be full of teachers and children alike, hitching a ride for a short distance to their approaches in town. At times, our drivers would get competitive and would have a race.

One time, my oldest brother, Joe, pulled the pegs out of the bunks of our cousin's wagon. He had the fastest team, so every advantage was necessary to win the race. With the teachers and kids loaded on the sleigh, away we went.

As we rounded the approach exiting the school yard, our cousin, Yves, was in the lead. While he was turning onto the road, the horses going flat out, his wagon came off the sleigh and slid into the ditch. Yves had the reigns around his back and was dragged for a few yards, skidding and rolling, trying to get up until the horses stopped. Dumbfounded and not realizing what had happened, he checked his sleigh and found the pegs had been pulled. While only his pride was hurt, he wasn't happy, but with his good nature, he got over it quickly and laughed. Everyone had a good laugh and was buried in snow. The next day, the principal informed us we could no longer have these kinds of activities going on, as someone could have easily been hurt. The Lord was definitely looking after us, but it was fun.

Throughout my school years, I always saw the disciplined ways of the school curriculum. We would line up in front of the school and enter our classrooms in single file. We always said the Lord's Prayer first, a passage from the Bible next, and then after singing, "O Canada," we sat down and proceeded with our learning experience. Hygiene was important, so we would show our fingernails, ears, and teeth to our teacher to prove we were clean. Mom was not doing her job, I guess. Parents then had the most control over their children and taught them the best way they knew how. We learned to do things and figure them out by using the gift of the mind to its fullest, no calculators and no guidance teachers.

We prayed at home as a family, which was very important to our values, and we were disciplined as required, sometimes harshly but most times fairly. We were disciplined by the teachers in the same way. To say the least, we were taught first and foremost about God, the truth, respect, responsibility, and honesty and to help and give of yourself whenever possible. These are the most important values one can have instilled in one.

As the years passed, I entered grade nine, so my father sent me to St. Vlad's college in Roblin, a minor seminary run by the Ukrainian Redemptorist priests. I was thirteen and afraid to leave. Not wanting to go, I rebelled. I had attitude and begged and pleaded, but to no avail. Our parish priest, I'm sure, had a say in what was going on, but no one would listen to my feelings. As a student up to grade eight, I did well in school. I was no different than any other student. I was disciplined equally with the others and did not expect it any other way.

As a thirteen-year-old in grade nine, having to leave home and my siblings, I was forced and made to go. I was defeated. I cried many times and wondered what this was all about. I wondered if I was even loved and thought if this was love, it sucked. At the time, I did not know what I was doing, but today, I realize my parents thought it was the best for me.

I did nothing in St. Vlad's. I did no homework, did not participate in class, and signed my tests without completing them. I was fighting with other students. I did everything I was not supposed to do. We went to church four times a day. Plus, we served mass for our parish priest when he came to visit. I even rebelled against God. I was forced to go to a church that I could not understand as everything was in Ukrainian. I was forced to study Ukrainian, learn the alphabet, sing in Ukrainian, knowing nothing of what it all meant. My parents thought it was okay.

In March 1968, my grandfather passed away. I thought the world of him because he would make us laugh with all the funny faces he made with no teeth. He smoked a pipe and would perform at times, curling up his lips with the pipe hanging out of his mouth, looking like the cartoon character, Popeye. I came home for the funeral and returned for the rest of the year.

When school was out for the summer, I would recite the Lord's Prayer in that language many times a day for relatives, friends, and whoever came to the house. I was also made to sing in Ukrainian. I was a shy person when I was young, very poor at speaking in front of people, and would get intimidated easily. This was not fun, but I survived and learned from it.

I continued to go to school at Goose Lake High in Roblin, repeating grade nine, and didn't do well. I was now fourteen and held resentment for being forced to do something I did not want to do. My attitude sucked. I didn't participate in activities and roamed the halls. I never could figure out the competitive side of our schools, like track and field, other sports, and trying to get the best marks. To me, many times, it led to some kind of disagreement and taught some kids to be more righteous than others. Kids are kids and do what they are told. This leaves a feeling of worthlessness in some children, who grow up in this environment, saddened they lost out, thus possibly causing some of the resentment we see today in adults.

It is used in many instances to motivate the kids who are good but not competitive and do not want to feel better than others. It seemed a negative, because our abilities are not the same, but we are forced to compete. We'll talk about this later.

I passed grade nine and was promoted to grade ten, but I felt restless, not wanting to go to school anymore. I hated what it stood for at a young age, making up my own mind about what we were learning: the past. We were forced to learn it or be a failure. We were reminded of the wars, conquerors, and the stupidity of mankind, instead of love, respect, how to survive, saving the environment, and getting along with all of mankind. Had the world been taught this, we would have no need for rules, enforcement, and jails, I used to think. Instead, we are taught all the manly things.

We had to get up, do our chores, travel for one hour on the school bus, go to school for eight hours, and then return home, which took another hour. We were putting in sixteen hours a day by the time we did our chores, ate supper, did our homework, and said our prayers. We were all just children and putting in a sixteen-hour day. Already at that time, the adults had secured an eight-hour workday. It seemed something was wrong with the system.

Economics, at whatever the cost, ruled over children and life, what it is and was. We were bussed to town on these polluting machines, through snow and poor road conditions, with little or no concern for our safety, having to attend when the temperature was forty below zero. We were forced to put in sixteen-hour days just to save a few pennies, the schools in the country had cost, without thinking of the environment, the kids and the long days. The larger schools and governments demanded we amalgamate.

Today, more money is required and much of it is spent for repairs on buses, which are escalating, extreme fuel prices, and escalating taxes beyond belief. Towns are dying out and country living nearly extinct; curling rinks paid for with donations and hard work are now in disarray. Halls are condemned with no money to repair them, and the infrastructure is nearly destroyed. Shouldn't we request the country schools back? Money: the root of all evil.

Maybe I was tired and rebelled. Maybe I was just lazy or worthless.

I quit school at sixteen years old, halfway through grade ten and went home. *Ha! Freedom at last!* I thought.

When I arrived home, I told my parents that I had quit school. I was afraid, but my mind was made up.

"If you don't want to go to school, you need to get out and get a job," my father told me. Even though I knew that, those words ring in my head still today. He didn't realize how much help we had given him in his store and on the farm, but he was supreme commander in chief. However, he was right.

He gave me twenty dollars. I packed what few belongings I had, bought a bus ticket to Winnipeg for six dollars and fifty cents, and left home. By the time I arrived in Winnipeg, I had about ten dollars left, but I had siblings living there who helped me out. Life wasn't too bad.

I found a job at a feed mill on Archibald Street and worked at this for two days. It was dusty, and my lungs filled up with dust until I was choking. Utilizing my power of choice, not wanting to work like this, I quit. This was my choice, and nobody could make me go back. I was proud I had that ability to make this choice. If someone else wanted to work like that, it was his or her choice. I didn't go to the government for a new regulation. If the grain company had had a conscience, they would have made it better without regulation. If we all thought about it and no one would work there, they would have to close their doors, without being regulated. The same goes for anything that we don't like. I knew God would guide me to something better. He always had looked after me, and I was sure he would again.

I got a job in construction as a laborer sweeping floors and cleaning up a high-rise complex. I was commanded to help this carpenter who was having problems putting up forms for a column, so we could pour cement. I held the form in place while he nailed it enough to hold, and then looking around, I found a hammer and proceeded to help him nail. That was a mistake. Immediately, the foreman came to me and fired me. I lasted one day on this job.

I asked, "What is the problem?"

He told me, "You had no business using a hammer on this site."

Confused, I asked, "Why?"

He said, "It is a union job, and you were hired as a laborer not a carpenter."

Still confused, I replied, "You told me to help him."

He replied, "I told you to help him, not to use a hammer."

I threw my hands up in a gesture of disbelief and left, disgruntled and confused, feeling cheated and with a hatred for this man. I wanted to beat him.

I was always taught to help wherever requested. Was I taught wrong? What did I do wrong? *Rules, rules, and rules equal Communism,* is what went through my mind, even though I did not understand what Communism really was. Then it hit me. *Power!* He had the power and abused it. What a sorry man. He also had the workforce behind him through the union, because they wanted their jobs secure. It didn't matter if it took double the time at double the cost or whether it took ten hours to do one hour of work. It didn't matter if I was fired and starved. I broke the rule, and by golly, I was a disgrace to the job site … because I had tried to help. I was judged immediately.

I jumped from job to job, from building swimming pools to diamond drilling, until I was seventeen years old.

On one particular job on the diamond drills, I was posted to the Perry River in the Northwest Territories. We used helicopters to move the drill and for crew change. Many times, we would see herds of musk ox and hover just above them. They would make a circle, the calves and cows with calves would be inside the circle. The bulls would jump up at the helicopter, attempting to scare us off. We posed a danger to them, but what an awesome sight! On other occasions, we would see an exodus of caribou a half mile wide and about two to three miles long, moving to another feeding range. What a spectacular sight to see these beautiful animals in the wild without any influence from man. They had no fear of us. They would herd around the drill in the evening, feeding without disturbance.

I came back home for a short while and was heckled about going to work or back to school. I found a job flagging on the road between San Clara and Roblin for a construction company repairing the road. I saved enough money to buy an old 1959 Buick LeSabre for $200.00 and headed for Alberta. It used a lot of oil, but you could find used oil anywhere. I had wheels. Yahoo!

I began working in the oil fields of Alberta. It was tough, dirty work, but I found I liked the challenge. I was helping people heat their houses, fuel their cars, and operate hospitals.

The crews were rough and tumble, drinking most of the time, showing their power to the world. We were young and foolish. Work hard and play hard was the motto. Work hard, we did, and play, we did harder. Drinking alcohol, doing grass, and buying fast cars was the norm. Finally, I had enough money for what I thought was freedom. That's what it's all about. I was nineteen and free.

I never forgot my values, however. I didn't go to church that often, but I was always spiritual. I always knew I couldn't possibly survive on my own without the grace of God. I drove my cars hard. I drank until I couldn't function. I fought if provoked or if I saw someone being mistreated or intimidated. I believed and still believe that no one should be subjected to belittlement or intimidation. If I could stop it or attempt to stop it, then I did what I felt was necessary. I earned a reputation for fighting because of what I believed and sometimes just because I could. Not many understood and would recognize you for a deed. Recognition only tells the world, "Look what I've done! I'm good!" which is something I never believed in.

At about this point in my life, I began to take some interest in politics and tried to understand what it all meant. I started thinking of the rules and regulations we were subjected to. I began to ask questions of my dad, as he was driven by rules and politics.

There were times when we were children that he and his brothers would get into some heated debates about John Diefenbaker and Lester B. Pearson. It was comical most times. They were poor people looking for a better solution to life. They were spiritual and held a fear of God deeply embedded in them by their folks. They were deceived many times by promises that the government couldn't fulfill and would bang the table with their fists while debating. They had pride in raising their families and held high in their hearts the values of trust, honesty, responsibility, and respect. Most of all, they believed very strongly in God and the importance of passing this down to their families and future generations.

Women still didn't vote, which was a big mistake. My mother put up with this. She was love, courage, nurturer, farmer, wife, mother, discipliner, baker, home-care giver, and more. She made coats, blankets, sheets, mattresses, clothing, and meals all with the love we needed. There were times I would look at her and wonder if she would be around long enough to enjoy life and relax. She would sing to us, looking after us fifteen children like a hen on a brood and never complained.

She had sad times like everyone else. Once while she was making a mattress, I observed her crying and could only give her a hug as I was too young to understand. Today, I understand. She had a big hole in her heart from losing two brothers in World War II for the freedoms they believed they were fighting for, for generations to come. Another brother disappeared for quite some time and was AWOL in the southern hemisphere but no one could reach him. Her father and my father did not get along so she had no family left, as her sister, who was a Christian sister, was in Rome and elsewhere doing the work of God.

Then Grandma died, and she really had no one for a time. We didn't ever know or see Grandpa and had met Grandma only twice. This is what power, hatred, and anger bring. It separates families and friends in peacetime as well as in war. It is evil. The chain needs to be broken, or mankind will not survive. Political power, oppression in any form, hunger, and hatred of other ethnic groups need to disappear.

Working in the High Arctic was one of the best jobs I had. We moved rigs with trucks, aircraft, and buggies. It was cold on rig moves, but once it was set up, it was great. On occasion, we would have to stay in longer than scheduled, because of storms causing whiteouts.

I met Barb in 1973 and fell in love with this beautiful young woman. I was still wild and carefree at the time, boozing and being an idiot. I was in Brandon visiting her and partied the weekend, as did most young people that age. I had to get back to work and left to catch the flight back to the High Arctic on Monday morning, around eight o'clock.

Speeding down the highway near Colonsay, Saskatchewan, I was picked up by the police and subsequently charged for impaired driving. I hadn't sobered up from the night before. I lost about four hours going through the breathalyzer and pleading with the officer that I would pay the fine immediately so I could catch the flight back to the Arctic. He finally agreed, but the other fellow I was with had to drive. It was the best thing that happened that day. I missed the flight by approximately a half hour. Unfortunately, the aircraft went down in frigid waters just short of the runway at Ray Point that evening. Thirty-one men were lost, and two survived. God was surely looking after me. It was such a sad day for all of us. Most of us knew someone on that aircraft and some of their families.

When I arrived in Ray Point the following week, camp was like a makeshift morgue. Coffins lined the walls in the theater room, and people were silent. No movies were being watched out of respect for the ones who had lost their lives. The room was being used for more important purposes. People were working hard trying to recover bodies from the wreckage. Diving gear was set out throughout the camp and storage areas. Divers went back and forth to the crash site, trying to recover whatever they could. Parts of the Lockheed Electra were sitting in front of the shop where an investigation was underway.

I quit the rigs and moved to Thompson so Barb and I could be together. We got married in 1975. My bride, Barbara Anne Grundy, is my soul mate, my wife, and the mother of my child, Tiffany, born in 1976. How I love her. She is one of the finest examples of kindness, love, peace, happiness, joy, trust, and charity, all the things that were sent to us through Jesus. That is the only way to describe her.

We see these messages in our churches but never heed them. She deserves a medal for putting up with me at times when I was astray with booze, drugs, and just plain stupidity. The only recognition she wants is to be loved and treated with respect. I understood this but didn't heed it until later on in life when our relationship was deteriorating. We sat down finally and talked. I quit drinking and taking drugs for a period of time, and we knew this was meant to be.

We prayed it would work, went to church, read a couple of articles, and talked, finally again believing in God and ourselves. It was a huge turning point, and life started to change, becoming excellent. I realized how selfish I was. God shone his light upon us and sent the Holy Ghost into our lives. What a blessing.

Tiffany was born in Thompson, Manitoba, where I was employed underground at the mines as a diamond driller. I didn't like being underground, and when the workforce went on strike, I took a job with the Canadian National Railway, trained in The Pas, Manitoba, and then moved to Gillam, Manitoba, to work as a plumber. I worked there until Tiffany was a year old but didn't like the isolation. The only way in and out was by train. I realized this when Grandpa Nabe passed away, and we had to wait for a train to get out.

We left Gillam, and I resumed working in the oil patch throughout Alberta, the High Arctic, and British Columbia. I had a family to support, and whatever it took, that was what we did. The patch was feast or famine, so we were never sure where the next paycheck was going to come from, but we managed.

With our daughter came responsibility. Since I was away at work most of the time, Barb raised our daughter—well, I must add. I helped out when I was home, but with a split relationship as we had, we had to be careful not to disrupt things, carefully dealing with situations. We were both independent and tried hard to be consistent in bringing her up.

We are able to have a drink in moderation now and enjoy our lives and company much more. There is nothing wrong with having a drink in moderation as long as it doesn't affect your relationship and the lives of others. We still get into disagreements, but they don't last too long. She always wins. Thank you, God, and please do not take the Holy Ghost away from us.

Tiffany was getting older, and we knew we would have to settle somewhere for her to go to school, but where? I still was keen on learning the oil patch and worked hard to improve my position. I started out as a roughneck and worked my way through the system until I became a driller at twenty-two years old. I asked a lot of questions and learned a lot of valuable information through the tool pusher and consultant. I read different material so I could understand the drilling aspect of the business. I pushed tools for a brief while in Canada and found there really wasn't anything steady enough to keep me here, so I started looking overseas for employment.

Chapter Two

I picked up the phone and dialed.

"Hello, Parker Drilling. How may I help you?"

"Hello. This is Patrick Carriere from up here in Canada. How are you?"

"I am fine. What can I do for you, Mr. Carriere?" was the reply in a Southern drawl.

"I am wondering if I could speak to the personnel manager for overseas employment. Could you tell me if you are hiring?" I replied.

"I'm sorry, but you will have to speak to Mr. Williams in Tulsa, Oklahoma. Let me see if I can connect you," came the reply.

I waited for a few minutes, nervous at what I was doing. Doubts started to engulf my thoughts as I waited.

"Hello, this is Williams. How may I help you all?" came this burly voice in a deep Southern drawl.

"Hello, Mr. Williams. This is Patrick Carriere up here in Canada. How are you?" I replied.

"I am fine," he replied. "Are you all related to a Bill Carriere from … geez … Medicine House or somewhere like that?"

Chuckling, I replied, "Medicine Hat."

"Yes! That's it," he replied.

"Yes," I replied. "I have a cousin named Bill from Medicine Hat."

"Well, we all just sent him to Singapore. Seems like he is a good fellow," came the Southern drawl.

"Well, I was just wondering if you were hiring for overseas. I would like to try something different."

"I need someone to go to Algeria. How much experience do you all have?"

"I am pushing tools up here in Canada right now and have six years experience from roughneck to present," was my reply.

"Do you all have a passport?"

My heart started to race, and I felt I was going to lose my chance because I didn't have my passport. I was thinking as quickly as I possibly could to save my opportunity.

"I'm sorry. No," I replied.

"Well, I'm sorry. We all need someone right away, and if you all don't have a passport, I can't send you," was the reply.

Feeling I had just lost, I stammered, "Ah! Okay. I could get a passport within a week if necessary and if the position is still open—"

"I'm sorry. We all need someone right away. I'll keep you in mind though, and when something comes up, I will call you all," he replied.

"Thanks for your time, sir," I replied.

"You all have a good day," was the reply.

"Okay, bye."

Feeling I had just lost the position, I hung up and hung my head, thinking, *Yeah right, he isn't going to call back.* Many thoughts ran through my head. *How much does it cost to get a passport? How long will it take? Ah, forget it. You have a job here; just go back to work and forget about it.* My mind was racing.

I talked to Barb about the conversation and said, "If I would have had a passport, I could have had the job."

Damned rules. Why can't we just go? Why can't I go anywhere in God's creation and work? Who makes all these stupid rules? Why are there all these borders? No wonder we have all these problems. My mind was racing. I was young and didn't understand all this, but I was aware of the strife in the world. I hadn't paid too much attention to it before.

Regaining my composure, I said, "Oh well. I guess it was meant not to be. I'll work in Canada and forget about it."

The next day, I packed my rig bag, jumped in my truck, and headed for Hinton. My rig was shut down, waiting on location, so we were cleaning, repairing, and painting. I had a skeleton crew, and we were just about finished with repairs. A few days passed, and I still had the desire to go but felt they weren't going to call me, so I forgot about it. I didn't know any other overseas companies, so I didn't call anyone else.

My phone rang.

"Hello, Mr. Carriere. This is Williams here in Tulsa. How you all doing? I just spoke to your wife, and she gave me your rig phone number, so I thought I would call you and see if you all got a passport yet?"

I was surprised and happy, yet dumbfounded. I was not expecting his call.

I replied, "No, I didn't get a passport. You said you didn't need me, so I didn't pursue it."

"Well, Gawd damn," came this Southern drawl. "There is a ticket at the Edmonton airport for you all. Do you all think you can have a passport by Monday?" he asked.

This was Tuesday, and I didn't know. I had six days to quit my job, get a passport, drive from Hinton, converse with my wife, and go. I had a decision to make, and it had to be quick.

"I'm sorry," I replied. "I wasn't expecting another call from you. I need to give this company notice that I would be leaving, get a passport, and settle things here in Canada before I can go. I don't know how long it will take. It might take a couple of weeks. If you could call me back tomorrow, I will see what I can do."

"Well, I got a ticket for you to come to Odessa, Texas, on Monday to attend a BOP course on ten-thousand-pound blowout-prevention equipment. It runs for a week, but you will miss the first day. We will honor your instruction as a full week course and send you to Algeria. Do you think you can make it? Apply for your passport and see if you can get one. While you do your course, they can process your visa for Algeria, and you could be ready to go at the end of next week," he replied.

"I'll see what I can do," I replied.

"Okay now. You all get your passport, and I'll talk to you tomorrow. Bye for now."

"Okay. Bye."

Happy but yet unsure, I picked up a cup and poured myself some coffee. My mind was racing. *I can't do this. I can't go this quickly. I can't just leave this company. I can't make this deadline. I have a big decision to make.*

While I was sitting and sipping my coffee, a thought popped into my head. I just thought; *I can't. I can't. I can't. Yes, I can. I can make this decision. I can go if I really want. I can get a passport. I can go, and nobody can stop me.* I was twenty-four years old, full of energy, and my own man. I had a family to feed. What was best for them? This could be a chance of a lifetime.

I finished my cup of coffee, picked up the phone, and dialed.

"Hello, Shelby Drilling," the secretary said.

"Hello. This is Pat. Is Wayne or Dave around?"

"Just a minute, Pat; I'll transfer you," she said.

Waiting and wondering, I thought maybe they would be disappointed with me for bailing out without notice but—

"Hello, Wayne here. What's up, Pat?"

Stammering, I replied, "Wayne, I ... ah ... have a chance to go ... ah ... overseas, and they want me to go by Monday next week. Ah ... Would there be a problem with that?"

A short silence followed, and then he said, "Well, it isn't much notice. We have Al off right now and not sure when he will go back to work. I could send him out today, and he will be there by tonight. Would that work?" he replied.

"I'm sorry, Wayne, but this is an opportunity I hate to pass up. If it is a problem, tell me and I will change my plan. I will postpone them if I can and give you two weeks' notice," I replied.

"No. That's okay. We will have Al on the road as soon as possible. If you need to go, just leave him a note explaining what is going on. All we have been doing is rig repair, and it looks like the rig won't go to work for a couple of weeks yet. You go ahead and do what you need to do," replied Wayne.

"Wayne... thanks! I really appreciate it. Thank you," I replied.

I was excited. I called my bride and told her the good news. I asked if she could get me an application for a passport.

I went out to the rig and said my good-byes to the crews, scratched a note, packed my rig belongings, and headed home, all within about two hours. I was pumped.

All the way home, thoughts raced through my head. *Is this the right decision? Are we going to be okay? What is Barb's mom going to think? Will she be disappointed? What will we do with our possessions? Should we sell everything? Maybe I should just stay in Canada.*

I wanted to go. I was driven by the opportunity to travel and see other cultures. I was interested in the way the world was. I wanted to see for myself what it was all about. There was so much negativity on television.

Is it really that bad? Will I be a target? Will I live to talk about it? I was scared but thought; *God will guide me. Algeria ... Where the hell is that?* I had forgotten my geography.

I arrived at home that evening and was exhausted but smiling. My mind was tired, and I was still skeptical. Barb and I talked about it with excitement, but we were reserved. We had no idea what we were getting into. We called her folks.

Unsure of what to say and the response we would get, I dialed.

"Hello." Her mother's voice always dragged the O on for a short while when she answered the phone.

"Hello," I replied. "How are you?"

"I'm fine. How are you?" she replied with a tone of concern in her voice.

"Well, we are okay. Just calling to tell you that I accepted a job overseas, and I have to go to Odessa, Texas, next week for a course. I'll be going to Algeria and Barb will stay back for two months, then, she will move overseas and join me," I got out.

"You're what? What are you talking about? You're going where? She was shocked somewhat. I'm sure she thought I lost my mind.

"Well, Barb and I have a big decision to make" I said. Her mother was always protective of her and had every right to be.

"Well, let me talk to Barb," she said still in shock.

I handed the phone to Barb and walked away. I was young and foolish like everyone else my age. I drank alcohol, drove fast cars, and did what young kids did, but at times I felt she had some difficulty with me, probably because of the way I conducted myself. I don't know. Thoughts were racing through my mind. *Well, maybe she is afraid she won't see us again. It's just a mother's intuition,* I thought. *She's just worried and shocked.*

I looked across the room and could see Barb talking on the phone. She was trying to let her mom know everything would be ok explaining things a lot better than I. It appeared she had convinced her somewhat and was somewhat relieved. She had a tear in her eye ... happy for me but knowing she would have to encourage her folks that everything was going to be all right. Finally, she said good-bye and hung up, wiping away a tear. She will be ok with it. I think we shocked her.

We talked a while longer and then went to bed. I couldn't sleep. Thoughts raced through my mind. I was anxious. I was happy for the opportunity. *Ah, I just won't go if it's going to cause problems. Do you really want to do this?* I couldn't sleep.

I got up and paced. *I have to go get my passport.* I started filling out the passport application my bride had picked up for me. *Who can I get to notarize my application?* I didn't sleep. I drank coffee and wore my mind down. This decision just got bigger.

The phone rang. Barb was up and answered it. "Pat, it's for you," she said.

I didn't want to talk. "Who is it?" I whispered. I was tired.

"I think Parker Drilling," she said.

Oh shit! I don't think I can do this, I thought. She handed me the phone.

"Hello," I said my voice shaky.

"Hello," replied Mr. Williams in that Southern drawl. "How you all making out there, Patrick? Did you get a passport?"

"Well, as best I can. I'm taking my application in today. If all goes well, I should have a passport by Friday. They told me it would only take three days," I replied. "Today is Wednesday, and there is a possibility I won't have it until Monday."

"There is a ticket at the airport in Edmonton with your name on it for 10:00 AM Monday. Are you going to make it?"

"I'm trying. I will get my passport picture taken, the application notarized, and take it to the office right away. It's the best I can do," I replied.

"We're all counting on you now. Do your best and we will see you

Monday night. I will pick you up at the Midland-Odessa airport. Talk to you Monday and have a good flight," replied Mr. Williams.

"Okay," I replied. "If all goes well, I'll be there. If a problem arises, I will phone you and let you know. Bye for now," I replied.

"Pressure," I said, "who needs it?" as I poured a cup of coffee. I looked over at my wife. She had this smile on her face that told me she approved, yet I could sense a little doubt. She came and sat down.

"Are you okay?" I asked.

"Yeah, I think so," she replied.

"Do you think we should do this?" I asked with some doubt in my mind.

"It's up to you. I will go with you anywhere. It's your decision, and I don't want to spoil your opportunity," she replied.

"Well, you're part of this too. I don't want to upset you or your family, but I also don't want to miss out on something and regret it later. Will your mom be okay" I asked?

"It's okay, honey," she replied. "You check it out for two months, and I will go home and talk to Mom and Dad. They will be all right."

Off to the passport office, I went. Once I was inside the office, it was clear. I was going. My bride approved of it, and that was all that mattered. We were going overseas, and that was all there was to it. I didn't care anymore. I wasn't going to let someone else tell me what to do. It really wasn't anyone else's business. I was my own man with a family, and we had to do what felt right for us. No, we couldn't listen to everyone else.

Everyone we told thought we were crazy. They were concerned about our safety. They were opinionated about other people and cultures, and most were negative. *They watch too much television,* I told myself. *How do they know how the other side of the world lives? They were never there. I'm going, and I will find out for myself. God will guide me.* I asked God for his help and was deep in thought sitting and waiting to be called up when—

"Mr. Carriere," this soft voice said from behind the passport office desk.

Startled, I jumped up. "Yes, sir … errr … ma'am," I said, stumbling for footing and words. "How are you?" I asked. "Sorry, I was deep in thought. This is the first time I've had to do this," I stammered.

She looked up, smiled, and then said, "The picture looks like you, and your paperwork is in order. We could have your passport ready by Wednesday next week. Would that be okay?"

"Oh! Oh! Is there any way I can have it by Friday if they put a rush on it? I have to go to Odessa, Texas, Monday, and Parker Drilling wants me to fly out from the U.S. as soon as I finish my course. Please! I really want this job, and I may not get it if I don't have a passport. They said they need to get me a visa for Algeria while I attend this course," I stammered.

"I think we can," she replied. "Come in at 1:00 PM Friday. Make sure as we close at 1:30 this Friday."

"Thank you," I replied. I wanted to jump up and click my heels. *We did it. Wow. I'm going to Algeria.* Happy thoughts were dancing in my head. I was so happy! Thank you, God!

The next few days were just a blur. Everything was happening so fast—packing, checking, unpacking what I thought I didn't need, and repacking again. We had no money to travel, but I didn't care. I would ask for an advance when I got to Texas. We were happy.

December 10, 1979, Monday morning came, and it was time to go to the airport. I was nervous and scared but determined. As we drove the twenty miles to the airport, thoughts raced through my head wildly. It was cold, minus 20, and clear. *How I love my bride! Will she come after the two-month probation is up? If she doesn't come, I will come back. Will she still be there for me?* How my mind raced. I wanted to cry, but I knew I had to be strong for her. She always kept her personal feelings to herself, and I had to guess many times.

I wasn't sure of myself anymore. *What's happening to me? Maybe I have lost my mind. It's too late. I have committed to this, and now I have to follow through. Quit feeling sorry for yourself and go. It's not the end of the world,* I told myself. My mind was playing tricks. I guess if you never had doubts, there would be no determination.

We parked the car, went into the airport, picked up my ticket, and checked in. We had about a half hour to wait, so we had coffee and chatted about what to do next.

I knew I would be on the flight to Odessa, Texas, in a few minutes and Barb would be on her way back home to New Sarepta.

We hugged and kissed for what seemed to be a long time, but in reality, it was just a few minutes then said good-bye. I headed for the boarding gate. Barb left with a tear in her eye. I was pretty choked up myself. *What the hell are you doing?* I thought to myself.

"You're okay," I told myself out loud. Realizing I had said this out loud, I looked around and saw a little lady, about forty, looking at me. I kept going to the gate. I was going and that was that.

Soon after, I was in the air and on my way to Texas, wondering if Barb had made it home. Even though we were used to being apart, this was something different. I was going for at least two months by myself, and we hadn't done this before. Three to four weeks was the longest I had been away.

I began to think of all kinds of things. What kind of people will I meet in Algeria? Will they accept me? I hope they don't hurt me in any way. I was skeptical of myself.

Chuckling, I began to relax and realized that it really didn't matter. *If I watch what I say and don't get involved in religion or politics, I should be okay. If I help them out and train them the best I can, everything will work out. What language do they speak? How do I communicate with them?* I didn't have time to think about this because everything happened so fast. *I guess I will learn.* I fell asleep.

I don't remember if I had to change flights anywhere. I woke up, and we were landing. Now that's the way to fly. I was not a good flier. The thrust of the engines on takeoff frightened the hell out of me, and I always said a silent little prayer and asked God to protect me. It comforted me, knowing he was there and always protected me. Thank you.

As I got off the plane, I wondered what Mr. Williams looked like. I had a picture of this big, burly man about forty years old with a gruff voice in my mind. I picked up my luggage and headed for the arrival hall. I looked around, and then I heard my name being called.

"Patrick," I heard and looked straight at Mr. Williams.

"Hello," I said. "How are you? I'm Patrick," I introduced myself.

"Hello to you all. How are you all?" said Mr. Williams. "Did you all have a good flight?"

"Yep; I had a nap for most of the way." I replied.

"Have you got everything?"

"I think so," I replied.

"Well, follow me. We all might as well go," he said.

I followed him taking notice of his size. He was a tall man, about six foot four, and weighed about two hundred and fifty pounds. He must have been near eighty years old and in pretty good shape. He walked straight, striding at a pretty good gait. The look on his face was pleasant, but I sensed he held respect high on his chart. He was friendly, and I felt quite at ease with him. We hopped in the car, and then he pulled a big cigar out of his shirt pocket and peeled off the wrapper. He bit the end off, spat the paper out, and lit up turning to me.

"Do you all mind if I smoke this awful thing?" he said.

"No, not at all," I replied. "Do you mind if I have a cigarette?"

"You all just do what you like," he replied.

I lit my smoke and sat back, making small talk as we drove. He explained I would have to get a medical and then go to my course in the morning.

I watched as he puffed that big cigar, and then he reached over without looking and flicked his ash off. It fell on the seat beside him, so immediately I went to brush it off in case it burned his seat. That was when I noticed his seat was full of burns. He was driving a big Cadillac Eldorado and had a beanbag ash tray on the seat.

"I miss that damn thing more often than I hit it," he commented.

Chuckling, I agreed with him.

Soon, we pulled into the Hilton hotel and stopped the car.

"You all will stay here for the week, so you all make yourself at home. I know most of these people here, and they all will look after you well," he said. "I'll pick you all up in the morning around nine. Be ready. Your medical will be at ten."

"Okay, sir. Thanks for picking me up. It was nice meeting you," I said.

He left, and I stood there for a minute thinking, *I hope the room is paid for or I will be sleeping outside.* I had about three hundred Canadian dollars between now and starvation. Chuckling, I went inside.

Once inside, I checked in and was relieved to find my room and meals paid for. I would survive for another week. I went to my room, put my bag on the table, and sat down. I was feeling lonely and lost, so I called home. Barb was home, and we talked for a short while, as money was really tight. If we were going to do this, we had to make ends meet and sacrifice some of the luxuries the Western world had. Again, my mind was working overtime and I was restless. I picked up my key and went downstairs to the coffee shop and had a cup of coffee. As I was sitting there, sipping a coffee, this voice called me. I looked in the direction it was coming from.

"Paddy, what are you doing here?" Some of the fellows with whom I had worked in the High Arctic used to call me Paddy.

I turned, and there was Steve. He had worked as an assistant driller for Mustang rig twelve when I was drilling in the Arctic.

"Well, holy shit. Steve! What the hell are you doing here?" I asked.

"I'm here to take a BOP course, then, I'm going to Algeria with Parker Drilling. What about you?" he asked.

"The same thing," I replied. "Parker has me scheduled to leave on Saturday."

We chatted for a while over a cup of coffee and then parted ways. He was telling me he had to sneak across the Canadian-U.S. border to get to Odessa. He had a record for impaired driving and got caught with a small amount of marijuana and of course rules, rules, rules.

How sad such a small infraction as that can control your life and take away your freedoms for a long time. I realize that we need law and order, and we do need to be structured in some way, but for something as minute as this? Is this not a form of suppression? Are we not free to make our own choices for such minute things as this? To get caught and pay a penalty for an infraction that society deems wrong is one thing. To be condemned and suppressed for it is another, and I don't believe it just.

I went back to my room and fell asleep, exhausted from all the excitement.

I awoke to the phone ringing. I rolled over and picked up the receiver. "This is your wake-up call," came over the phone.

I stumbled out of bed and fumbled with my shirt looking for a smoke. I pulled one out and lit it. Rubbing my eyes, I thought, *where am I?* Immediately, it came back to me. Odessa, Texas. Looking at my watch, I saw that it was 7:05 AM. Mr. Williams would pick me up at 9:00. I had time to relax and have a coffee.

Mr. Williams came and picked me up at 9:00 sharp. *He is very punctual,* I thought.

"Good morning, Patrick. How are you all being treated" he asked?

"Great. How are you?" I replied.

"I'm having a great day," he said. "Did you have some breakfast?"

"Not yet," I replied. "Do we have time yet?"

"Well, I think so. It's only a few minutes from here to the clinic," he said.

We hopped into his burned-seat Cadillac and headed for the restaurant, making small talk as we drove. We pulled into the parking lot and went in.

"What do you all want to eat?" he asked.

"Bacon and eggs," I replied.

"I think I'll have biscuits and gravy," he commented.

I hadn't heard of this and thought it was quite out of the ordinary. Who was I to say anything?

"You know, Patrick. I think you are a pretty good fellow," he commented. "That cousin of yours, Bill … he sure likes his beer," he said grinning.

Chuckling, I replied, "Yeah! So do I".

"We went for supper when he came up, and he drank four beers with his supper. I paid the bill," he said grinning.

"You're lucky. You actually got away cheap," I replied. "Do they serve beer with breakfast?" I asked jokingly.

"Do you all have a drinking problem?" he asked more seriously.

"No, I don't," I replied. "But I do go hard sometimes."

"You know, that stuff ruins a lot of good people," he offered.

I hadn't thought of it as ruining anyone before, so I thought about it and replied, "You're right. It does."

We finished our breakfast and left for the clinic where my medical was to take place. We drove in silence. I was thinking about what he had said. *He is a pretty intelligent man,* I thought and then forgot about it.

Other thoughts began to surface. I had had a couple of hernia operations when I was twelve years old and feared that the medical might say I was unfit to work for them. I began to get worried, but I was there so I had to do it. Again, I was being forced to do something I really didn't want to do. *I'm okay to work in Canada, so why should anyone stop me from working overseas?* I didn't have to take a medical in Canada to get a job. *What if I fail the medical? What now?* Thoughts raced through my mind.

"Well, we're here. I will leave you here, and someone will pick you up later," said Mr. Williams.

"Thank you, sir, and thanks for paying for breakfast," I replied thinking, *what a nice person.*

I proceeded into the clinic and checked in with the front desk. The medical went well, and I thought, *you worry too much,* but still, I didn't like being forced to do something I didn't want to do. They did comment on the hernia operations and said I should be okay.

I was picked up and taken to Parker Drilling's school for well control. The class was informative, quite the same as any other well control course. I knew my math and equipment well enough that it was really a waste of time, but we were forced to do it if we wanted to work for the corporation. I thought; *corporate dictatorship. Is this what the world is coming to? People will be dictated to in order to make a living. Manipulation of words can make it sound like help. No, surely our people will not tolerate dictatorship.* I brushed it off as anxiety.

We finished the course on Friday at 4:30 PM. I got an advance, went out, and had a beer or two, visiting for a while. I had to leave at 11:30 AM the next morning, Saturday, for San Francisco, and fly out of there the same evening, but my destination had changed. They were sending me to Singapore. We sat around and had a few more beers.

After drinking the extra beer, I needed to go to the boys' room and relieve myself. While standing there, I observed a couple of local boys chatting and showing each other their pieces. They had handguns in the bar. I finished my business, took an about-turn, and walked out. Wow! Those guys meant business. It frightened the hell out of me.

I began to wonder if they really needed to have these kinds of things in the bar. They could hurt someone if provoked. *What the hell do they really need these things for?* They should pass legislation on these things and keep the public safe. Really, I could not see the need for these kinds of things, especially in the bar. *The power of choice,* I thought. *Guns used to hunt for sustenance is okay, but why in the bar? Who were they hunting?*

What were they hunting? I didn't feel safe. Only in America, went through my mind.

Why didn't the education system educate these boys properly? Maybe they would have used their choice wisely, left those things at home, and enjoyed themselves without violence on their minds. Maybe they felt a need to protect themselves because others were not educated properly. The excuses went on. I was still young, and I would learn. I went back to my table, finished my beer, and left.

I had a wake-up call for 8:30 AM, and my ride to the airport arrived at 9:45. I was taken to the Midland-Odessa airport. I checked in and went to have a coffee. Sitting there, I thought about the day. I would get to San Francisco, hop another aircraft, and head for Singapore. I had heard of it but knew nothing about it. *What is it like? What nationality are these people? Where is it? What part of the world is it in? Wow, Singapore. At least I will know my cousin Bill, so it won't be so bad.*

I heard, "This is your first call on flight so-and-so to San Francisco. All passengers please proceed to gate …"

I immediately picked up my bag and proceeded to the gate called out. I certainly didn't want to miss my flight. Soon, we were in the air and headed to San Francisco. It was a good flight, smooth without incident. We had a lunch and a beverage, and then we were landing.

Well, this is it. Thoughts were racing through my head. *Do I really want to go? Am I crazy like the people were telling me? What the hell are you doing?* I became sad and felt like crying. I was leaving my wife and child for two months and really hadn't had time to think about it properly. I hadn't been given any details on Singapore or for that matter, where I was to go when I arrived there. I was told that someone would pick me up at the airport. I had a couple of hours left to make up my mind. It was not too late to change my mind. My bravery was diminishing rapidly. I thought about Barb and Tiffany.

We touched down, taxied to the loading ramp, and filed off the plane. I went to the nearest phone and called Barb.

"Hello," she said in her soft, sweet voice on the other end of the line.

"Hello sweetheart. How are you making out?" I asked.

"I'm fine. I miss you," Barb said. "How was your school?"

"It was a breeze. Kind of a waste of time, but that's the way it is. So … are you still okay with me going overseas?" I asked.

"Of course I am. I'm looking forward to going myself. What about you?" she asked.

"Yeah, I'm okay with it. I'm going to Singapore instead of Algeria," I said.

"Really?!" was her response. There was excitement in her voice.

"Yes. Bill is over there someplace working out of Singapore. I will try to get in contact with him when I arrive," I said. "Have you talked to your mom?" I asked.

"Yes. I talked to her, and she is coming up to help me pack. She's going to be okay, honey. I think we just shocked her," Barb said.

"I am so relieved. I wasn't sure at first though. Honey, I love you so much," I told Barb.

"I know. I love you to. When do you fly to Singapore?" she asked.

"Well, I'm in San Francisco now, and I will fly in about two hours. I go to Taipei then to Singapore. It will take about sixteen hours of flying time, and I don't know how long we stay in Taipei. We cross the International Date Line, and I will lose a day. That is a bit confusing, but I will call you when I can from Singapore. Will you have enough money and everything to last you while I'm away? Just sell everything and use whatever you need to get here. I miss you already," I was babbling and wanting more reassurance.

"I'm sure it will be fun. I am looking so forward to seeing you in a couple months," she said.

"Well, honey. This is costing money we don't have. I better go or we will be too broke to pay attention," I joked. "I love you and miss you. Bye for now, honey," I said with a tear in my eye. I hated saying good-byes.

"Bye, honey, I miss you too. I'll see you in a couple months. I can hardly wait. I love you so much," she said. "I love you."

"Honey, I love you too," I said and hung up. A tear rolled down my cheek, and I wiped it off regaining my composure. I was nervous and a bit afraid.

Chapter Three

"This is your first boarding call to Singapore on Singapore Airlines via Taipei. Please go to your designated gate and proceed through the check-in," came over the speakers at the San Francisco Airport. I went to the boarding gate and proceeded to check in. I sat down and waited, striking up a conversation with the gentleman sitting beside me. I found out he was going to Taipei on this flight. It stopped there for fuel, and we would be held in transit for about an hour. We talked for a while, and then it was time to board for our journey. It was around fifteen hours to Taipei, and I wondered if there was enough fuel on board to make it. I hadn't been on a transoceanic flight before and hadn't seen a Boeing 747 aircraft before.

It was a big bird indeed, holding around three hundred people onboard when full to capacity. I remember reading the safety features in the pouch in front of me and thinking; *how do they come up with these goofy things to make you feel comfortable? If this thing were to fall out of the sky for any reason, all this crap would be for nothing. How stupid do they think people really are? If you were at 44,000 feet above sea level and the engines quit, what would you do? Jump? Where would you run to? I guess on takeoff, if your speed wasn't too great and something went wrong, you'd have a chance, but if you were off the ground at five hundred miles an hour and something happened, you probably don't have a chance.*

Taxiing to the runway, I observed the plane was half empty and a lot of seats were available. When we leveled off, I moved to where I could stretch out and fell asleep. I was awakened by the stewardess and asked if I wanted something to eat. I declined and went back to resting. It was a long flight, smooth, with the sounds of the engines purring steadily. The cabin was dim. Everyone was watching a movie now or listening to music; with their headsets on, oblivious to their surroundings. I woke up a few hours later, got up, stretched, walked to the back of the plane, sat down, and lit a smoke. I dragged on my cigarette and was lost in my thoughts when over the intercom the pilot announced we were crossing the International Date Line, explaining it was now the next day. Ironic as it may be, I lost nearly a full day of my life in a short time.

A few hours later, we were landing in Taipei for fuel. We were allowed off the plane and went into the transit lounge for about an hour and fifteen minutes. How good that felt to be able to walk around and stretch. Freedom!! It seemed like an eternity not being able to walk for any distance on that flight. Soon, we were back on the plane and headed for Singapore.

The flight was uneventful with everyone watching the movie. As we approached Singapore, all the people sitting at the windows were looking for the lights, probably glad the flight was near an end. As we touched down at Paya Libar Airport, a cheer went up and everyone started clapping. A few people sitting near me made the sign of the cross and looked up thanking God for protecting them throughout their flight. I too thanked God for allowing me the safe trip and the ability to make my decision to go there. It was not as pronounced as most, but I was just as thankful.

We filed off the aircraft as normal, the executives and business class first and then the cattle section last. I could never figure this out. They paid double the price for a little better service, boarding first, a slightly more comfortable seat, a glass of wine or spirits when waiting for the rest of the people to board, and they left the ground one millisecond before me and got a trinket worth about five dollars. What a cost! They arrived one millisecond before me and got off the plane first, but I still was just behind them through check-in at customs. I also observed them reading the newspaper, not smiling. Some looked at us like we were worthless. They didn't say hello and even asked if the curtain could be drawn so they didn't have to see us or so we couldn't see them. This is accepted and tolerated segregation of the rich and poor.

We got through customs and proceeded to get our luggage. To my surprise, some of it didn't show up. I had a duffel bag with winter clothes in it, because when I left Canada, I was informed it got cold in the desert in Algeria at night and I should bring some warm clothes. When I got rerouted, I didn't know what I was supposed to do with all these winter clothes. I couldn't afford to just throw them away. I spent two hours waiting and going through the steps with the local ground staff, trying to locate my luggage, but to no avail.

"We will put a tracer on it, and hopefully, you will receive it in a couple days," I was told.

"What about my necessities like toothbrush, deodorant, shaving gear, and everything else? My underwear and socks" I proclaimed.

"We will do the best we can for you," I was told and handed a small bag with essentials. "Where can we send your luggage when it arrives?"

"I am going to work for Parker Drilling. I have no idea where I will be staying, sir," I replied. I had no idea where Parker was going to put me up, and I didn't have Bill's address. I was at a loss. I was at their mercy.

I looked around and thought: *Where am I going to get something to wear and change into if my luggage doesn't arrive? These people are quite a bit shorter than I am. What size and how big is their large?* I began to chuckle but knew this was going to be a serious challenge. I didn't have a lot of money to spend.

I walked into the arrival hall and looked for anyone wearing a Parker hat, holding a sign ... anything. No such luck. Did my ride go because I was too long attempting to find my luggage? Did they even send someone to pick me up? It was 2:30 AM and hardly anyone was in the airport. I didn't know what to do, so I picked up my duffel bag, found an empty row of seats, sat down, and waited, a little upset with Parker Drilling for hanging me out like this. It was hot, humid, and muggy. I was wearing a long-sleeve shirt and was sweating profusely. I had just left cold weather in Canada, and my body needed to adjust to the climate. Taxi drivers hounded me for a fare, but I didn't know where to go or where they would take me. They were speaking in their language and laughing.

They sensed I was new and didn't have a clue what to do. They seemed to be taunting me somewhat. I was tired and just wanted to get a room to sleep … but where? I didn't know any names of hotels.

Putting my bag on the seat, I looked around and then lay down on the seat using my bag for a pillow. I thought about all kinds of things until sleep overcame me. I awoke at about 07:00 hours and tried to phone Parker Drilling's office. There was no answer. I decided to check out the airport and see if someone was looking for me. A taxi driver saw what I was doing and came up to me.

I asked, "Do you work for Parker Drilling?"

He replied in broken English, "Yah, me work Parker Drilling. This good company."

"Do you know where Parker's office is?" I asked.

"Yah, me know Parker office. You need go to Parker office?" he asked.

"Yes," I replied. "You can take me?"

I followed him to his taxi and jumped in but was a little apprehensive because I wasn't sure if this guy knew where I wanted to go. We were just about to get onto the motorway to downtown Singapore when he asked, "Where Parker office, mister?"

I looked at him in disbelief and replied, "Turn back to the airport and let me out." So he did.

He wanted me to pay him for our little tour of about two kilometers but I was standing firm. "You told me you knew Parker Drilling's office and promised to take me. You lied so I'm not paying you for a joyride."

"Oh, you muss pay. I am taxi," he replied as we were getting my bag.

"No," I replied. "You must not lie when I asked you about Parker Drilling."

I picked up my bag and went inside the airport with him on my heels, grumbling about me having to pay. I was about to sit down when I noticed a Singaporean policeman approaching him. I froze with fright thinking I was going to be arrested and charged with something I really had no control over. Many thoughts raced through my mind in the few seconds it took for the policeman to arrive on the scene. This taxi driver was hell bent on telling the cop how I had deceived him for a taxi fare. The policeman was very fair when I told him my side of the story and understood. He spoke English very well. He told the taxi driver to leave immediately with no further adieu or he would make sure he would not be allowed to pick up people at the airport. As the taxi driver left, rather hurriedly, the policeman smiled. I thanked him for his help and understanding.

I had learned something very important about that little episode. I had to make sure the people I spoke to from then on understood me clearly before I could accept anything. I also learned our media hype about other countries and people, was completely wrong. You can trust other people and cultures to be fair when problems arise. Not everybody is like the negative portrayal our televisions tell us. I would find out many things as I traveled.

I went to a pay phone and dialed.

"Hello, Parker Drilling. How may I help you?" said this voice in slightly broken English.

"Hello. This is Patrick Carriere. I am at the airport and have not been picked up yet. Is someone going to pick me up?" I asked.

"Oh! Mr. Carriere. I am very sorry. We forget to tell driver to fetch you. How long you wait for?" she asked.

"I arrived here at 2:30 this morning, and it has been quite interesting," I replied.

"You wait. I send driver right away and get you to hotel," was her response. "It takes maybe thirty minutes."

"Okay. Thank you," I replied trying not to sound too disappointed.

I sat and waited for my ride. *I guess things will be all right,* I thought. I was thinking about Barb and how she was doing. She had a lot of things to sort out before she could come to Singapore. Was her mother going to try to stop her? Was she going to come? Was I going to be by myself, and would I have another big decision to make? I started feeling the pressure building as all the doubts began to unfold again within me, and then the driver arrived.

"Hello, Mr. Patrick. I come to pick you up and take you to hotel," this finely dressed gentleman said. "I am driver for Parker Drilling."

"Hello to you too," I said. "I am pleased to meet you. How are you?"

"I am fine. Sorry no one pick you up last night, but they don't tell us and I not know," he offered.

"That's okay. I guess there was a little miscommunication problem. Are we going to Parker's office?"

"No, I will take you to Pink Flamingo. This is place Parker uses for their people. Are you ready to go?"

"Well, I have a small problem," I replied. "My luggage is lost, and I don't know where to get it sent to."

"Oh! I see if I can help you. Let's go to talk to baggage department and see what can do."

We went over to the lost and found area and spoke to the ground staff. He explained what I had just told him, and in no time, it was arranged that he would pick up my luggage and deliver it when it arrived. He gave them a phone number to contact him, and then we left.

As we drove, it appeared Singapore had quite a different way of life, and things looked awfully crowded. High-rise apartment blocks, full of people, lined the streets, with laundry hanging off of every balcony on bamboo poles protruding over the balconies. Bamboo scaffolding was crudely put together around work areas, with people going up and down these things with ease. Cranes pulled cement buckets up above, while people walked on the street below, crossing everywhere and moving around, with no barriers to stop them. It was quite different from what we were used to back home, but the job was getting done and no one was complaining. Dredgers were going at full speed, dragging dirt from the ocean, reclaiming land, and expanding the country.

Regulation and rule didn't seem as apparent or stringent. Traffic was moving fast, cars weaving in and out, horns honking with drivers jockeying to get to the front of the line, pulling in between and around other drivers if there was enough space to fit their cars at the traffic lights. A two-lane road became a four-lane, when traffic was stopped at a light. No one seemed to mind, and we saw no accidents. Even the police drove like this. I was completely amazed at the culture and how they operated. With twenty-one million people on a twenty-six-mile island, things were done differently. When the lights turned green, it was a speedway, traffic moving faster than I had ever been exposed to, bumper-to-bumper. Chuckling, I thought, *the road and lane divider lines must mean no parking.* It was great to be there. I felt a sense of relief knowing that I was going to be able to go to bed finally. It seemed like I hadn't slept in two days.

We arrived at the hotel and went in. The driver explained to the staff at the hotel that I had a reservation and booked me in. They were pleasant and very accommodating. "If you have concerns, please feel free to ask us for assistance," I was told. "Enjoy your stay with us."

I thanked the driver for all his help and professionalism. He left, telling me he would pick me up the next morning and take me to the office. I went up to my room, dropped my bag on the floor, jumped in the shower, and cleaned myself up. I had nothing to wear. It seemed like a long time since I had had a shower or a shave. I must have looked pathetic but … oh well I was there and had a feeling of some sort of stability. I lay on the bed and slept for what seemed to be a long time but, really was a couple of hours only. I awoke and looked around not knowing where I was for a brief minute, then remembering where I was, I got up and looked out the window. Singapore!

It was hot and humid. I was sweating even though I was naked except for my underwear. *I have to get used to the climate before I can go to work,* I thought. *This will kill me if I don't.* It's funny how the body reacts when coming from a different climate, with so much change in temperature.

As far as I could see from my room on the tenth floor, there was apartment block after apartment block. It didn't matter where I looked; there were clothes stuck out over people's balconies on bamboo poles. Many different colors of buildings and rooftops could be seen for blocks. All around these buildings were palm trees of one kind or another. Fan trees, spreading their foliage broad and wide, some as much as thirty to forty feet, in a big arch stood out amongst the other palms. Birds were chirping everywhere, making different sounds than the birds at home in Canada. People were moving around on the streets like ants, shoulder to shoulder, some bumping into each other, everyone accepting and tolerating it as normal. Elderly people and young people alike were sweeping streets and corridors everywhere, doing all kinds of jobs to keep their city clean and as a source of income. *What a bustling city with so much culture,* I thought. I turned around and saw a lizard scamper across the ceiling and then duck outside. The windows had no screens on them, and the louvers were left open. There was no air conditioning.

I got dressed, went downstairs to the restaurant, and ordered a meal ... and of course a beer. I sat there and ate in silence, observing everything around me. I was culture shocked yet impressed with the situation I had gotten myself into.

I met a gentleman from New Jersey who had been in Singapore for a while. I struck up a conversation and asked a lot of questions. He informed me about the lizards. I found out they were accepted by the locals as good, because they ate mosquitoes and other insects. I got to know them as chitchats because of the noise they made, sounding as just that "Chit chit chat." They were everywhere, in restaurants, running up and down walls, in the kitchens and in everybody's homes. If they were threatened, their tails would fall off and wiggle, so predators would stop and eat that portion while they got away, growing a new tail repeatedly for their defense.

It was a far cry from our perception of life and cleanliness. We would have had them exterminated to extinction. How sad.

Cockroaches as big as three to four inches roamed everywhere and the locals would walk past them as if they didn't exist. They were accepted and tolerated.

"People sweep the streets," my newfound friend from New Jersey said, "instead of collecting welfare, unemployment, and old-age pension for a living." I found out later this was true. There were none of these handouts as seen in our society. What a good idea! Very few machines were used to do the work, and people seemed proud, appearing to have a sense of being and worthiness.

We had about four or five beers, and I felt sick to my stomach. I went to the boy's room and vomited. *I have never gotten sick on a few beers,* I thought. *It must be the climate change.* I felt better.

I went back to my room and tried to relax, but my mind was working overtime. We are getting into another phase of advancement: technology. *What will that bring? What will we use it for? Will we have a better world? How will this control us?* Many thoughts were running through my mind.

Then back to the good stuff, my mind told me. *I should phone Barb and let her know I made it. No, I better wait until tomorrow. I will have more information to tell her.*

Satisfied with my decision, I fell asleep.

The driver picked me up and we drove through the streets looking for Parker's office. High-rise offices and apartments looked alike except for the clothes hanging out the balconies indicating where someone lived rather than worked. I arrived at Parker Drilling's office and met the staff. I met the drilling superintendent and was informed I would be going to rig 125 in central Kalimantan. My day push was Troy; but everyone knew him it seemed as Hap. I had no idea what he looked like or how we would get along. I hung around Singapore for a few days while Parker had a visa processed for Indonesia and just got to know my way around a bit.

I asked the staff for Bill's address, and they gave it to me. I was informed he was at work and wouldn't be home for a week or so and I would probably be in the field when he got out.

I left the office and headed for the Jockey Club for lunch and a beer. I looked around and saw many expatriate personnel sitting around and having fun. I noticed this one fellow watching me like he knew who I was so I approached him, because I too thought I knew him.

"Hello. Do you mind if I join you?" I asked him. "I'm Pat. Patrick Carriere."

"Well, I thought it was you. How are you? What are you doing in Singapore?" he asked.

"Going to work for Parker," I replied. "I should know you too, but you'll have to excuse me. I'm not sure of the name," I replied.

"John. John Peebles," he introduced himself.

Was I surprised? He hadn't changed a lot, but I never expected to meet him on my second day in Singapore. I hadn't seen him in quite a few years. We had worked on Gustavson rig 14 in the Arctic.

"Well, for Christ's sake," I replied in disbelief. "I would have never guessed I would run into you here. I haven't seen you in years. How have you been?"

"Okay, I guess. My wife and I split up, and here I am," he replied.

"Oh! I'm sorry, John," I said in disbelief. I went silent for a few seconds.

"You know this business. It's hard on women," he said smiling.

"Yes, I know," I said thinking of Barb, glad I still didn't have those problems.

We had a beer and chatted for a while, and then I left, flagged down a taxi, and hopped in.

"Where you go to, sir?" the driver asked me.

"To my cousin's place on Orange Road in Bedok… You know where that is?" I asked.

"Nothing sure, but I know Bedok. Maybe I find for you," the driver said.

"Okay. Don't drive too fast though. You people drive crazy," I said chuckling. I meant no offense, and he understood.

"Yes! Too much jappat, jappat! Everybody jappat!" he said.

I had no idea what he meant but laughed and agreed with him. I thought he meant crazy, but you will see I was wrong.

We drove in silence for a while, and then he said, "This Bedok. Now find Orange Road."

I started to pay attention to where I was and look for the road sign when he announced, "This road. Me know that. What house?" I looked on the paper I had and told him. He stopped, and I paid him twenty or so Singapore dollars.

I was walking toward the step when Tammy came out smiling and said, "I thought that was you. You look just like your dad with those glasses on," giving me a hug.

"Hello," I said smiling. "How are you? I just got my glasses before I left so I didn't realize what I looked like."

"Come in. It's good to see you. How was your trip?" She was inquisitive. I really didn't know her that well. I had met her in Canada a few times briefly, and that was all. I kind of felt out of place for a minute and then relaxed.

"Everything is good. How do you like it here?" I asked.

"Well … It's different. I've gotten to know a few people here, and it's getting better. The kids have adjusted okay. They are running around with no clothes on half the time because it's so hot here," she said laughing. "How long have you been here?"

"This is my second day. It's quite different," I said thinking about what I had seen the last couple of days. "These guys drive pretty crazy," I offered. "We'll have to get used to this."

She poured us some iced tea. We chatted for about an hour and a half, and then I announced, "I guess I should get going to my room."

"Where are you staying?" she asked.

"At the Pink Flamingo," I said.

She looked at me a bit bewildered, and I knew she didn't know where that was. They had been in Singapore for only two months and had not seen all the local attractions. "It's right downtown. Walking distance to the office," I said.

"Oh! We probably saw it, but I can't remember," she said. "Do you want to stay for supper?"

"I really don't want to bother you," I said.

"No! Really, it's nice to have someone from home to talk to. Stay if you like. I'll get some Chinese food or whip something up," she offered.

"Well, if you insist, then okay," I said somewhat hesitantly. I hated bothering people.

"I would like that," she said.

I stayed for another hour, ate, and then left. I really didn't know her well, but I liked her. *She was sure pleasant,* I thought. The kids had played, and there was a lot of hollering and chaos. They seemed to have fun for a while, and then all hell would break loose, and the crying and hollering would distract her for a while. She would come back and sit down as if nothing had happened. She seemed to tune out all of this. It must have been normal for her, and she was used to that. Tiffany never acted like that, probably because she was an only child. *They seemed to manage quite well for themselves,* I thought.

Once in my room, I phoned Barb and explained to her what had transpired. We chatted for a while about little things and then hung up, and I went to bed, falling asleep immediately and sleeping until morning. It was the first good sleep I had had since leaving Odessa, Texas. My biological clock had settled into the routine across the International Date Line and seemed to normalize, in tune to time across the pond.

I spent a few more days in Singapore, bumming around. I found a tailor who could make two pairs of pants and two shirts while I waited for my clothes to arrive. I had checked out some of the shops and found their large was too small for me, with shirt sleeves coming halfway to my elbow.

I got up at 4:30 AM and left my room at 5:00 to catch my flight to central Kalimantan, which left at 6:30 AM. The driver picked me up, drove me to the airport, and waited, making sure I was okay before he left. I boarded this aircraft that looked somewhat like a Lockheed Electra and sat by the window, looking out at the engines. The engines had Rolls Royce on them. Remembering Rolls Royce was a good manufacturer of this type of equipment I felt somewhat safer, but prayed silently and asked God to protect me from harm. The inside of the plane was old and somewhat deteriorated but not too bad. I wondered if they maintained these engines to the manufacturer's specifications. It was a turboprop aircraft so we shouldn't have too much of a problem. I was still a bit antsy, but I needed to work. I thought, *this is better than lying around in my room.*

A young woman boarded and sat in the seat next to me. Smiling, I said, "Hello! How are you" not thinking of the language barrier?

She replied in somewhat broken English, smiling, "Hello. How … ah … you? You go to Kalimantan?"

"Yes! I go to work for Parker Drilling," I said catching myself speaking just like her and feeling a little embarrassed.

"You from America?" she asked. She didn't pick up on my broken English. I was relieved. The last thing I wanted to do was cause a problem in a foreign place. I had had my scare at the airport when I arrived. That taxi driver had taught me something, even though it all worked out.

"Well, Canada," was my reply.

"Oh! Canada! I want go to Canada sometime," she replied.

"It's very cold there now," I said.

"Oh! How much cold?" she asked.

"About minus 20 when I left. Now, maybe it's minus 30 or 40. It gets really cold sometimes," I replied.

The plane started to taxi to the runway, preparing for takeoff. I looked around and saw people making the sign of the cross; some were kissing the medals around their necks while others were just talking. I said another silent prayer and tensed up as the plane thrust forward.

It's too late to change my mind now, I thought. *Just relax. It will be okay.* We got airborne, the plane rocking slightly as it left the ground. I convinced myself everything would be all right, knowing I was afraid and hated flying. If I wanted to work over here, I had to get used to it. I was fighting with my fears, finally relaxing for a period of time, and then we would hit an air pocket or turbulence and my heart would speed up. I would look out the window to see how close to the ground we were.

She must have known I was afraid and asked, "You no like to fly?"

I replied in the bravest tone of voice, "Its okay," and nothing else would come out.

"I no like to fly. Too much problem with plane in my country," she offered.

Didn't that make me feel good? I looked over at her, and she was smiling.

"What kind of problem with the plane?" I asked bravely.

"Oh! Too much people all the time, and sometime I stay back for two day waiting for airplane to take me," she said. "Sleep in airport and wait. No place to wash sometime."

I felt a relief this was her only problem with flying. I felt sorry for her. *But that's the way it is over here,* I thought. *We are so lucky we don't have this problem at home.* But I didn't know for sure. I hadn't flown much in Canada, and maybe I was naive.

"I'm sorry. How many people are in Indonesia?" I was inquisitive.

"Maybe two, three hundred ... how you say ... millon" she asked?

"Million," I said, correcting her.

"Yeah: Million! Too much people; in city, too much," she said in broken English.

I understood. I had seen the amount of people in Singapore, with the streets full most of the time. They had ten-foot sidewalks and were still getting bumped off into the street at times. We would try to dodge them in politeness, but soon, you learned if you didn't want to get hit by a car, you did the same. Walk straight ahead. It was normal to bump into each other. It was tolerated, and no one made a fuss about it. They would continue on their way as if nothing had happened. I noticed in the few days I spent there, with so many people, it was a way of life. They were always jockeying to the front of a line, speaking, at times, interrupting you when purchasing items. I was amused at this because they did this all the time. Many would think it rude, but if they wanted to get anything done, they had to be aggressive.

We were told to fasten our seat belts and prepare for landing. Looking out the window, all I could see was jungle. With no town anywhere in sight and the rain just starting, I became frightened again. Straining my eyes, looking for some clear ground where we could set this bird down, I saw nothing. We circled a few times and then were told we were in the final approach and to please ensure our seat belts were fastened. I checked my belt, pulling on the end to make sure I would not come out of it on the first bump. We were close to the top of the jungle canopy now and still coming down.

I tensed up and looked away for a minute, and then thump, bounce, and thump again. I looked out. We had landed on pavement in the middle of the jungle and were going pretty fast. The reverse thrust of the engines kicked in slowing us rapidly, and then the plane settled and taxied to the end of the airstrip. I said a little prayer, asking God to forgive me for what I was doing and thanking him for the safe trip.

I watched out the window as we turned around and couldn't see any control tower or airport. We had landed. We made it. That was all that counted. Soon, we stopped. A crudely built staircase was pushed up to the door of the aircraft, and we were told to disembark. We were filing off one by one, when my friend said, "Hope to see you again. Have good day."

I replied smiling, "You have a good day too. It's been a pleasure talking with you. Bye and I hope we cross paths again."

"What you mean?" she looked puzzled but smiled.

"Oh! Hope to see you too," I replied. "You have a good day."

I never did see her again, even though I did keep an eye out for her in my travel back and forth.

We entered the little building used as the air terminal. It was small, about a hundred feet long and forty feet wide with a concrete floor and sides about three feet tall. Poles, about eight feet tall, stood upright on the concrete floor along the outside and in the middle of the building holding up the framework of bamboo wood. A thatched roof of palm leaves hanging over the frame approximately two feet on either side held out the rain. It was divided into three sections with wood and cement divider walls that had not been painted or sealed for some time. The entrance was an opening in the concrete with a run-down wooden frame in need of paint and minor repair; the customs office was five feet inside. A desk and chair stood in the open, and passengers lined up to get their passports stamped for entry into Indonesia. The public was blocked off with a piece of rope strung across on two steel stands, dividing the customs and public access. People were talking and laughing while waiting for their loved ones and friends, who had just returned from the city with survival goods. Boxes of food and clothing were brought into the terminal by local workers and placed in the arrival area to be picked up and checked by customs. People were holding up signs with company names written on pieces of cardboard attached to a wooden stick guiding passengers to them. They walked back and forth hoping to find their passengers. It reminded me of Wile E. Coyote and the Road Runner from my childhood days. I spotted a Parker sign and waved at the driver. He smiled, acknowledging me, and patiently waited until it was my turn to speak to customs. Everyone seemed to be in harmony, enjoying themselves. I saw no rudeness toward us, pushing, shoving, or squabbling. Everyone was happy, patient, and seemed to accept us in this small community, unseen by many in our society.

I approached the customs desk and was greeted politely by the officer. The interpreter, holding a Parker sign, came to my assistance, explaining that I was going to work and would be there for three weeks. The customs officer accepted our explanation, smiled, and waved me through with no hassle. I picked up my duffel bag and proceeded to get checked out at customs, putting my bag on the table for inspection. The officer looked at it, opened the zipper, made a gesture as if he had searched it, and waved me through. He didn't look inside. *Pretty trusting,* I thought. *I shouldn't have a problem here in Indonesia.* I picked up my bag and entered the waiting area, looking around for a table. I found the coffee and poured myself some.

I looked around and then asked a man standing nearby, "Where do I pay?"

He didn't understand me so he smiled, shrugging his shoulders in a gesture of not understanding. The interpreter, who was at the customs desk, came to my aid. I asked him the same question.

He smiled and told me "Compliments of Borak Airlines and Indonesia. Welcome!" he said jokingly in broken English. I saw he meant it in a pleasant way and smiled broadly.

He was to drive me to the helicopter pad so I could get out to the rig, I found out. "I come back in few minutes," he said.

I sat down at a bamboo table with a couple wicker chairs placed neatly around it and set my coffee down. I looked around at all the commotion going on and smiled to myself. What a bunch of nice people. They didn't search or harass me and didn't try to take advantage of my situation, with me not speaking or understanding their language. *Instead, they welcomed and accepted me with open arms and politeness,* I thought, wondering what our country was becoming, knowing how negative our media was and how regulated we were.

Waiting for the driver to finish his visiting with people he knew, I sipped my coffee. I sensed it was different from what I was used to. It was very strong, and no amount of sugar could take the bitterness out of it, but I thought, *Thanks for giving me that coffee.* I was really appreciating how they treated me. I thanked God for giving me the opportunity to see this. I felt quite relaxed.

I was thinking; *I can't see what people at home are so worried about. There isn't any threat. People from Canada need to travel and find out for themselves. The media is too negative.*

"Okay, Mr. Pat. We go to heliport now. Your flight maybe one hour from now," the driver said startling me. I was deep in thought.

I smiled, picking up my bag, and asked, "How far to the helipad?"

"Maybe twenty kilometers," he replied. "No too far; maybe, thirty minutes."

We loaded my gear into the old Toyota Land Cruiser and left the airport.

It was still raining a bit, and the roads were somewhat slippery. We drove down a winding dirt road with barely enough room for one vehicle and no gravel on it. The Toyota was doing some sliding around. I reached for the seat belt and fastened it. The driver looked at me and smiled. "Safety," he said and kept on driving without buckling up himself. He probably saw no use for the belt as we couldn't drive very fast, but I saw a need. If we met a vehicle on this muddy, slippery road, we could slide into the ditch that was full of water.

We drove about four miles through forests of bamboo and palm trees and then came to a settlement with crudely built houses that stood high above the ground on pillars about eight to ten feet tall with stairs descending to the ground. The roofs were thatched with palm leaves in the same way the airport was, and the walls were built of boards running up and down, cracks visible between each board. There were openings for windows, and doors were hand built of the same boards with one-by-four supports to hold them together. Some windows had glass, but most didn't. A man sitting on a crude platform built around the front of his dwelling with no handrails waved as we drove by.

"My uncle," the driver offered in our silence.

Kids were dirty, playing around in the mud, laughing, and seemed to have no idea we were driving through their community. It appeared so relaxed, with nothing but time to visit and play. At first, I felt saddened for them. They seemed so poor, but as we drove, I relaxed my thoughts and accepted their lifestyle as they had accepted me. *These people have a wonderful life with not a care in the world, probably not knowing what goes on outside their community,* I thought. My mind was racing with all the positive things they had: no cars, no store, no chemical plants, no elevators, only natural landscapes. A lucky few had a horse tied to a bamboo tree.

I asked, "Why do you build your houses so high off the ground?" not knowing their reasoning.

"Too much rain; when rain too much, how you say ... *olar* ..." he said motioning with his hand zigzagging, indicating a snake. I understood their thinking.

We drove another mile through the settlement and crossed a bridge with a river flowing beneath. I looked down at the river and noticed along the bank women washing clothes on a scrub board, using sand to get them clean, while children swam.

"Indonesian washing machine," he said laughing.

My mind drifted back to home. Mom had used those same washboards not that long ago. They were not that far behind the times. *They sure have it good. Simple,* I thought.

What seemed like a long journey took only thirty-five minutes. He was pulling into the helicopter port before I knew it.

"This where we need go, Mr. Pat," he pleasantly explained in broken English.

"Right on," I replied. "I enjoyed the ride and found your lifestyle to be very interesting. Thank you for picking me up and helping me through the airport."

"No problem," he replied. "If you need something, Mr. Pat, you come get me."

"Thanks again," I offered.

We went into this little building, and the driver introduced me to the girl at the desk. She asked us to sit down and wait, informing us that they may not be able to fly the chopper to the rig. It was on standby at the rig site due to rainy weather. She got up and poured us a coffee, talking to the driver like they had known each other for years. They probably came from the same settlement. It was 11:00 AM, and we had lots of time to waste while waiting for the helicopter.

I went outside and walked around for a while. The jungle seemed to be screeching with noises. I had never heard this kind of noise, a steady screeching and humming that would die down briefly for a second, and then start up again with a vengeance. It sounded like crickets, but I had no idea, it being my first jungle experience. As I looked around, a frog jumped out of the grass and frightened the daylights out of me. I was nervous and didn't expect it. It was different from any I had ever seen, green and red with some yellow spots on its belly. It jumped again, landing on the side of the helicopter office, and then it started to walk up the side of the building effortlessly. I was amazed and thought I was hallucinating, being tired from the trip possibly. I questioned myself and brushed it off as a new experience, and then thinking about it, I smiled.

"It must be a tree frog," I said to myself out loud. I didn't know they could walk up the side of a building. Entranced with this creature as I watched it disappear under the roof leaves, I thought, *I better not say anything just yet. Maybe I am seeing things.* I kept my mouth shut for once. *I hate making a fool of myself,* I thought.

Just then, an insect I hadn't seen before came flying toward me. It was huge, and I, a big brave oil rigger, afraid, knocked it out of the air, and then bent down to see what I had discovered. It was about an inch and a half long and three quarters of an inch wide, supporting what looked like two horns on the bottom and one horn on the top of its head. It was black as coal with brownish legs sticking up and moving slowly like it wanted to right itself. Its beady eyes protruded from each side of its head. The devil crossed my mind, but I wanted to inspect this thing so I picked up a small piece of a twig and rolled it back onto its legs.

It stood up appearing dazed and disorientated, and then stumbled around in a circle as if trying to get its bearings straight. As it walked, I concluded it looked somewhat like a rhinoceros, but I wasn't sure what it was called and was definitely not brave enough to pick it up in my bare hands. *Strange shit here,* I thought. *What should I call this bug?*

"Mr. Pat, the chopper will be here in ten minutes," I heard from behind me. I turned around startled, as the driver picked up my bag getting ready to take it to the helicopter pad. I was caught up in the world of nature, observing everything in this part of creation.

"Okay! I will be right there," I replied. "Thank you." He was such a good fellow. *Look at him, he's got my bag and it's nearly as big as him.*

The Indonesian people are of a smaller build and not very heavy in body weight. Maybe it was because they ate properly. They didn't eat a lot of chocolate and candy like us. Most of their food was rice and chicken, free-range chicken. Everywhere you looked there were chickens, I had just realized after driving through the settlement. There were a lot of chickens walking around pecking insects and whatever else they ate. I hadn't noticed any grain bins or elevators. A small little shack in the backyard for them to roost at night was all I had noticed. From a distance, I heard a rooster crow. Did they even feed them grain? I wondered as the helicopter approached the pad.

The chopper landed. After cooling down the engines for a minute or so at full throttle, the pilot slowed them to an idle. He waved us forward. I approached, ducking lowly so I wouldn't get caught in the rotors, using the skills I had learned to approach a helicopter when I worked in the Arctic. I threw my bag on and hopped in. The Indonesian pilots were smiling as I jumped onboard.

Turning around with a grin on his face, one of them said, *"Salumat paggie."* From the expression on his face, I knew he meant hello.

"Hello," I said smiling equally as happy. "How are you fellows?"

They both nodded in a friendly gesture and said, "You Mr. Patrick?"

They always used first names, I observed. It must be a tradition. I would find out.

"I am Patrick. Is my bag okay here?" I had put it on the floor beside me.

"Bagoose," one said. I attempted to move it, and he repeated, *"Bagoose, bagoose",* gesturing with a downward motion of his hand. Again, I guessed it must be all right.

The engine sped up as I buckled my seat belt. We lifted straight up, above the jungle, and then moving forward slowly, we started to pick up speed. They were busy monitoring their gauges, while I looked out the window. We were very close to the canopy of the jungle. I was looking for monkeys and other wildlife I had heard lived there. The rain subsided as we climbed higher above the canopy. I could see jungle top for as far as the eye could see. We traveled for a few minutes and came over another little settlement with thatched roofs. People were walking around, along with a dog or two, but I couldn't make them out very clearly because of the altitude we were at. I looked out the window for about twenty minutes, straining my eyes to find a monkey, but it was not to be.

Off in the distance, I could see a bit of smoke rising from the jungle floor and thought maybe it was another settlement. The pilots turned to me saying we had about five minutes and we would be at the rig. I checked my seat belt, realizing I hadn't been afraid to fly in this helicopter. Strange, but I must have been concentrating on seeing a real live monkey in the wild for the first time. I spotted a camp and saw the drilling rig. "Parker Rig 125" was stenciled on the side of the doghouse. *This is where I stay for three weeks,* I thought.

Water was all around the location, and it looked muddy from the air. I could see the rig was sitting on a wooden pad covering the whole lease. Even the extra pipe and equipment sat on the pad. I observed a boom cat sitting behind the rig where the mud tanks were. I hadn't seen that much water lying around a rig in Canada. I hadn't realized the jungle was mostly rain forest. It rained a lot of the time. We came in straight ahead and landed on a small wooden pad. The engines were cooling down when I spotted a local man standing ahead of us waving his hands. He had guided the chopper in, I guessed. The pilot slowed the engine down and turned to me saying, "*Bagoose.* You get out now, Mr. Patrick."

"Thanks. Have a good day," I replied smiling.

The fellow who was waving his arms came up to the helicopter and opened the door to let me out.

"Hello. Stay down," he warned me.

I exited the chopper, ducking in the same way I had when I boarded, grabbed my bag, and walked away from the helicopter. The gentleman grabbed my bag from me and continued toward the rig. They put a huge effort into serving us, I observed.

"You Mr. Patrick?" he asked.

"Yes," I replied. "What is your name?"

"Said" he said; pronouncing his name sa-eed. "Welcome."

I always felt good when they said welcome. They were genuine when they said it, smiling and looking right at you. They all seemed very friendly and happy.

The chopper engines whined as they were brought up to full speed. Turning around, I watched it leave. *I've made it,* I thought, looking at my watch. It said 3:30 PM. The long day made it seem like it should be more like six o'clock, but I guess I was somewhat exhausted from the early start.

The rig crews were standing around looking over the handrails, observing me come toward the rig shacks. Some looked on in bewilderment, possibly because of my walk or whatever, and some waved in a friendly manner. They all seemed to be concentrating on me arriving. They looked like a curious bunch. I waved and proceeded to the rig manager's office, knocked, and went in. Said put my bag inside while he waited outside.

Chapter Four

I was removing my shoes when Troy said, "Come in. Don't take your shoes off."

"Hello, I'm Pat. How are you" I said walking across the little office, sticking my hand out to greet him with a handshake?

"Hello. I'm Troy. Everybody calls me Hap," he offered. "Would you like a coffee?"

"Yes! Sure, I'll have a coffee" I said.

We talked, getting to know each other for a while. "I guess I will be your night guy for a while," I said.

"Well, the rig seems to run fairly well, but we need to do a lot of work to it. The mud system needs a lot of work, so we're bringing more welders in on rig move to do that" he said.

"I guess that is a step forward. If the equipment doesn't work properly, then it makes it hard to get our jobs done properly." I was trying to be accepted as a leader and show diplomacy, I guess, but it was true.

"It sure does. We have been trying to get our mud system working for the last couple of moves but seem to run out of time and accomplish nothing. We need to repair the suction valves, the high-pressure jet lines, the mud guns, leaks, and just about everything else. We have a lot of work to get the rig up and running when we tear it down and put it back together. It's broke down into four-thousand-pound loads to move so you can imagine all the seals that need to be replaced just to stop the oil leaks when rigged up," he said relaxed but concerned. "How old are you?" he asked.

I must have looked young. "I'm twenty-four. I pushed tools in Canada for the last six months and drilled for two years," I offered.

He sounded tired and somewhat frustrated at the operation, but I thought we could help and get it right. I was young, new blood, and could possibly see things from another perspective. Troy was around fifty-two years old, I guessed, and graying a bit. He was tall, about six feet six when he stood up. When he walked, I would take two strides to his one and had to move pretty quickly to keep up with him. He seemed kind and genuine in his tone of voice, but something didn't seem right. He looked tired. I could tell he was working hard to get his rig in shape. We chatted for about an hour and exchanged ideas.

He had an American accent that sounded somewhat like the rest of the guys I had met from the States. He said, "You all go to camp and get some rest. You had a pretty long day. You can come out at midnight tonight, then we will get us on a regular twelve-hour shift tomorrow, from six to six," he said. "Said will take you to the camp and get you a room." He pronounced the name, "said." I kind of chuckled under my breath.

Said took me to the camp and made sure he carried my duffel bag. It was heavy, but he would not let me help when I offered.

"This no problem, Mr. Pat," he said.

We arrived at camp, and I settled into the room that was going to be home for the next three weeks.

The walk to camp took about ten minutes. A crudely built walkway, about four feet wide and made of lumber, had been built from the rig to camp. Posts were driven into the jungle floor, sticking up above the walkway about four feet, ten feet apart. There was water on both sides of the walkway. A rope used as a handrail was strung along both sides of the walkway and hung loosely down about a foot or so at the center between each post. Some planks were missing; some had been repaired crudely with whatever lumber was available, causing tripping hazards, but everybody was aware of and accepted it. Upon entering the camp area, I saw a huge deck supporting the camp shacks, which were made of fiberglass and ten feet by sixteen feet long. They were lined up forming the L-shape figure in which the camp was positioned. While I was observing my new surroundings, Said set my bag down on the deck.

The kitchen consisted of two of these buildings put together end to end and used for the cooking area and mess hall. It was painted blue and white, Parker Drilling colors. They seemed to fit in with the jungle somewhat but would have blended in better if they were green, I thought.

The shack I was awarded had a bed at one end and a closet about two feet wide with a small table attached. I had to fit all my gear into this little closet, along with my personal belongings, such as shaving gear and towels. The washroom, about six feet long and the width of the building in the center, consisted of a shower, a toilet, and two sinks. Another bedroom the same as mine was on the other end. We had about seven feet by ten feet in total to live in, after hours, when done on the rig. A wall-mounted air conditioner, installed in an opening where a window should have been, hummed and rattled, working hard to keep this uninsulated shack cool. Said went out and got my bag from where he had dropped it and set it down in my room.

I gave him a U.S. dollar for his hard work. He accepted it like he had won a jackpot.

"Oh! Thank you, Mr. Pat. You good man," he complimented, without knowing me for more than a few minutes.

"You're welcome. That looked like hard work," I said smiling and meaning it.

"For you, Mr. Pat, no problem," he said.

He was genuine in what he had said. Was I the only one who was treated like this? I didn't think so. They appeared to accept others with kindness and were willing to serve, without stipulation. I didn't know anything about their governments yet. In fact, no one seemed to talk about them. Was it not a concern or important?

The nationals were living in a compound built of rough lumber.

The ventilation consisted of a one-foot space below the soffit at the top of the wall, with a bug screen nailed to the framework. A makeshift door was used as their entrance. Once inside, I saw that a row of single beds with mattresses, pillows, and blankets lined the outside walls. Curtains made of old sheets shielded them from the kitchen area. The floor in the compound, constructed of rough lumber in the sleeping area, was strewn with clothing. The kitchen area where they cooked had a dirt floor. Inside the kitchen were a cook stove and a few dilapidated tables and chairs. About forty to fifty of them lived in this kampong.

Toilets, sinks, and a few showers inside a building that was refurbished to a standard slightly better than standing outside in the rain accommodated their hygiene needs. Everyone seemed to accept it and smiled whenever we went to inspect the camp.

Was it better than their home? I wondered.

The weather was hot, humid, and muggy. It was about ninety degrees in the shade. Tarantulas as big as three or four inches when stretched out roamed freely on the deck, scampering away when the lights were turned on or when we approached the kitchen for our daily bread. No one, it seemed, tried to kill these pests.

It is the price one pays for helping to supply fuel for all the cars, aircraft, and homes throughout the world, and complain as we may about the price, I dare anyone who complains to go and try this kind of work. Their attitude will change immensely when they too have to spend Christmas, New Year's, birthdays, statutory holidays, anniversaries, and the like missing their loved ones and wishing they could be there. No one thinks twice about paying twenty-five dollars for a liter of whiskey, two dollars for a half-liter bottle of water, or thirty-five dollars for a haircut every two weeks. I think we earned every dime we were paid; however, I agree, corporate and government greed has escalated the price of the commodity far beyond what it needs to be.

Not many corporate and government czars miss these types of holidays and are away from their families for extended periods of time. They can drive the best of vehicles, fly in the best of privately owned aircraft, eat caviar in the finest of restaurants, stay in the best of hotels, free of insects, and write off many personal costs through the tax system. Did they really earn this? Maybe a lot of the money we waste on selfishness can feed a lot of poor, hungry people around the world. Maybe we can spend a lot more on educating the people of our nation and the world to get along. Maybe we can spend this money on kindness and stop the killing fields of war and self-righteousness of each and every nation. *Will it continue to get worse?* My mind raced as I observed my surroundings.

I got myself a coffee from the kitchen and then went back to my room and started to unpack. I had been warned not to leave anything lying around as these people would steal it. I had a hard time with that because they treated me with the utmost kindness and respect. I thought there were times I lost smokes and a few small items in Canada from my room also. Already, I was learning to distrust them, and they had done nothing to me.

I put my things wherever they would fit and checked my bed for insects. Cracks around the door and air conditioner would allow bugs to get in.

I tried to stuff paper and old rags into the cracks, and when it felt safe, I locked my door and lay down. I could hear the crickets and other jungle insects making all kinds of screeching noises and listened for what seemed a long time. Sleep crept over me as I relaxed, and I didn't wake up until 10:30 that evening.

I got dressed and then went to the kitchen and had lunch before going out to the rig. What I had were leftovers from supper that night and a coffee. I sipped on my coffee on the deck and listened to the crickets singing. The noise from the rig could be heard at a distance. The banging and clanging of pipe being pulled out of the well and being racked back in the derrick indicated they must be pulling out for a bit. It was dark with just a few small yellow lights glowing in the deck, so the insects wouldn't be attracted. *Indonesia ...* I thought.

Barb wouldn't believe the noise out here. A steady humming was what it sounded like with the odd screeching noise.

A frog hopped in front of me on the deck and immediately caught my attention. I watched it until it disappeared through a crack. Insects flew around the lights. I had been inoculated for the diseases Canada had warned me about, such as yellow fever, diphtheria, tetanus, hepatitis, and malaria, and was taking some chemicals for malaria.

I went to my room, put on my work boots, found some gloves, and headed to the rig. It was time to get to work. As I walked through the jungle on that old rickety walkway, I was thinking of the pythons and creatures that could really hurt me. I was watching intently for the snakes I had been told lived in the jungle. I could hear tick, tick as I walked. I stopped periodically, concluding this to be insects hitting the walkway. I was brave and kept moving forward, telling myself that

I could do this. The banging and clanging from the rig had subsided, and I wondered if they were out of the hole.

Upon approaching the rig, I could see insects flying around all the lights, which appeared to be blocked out from time to time, there were so many. I could see bats swooping down, doing their acrobatics through the air, having a feast. I entered the office and discussed the operation with Hap and then told him to get some rest. I would look after things for the night. I went to the rig floor and met the company man and crew. The driller appeared somewhat agitated about having to pull the pipe out of the hole; he grumbled while inspecting the bit with the company man. It was worn out but all the moving parts were intact. The crew was cleaning the floor, preparing to run in with the new bit.

I helped them organize and make up the bottom hole assembly. It seemed to take forever, but it got done in about two hours. The insects were so bad we could hardly talk without them getting in our mouths. The stench on the rig floor was something I hadn't witnessed before, but this wasn't the time to ask. We needed to get the pipe back to the bottom as quickly as possible. The Indonesian men being small had a hard time lifting the heavy equipment we used to drill with. They used an air hoist for everything, which took longer, compared to the way we did things at home. They gave hand signals shouting excitedly with concern, so as not to hurt anyone. There was so much excitement I had to tell them to slow down at times. I didn't understand the language, but through the hand signals, I could tell they were saying up and down as the air hoist moved the equipment in these directions. The derrick man used a mule line attached to the air hoist to get the pipe into the elevators. It was time-consuming, but nobody got hurt, I thought after I left the floor.

It was frustrating. The driller cussed the crew out for everything, causing confusion most times. I could see he had a hard time with the language, trying to explain the procedure and work the crew. Some of the things he said were unpleasant and not called for, I thought, but said nothing as this was my first night. I would ask Troy if this was how they always talked to the crews.

I went to the office, poured a cup of coffee, and then stood outside, watching the pipe being run into the hole from a distance. The company man had gone to bed already, and I was responsible for the rig until morning. I was curious, wanting to know what the smell was coming off the rig floor.

I went back to the floor and started to inspect the rig. I wanted to know what equipment I had to work with and was making notes in a small pocket pad I had brought with me, jotting down things I saw that needed to get done. Looking around, I noticed insects about three to four inches deep, some still moving around in the derrick legs. I had found the cause of the stench. They were rotting; some had been trapped for a few days, piling up in the beams of the derrick. There were all kinds of strange-looking creatures lying there, such as praying mantises, rhinoceros beetles, rice bugs, bees, and spiders of every kind. I was amazed at the different kinds of insects I saw that we didn't see at home.

Big fans behind the driller and across the floor, called bug blowers, were humming constantly, with forty-mile-an-hour winds blowing out of them, in an attempt to keep the insects off the crews while they performed their duties. Life in the patch was different, I thought.

At about five in the morning, we reached bottom and more confusion. The crews were trying to get the pumps going and were having difficulties priming them. The driller was shouting from the rig floor, cussing at the crews to get the pumps going. I went to the mud tanks and observed very little mud in the suction tank. Valves were being switched in an attempt to fill the suction from another compartment. After about a half hour of playing with valves, we got the pumps pumping, reamed the last joint of pipe to bottom, and commenced drilling.

I walked back to the rig floor and asked the driller, "Do you always cuss these guys like that?"

"They're all brain-dead," was his reply. He was angry at them.

"Maybe if you explain things in a better way, more calmly, they would understand you better," I said trying to keep my voice calm.

"You stay a while and work with these assholes and you will get just as frustrated. They don't have a clue how to work these rigs, and we have to put up with this all the time," he said frustrated and angry.

"You don't have to put up with anything," I told him. "If this is getting to you, you can go home rather than put yourself through this kind of punishment." I was giving him a choice.

"Are you all running me off the first night you are here?" he asked defensively.

"No, I just don't think it's worth all the pressure you are putting on yourself. You can do things more calmly and try to work with these guys rather than yell and cuss them out all the time," I told him. "It's up to you."

He was adamant he did nothing to cause me to question him on his experience. He was frustrated, right, and had every right to be angry at me and the crew, so he thought. Rather than get into a conflict with him, I said, "Calm down. Everything will work out. How long have you been in here for?" I asked.

"Too long; it's been about three weeks already. I have no relief for another week, so you will have to get used to me," he said sarcastically.

"Are you taking this out on the boys? If you're angry because you have to stay, maybe Hap will let me drill and you can have your days off. I can drill on this rig and get to know it better if you like. I'll talk to Hap when he gets up." I was confident he was disgruntled and was being an asshole himself but tried to smooth things out.

"No," he replied. "I told Hap I would stay already."

"Okay. You will have to calm down though, and we will get along just fine," I replied. I had the ability to manage this situation with calmness and fairness. He calmed down and apologized. My first night and we had a problem. *Is this why the Singapore office warned me and said we need to make some changes?* I wondered. *Is he a buddy of Hap's?*

The crew saw what happened, and when I left the rig floor, some of them approached me and began talking to me. A couple could speak broken English and informed me the driller was like that constantly. The last night manager had quit and left because of this.

One of them, gesturing with his finger up around his ear, making circles said, "This man crazy." I chuckled at his motions and walked away. I would talk to Hap.

I lit a smoke and stood by the push shack for a while and smoked my cigarette. I thought about what the fellows had said, trying to think of a solution to end this problem. I could see this probably would continue and needed to be dealt with. How was I going to talk to Hap? What was I going to say? Was my intuition about him being Hap's buddy right? My thoughts were all over the place. Would I get fired if I pushed the issue? I decided I would let it ride and wait until I had a couple of shifts behind me. I knew I would have to prove myself first. It was 6:00 AM. Troy would be up soon.

Daylight was breaking, and I would be able to check things out on the rig when I could see. I was somewhat apprehensive about going behind the mud tanks in the dark. I was afraid of the snakes. Some were forty feet long, I was told, and although I wanted to see one, I was afraid of being strangled. I went behind the tanks and observed that they had been patched numerous times and were in rough condition. Small pieces of wood had been pounded into the sides to stop the leaks where holes had rusted through. Through rusted-out cracks, small streams of mud trickled out beneath. Gel was mixed with water and smeared over the leaks that appeared throughout the whole system, attempting to save our mud. I jotted this down and moved on. It was drizzling rain. The de-sander was spewing out liquid. Peering at the gauge, I found it to be too low and adjusted the valve. A pair of vise grips hanging off the valve stem was used as the handle. I peeked under the sub and spotted oil drums with oil dripping into them from the guards on the rotary chain, and then walked over to the pumps and found they were filthy and had not been cleaned for some time. Oily rags lay around, spills visible, with the pump rod cooling system flowing over. Oil was leaking from a seal on the bull gear. We had our work cut out for us, I thought, looking over at the tool rack, which was in disarray and needed to be sorted out. *This rig needs some TLC.*

I peered over at the rig office. Hap was sitting at the window sipping on a coffee. I walked over and went in.

"Good morning," I said with a smile.

"Good morning. How was your night?" Hap asked.

"I think we did okay," I said thinking about the driller.

"Good. What do you think of the rig?" he asked.

"I looked around a bit and wrote down some things I want to work on over the next few days," I replied knowing it would take longer.

"I am going to get the boys to clean today and maybe have the mechanic fix some of the oil leaks before we get in too much trouble.

The company man has been on our ass for a few days," Hap offered. "He's a pretty good guy to work with though."

"Where's he from?" I asked.

"From where you are, Canada," he said grinning.

"Who is it we are drilling for?" I asked.

"Arco," he replied. "They're from the States."

We chatted for a while longer and discussed our plan forward. I met the daylight driller and mechanic when they came to work. They were joking around and making comments about the work that needed to be done. They had just finished the rig move a few days ago and needed to catch up on some repairs. I yawned and told Troy I was going to camp for breakfast. "Do you want to join me?" I asked.

"I don't eat breakfast," he replied.

"Okay. I'm checking out and going to camp. See you tonight," I said.

"Catch a good sleep," Hap said.

I was walking out when the night driller approached the office. I closed the door, and he stood there for a minute.

"Did you tell Hap about last night?" he asked.

I replied, "No. I didn't think it was important."

"Thanks," he replied.

He had a smirk on his face. I thought, *He will talk to Troy, and then I can speak up on what happened. I wonder if he is a buddy.*

I left and went to camp, ate my breakfast, and was sitting outside sipping coffee when the night driller came up. He walked past me and said nothing as he went into the kitchen, had his breakfast, and then came out grumbling about his meal. *This guy has an attitude problem,* flashed through my mind.

I went to my room, showered, and got into bed. I was tired and fell asleep. I woke up at 2:30 that afternoon, feeling I had slept well. I got up, had another shower, and went outside. The jungle still hummed and screeched as I went into the kitchen, poured myself a coffee, grabbed a cinnamon bun, and went back out on the deck. It was humid and hot. The sun was shining, and there was no rain. It was a beautiful day.

I was sweating profusely, sitting around drinking my coffee, having a hard time with my body getting used to the climate.

I went back to my room, had another cool shower, got dressed for work, and went in for supper. It was a quarter to five. I wanted to get to the rig early so Hap could go to bed and get some sleep.

Hap was sitting there, and I could tell when I walked past his window he was in deep thought. He sat there looking out at the rig and had a blank expression on his face.

"Good evening," I said pulling up a chair.

"Good evening. Did you get a good nap?" he asked.

"Yes! Pretty good; I was up at two thirty though," I replied.

"The driller came in this morning and told me you were going to fire him," Troy said, concern on his face. "He's a good guy, you know."

"Really" I said, thinking, *A good guy wouldn't come to you and lie.*

"Yes," Hap replied. "He's been here for about a year now."

"I didn't tell him I was going to fire him. He was cussing out the hands and angry that he had to stay over. He complained he had to put up with these guys not knowing what to do so I told him he didn't have to put up with anything, showing him he had a choice. He could leave or put up with these guys. Basically work with them instead of cussing them out all the time," I said.

"It gets pretty frustrating trying to teach them when they don't understand English very well. I know his frustration because I speak the language and I've been here for a while. I still get frustrated," Hap said.

"I realize that, but I didn't say I would fire him," I said.

"I understand," Hap said.

"Is this why your other night guy left?" I asked disappointed in what I was just accused of.

Silence, then, "I don't know. I talked to the driller before about this problem and thought we had worked this out. I guess I will have to talk to him again," replied Hap.

I wanted to say more but decided to leave sleeping dogs lay. Thoughts of losing my job, not being allowed to do my job and this guy trying to cause problems and lying crossed my mind.

I would take whatever action I needed to fix this problem myself. My mind was made up on what I was going to do. *I can get it,* I thought, as I finished drinking my coffee and discussing the plan forward for the night. I went to the pipe racks and lit a smoke. I pulled my notepad out of my pocket and counted the drill pipe and drill collars on location. It was important we count this, knowing what was on location in case we had any down-hole problems. We needed to know where we were at in a predicament.

The driller came from camp and went to the office. I could see through the window Troy was telling him something, so I waited, looking around to see what else I should count. I looked at the crossover subs and put a protector on a pin end exposed to damage. *We need to straighten this bin up so we can see what we have,* I thought, writing in my notepad. Doug had taught me this when I worked with him in the Arctic. He was pretty sharp and tried to take care of his equipment. "You never know when you will need them," he told me one time.

The driller walked out of the office toward me. "You said you didn't tell Hap," he said.

"I didn't," I replied. "You must have said something this morning when I was having breakfast."

He turned and walked away. He was caught up in his own trap. *Why would someone make a story then blame me?* I wondered. Did he not like being treated fairly? I knew the problem wasn't over but felt confident he had learned. I would treat him fairly, but if this happened again, I would take action. The Indonesians were trying hard to get the job done and were being treated like nobodies. We needed to work with them respectfully and get some of my list done tonight.

I approached the rig calling a couple of the hands over and then went to the doghouse and held a safety meeting, discussing housekeeping. They had funny names like Mahiddin, Ammirudin, and Daud.

When the meeting was over, I asked a couple of them to help me clean the pump house. They willingly came with me and worked their butts off. We cleaned the pump house and sorted and cleaned the tools; then I asked them to clean the derrick and get rid of the stench.

One of them complained, "No use, Mr. Pat. In one hour, same, same," he said. This was how they spoke when trying to communicate. They had been taught by the expatriates. It was funny, and they got their point across.

"Let's try to keep it clean. It would be nicer to work up there without that smell," I said through the interpreter.

"Okay, Mr. Pat, we clean but you see," replied the fellow.

"Maybe every day we wash the derrick and get the bugs off," I said. They looked surprised that I would ask them to do it every day but agreed.

Things on my list were getting done during the day. The mechanic had fixed a few oil leaks, and some washing on the substructure was done.

The company man came out to see how the rig was operating. We talked for a while and then he went to bed.

After I lined the boys up, we started to clean the rig. I would help them for a while and then go for a smoke, leaving for an hour, letting them work away at what I gave them to do; then I would compliment them on how good the rig was looking. They would smile and give me the thumbs-up.

"*Bagoose,*" they would say.

I would reply, "*Bagoose.*"

They chuckled, complimenting me. "You speak Indonesian good."

We drilled all night and encountered no problems. I went to the rig floor and checked on things, periodically giving the driller a break so he could have a coffee and his smoke.

He wasn't very talkative but did his work and tried to get the men working with a calmer voice. He had changed somewhat, and the next couple of days went smoothly. I guess he was just trying to test me to see what he could get away with. I was giving him the benefit of the doubt. He did his job, and that was all that mattered. Personal vendettas were not taken to the job as far as I was concerned, and he was leaving for days off the next morning. *I'm sure he'll be all right,* I thought.

I finished my tour and was sitting having coffee on the deck when the driller approached and pulled up a chair. He wanted to talk, I guessed, as he hadn't said too much since the first night working with me.

He apologized and asked if he was coming back to the rig after days off. He wanted to know what my plans were for him, but I hadn't thought about it too much.

We had worked hard for the last few days with substantial evidence in our progress. We fixed quite a few oil leaks, repaired the seal on the pump, and cleaned up most of the rig. We still had the sub basket to clean as well as under the sub base. The crews seemed to jump at the opportunity to show us they were capable of working without being yelled at. The company man was happy and complimented us on our hard work.

"I have no problem with you coming back. You have done a good job, and you're not angry at the hands anymore. Tell me. Is it easier?" I asked.

"Yes! I guess I've got to control my temper," he said.

We chatted for a long while and then I went to bed. After waking early, I went to the kitchen, poured a cup of brew, and sat on the deck. The jungle never slept. The humming and screeching was very apparent. As I was sitting there, a monkey was creeping through the trees, getting closer to camp, so I watched closely to see what he would do. He came closer and closer, not afraid that I was sitting there. I didn't want to move and scare him. This was my first wild monkey, and I was curious to see it. He jumped down on the deck and stood fidgeting for a moment, as if to say, "Catch me if you can." He was silent, watching me intently, and then he moved closer to get a better look.

Just then, the cook came out from the kitchen, unaware I was watching this creature and scared him off. With a leap, he disappeared into the treetops, squawking as he left.

He was a small fellow about two feet tall and skinny. His face was lighter brown with a flat nose and dark eyes, which were very concentrated on what he was looking at. He had a darker brownish, almost black coat with a tail to match, about two feet long. Small ears protruded from the top of his head. He looked almost human, I thought.

"What you look at, Mr. Pat?" the cook said.

"There was a little monkey here," I said.

"Oh yes! Too many monkeys here in Indonesia. Some are very big not too far from here. Everyone too much scared of big monkey," he offered in broken English and then went inside as if afraid himself.

I sipped on my coffee and enjoyed the warm weather. I was getting used to the climate but still had to go inside an air-conditioned place often. It sure was muggy here all the time, with all the water and rain we were getting. We didn't have a day since I arrived without some rain. It seemed to rain every day around six in the morning or between five and six at night. Sometimes it would pour so hard the location would flood and things would float into the jungle. We were always picking up garbage and wood washed away by the rain.

We worked that night, and the following morning, the driller went on days off. The new driller came in. He was much younger than the one that had just left. He was pleasant and not so set in his ways. The daylight driller came on nights with me, and we enjoyed ourselves working together. He told me that the rig looked much better than it had in quite some time, and he was enjoying working more.

"It's nice to see things getting organized," he told me.

"Well, it's a team effort," I told him. "If we all pull our weight, we can have a pretty good operation."

"What do you think of the hands?" he asked.

"They try hard. I think most of our problem is they don't understand us and we get frustrated with them. We cuss them out, and who wants to work for someone who is angry and venting all the time? I think that is demeaning," I told him.

"Yes, Pat. But sometimes they get lazy and won't do anything also. That's when it gets frustrating," he said.

"Do you know what they get paid?" I asked.

"Not very much," he said. "Some make about sixty dollars a month and some make up to one hundred, depending what they do. The assistant drillers make the higher dollars so they're not too bad."

I thought about this for the night, wondering if I would work very hard for sixty dollars a month. I sympathized with the hands. That wasn't a lot of money in 1980, and they had families to feed. I wondered what their cost of living was and what it cost to buy a home in Indonesia. Some of these hands were sixty plus, probably wanting to take it a little easier but had nothing to depend on for their livelihood. I was inclined to think they were going to work till they passed on, just to feed their families. We were making forty-two hundred a month U.S. at the time, plus a 10 percent bonus if we stayed the full year, and we had no expenses at the rig. We ate for free. Our laundry was done for us. Towels, soap, linens, everything was supplied and cleaned. Even our work clothes were ironed. I couldn't believe they would take the time to iron our work clothes. Now that was service.

The camp staff made even less. They made forty-five to fifty dollars a month, depending on seniority. I asked Hap about this in the morning.

"Hap, these guys don't make a lot of money in a month," I said trying to find out some way, maybe, to get them more.

"I know, Pat. We tried to get them more, but the government has regulations on what we can pay them."

"Really" I couldn't believe what I was hearing. "They can do that?" I asked in disbelief.

"Yes. When they negotiate their contract, everything has the cost of labor included. They have people who supply the hands on a labor contract," Hap said.

I said no more but was thinking; *this is nearly slave labor. This isn't right. Slavery went out a long time ago. I'm glad Canada isn't like that. Yet* ... I added in my mind, *there is nothing one can do.* No wonder these people were thought of as lazy, I thought. I sure as hell wouldn't work my ass off for sixty dollars a month. My mind was racing. A thought came to my mind. *Will Canada get like that with corporate business?* A fear came over me, and I felt some disgruntlement toward the system I was working in. *That's not fair,* I thought. I finished my coffee in silence while Hap did his morning report.

"I'm going to bed," I announced to Hap.

"All right, Pat. See you tonight," Hap said.

As I walked slowly to the camp over the rickety walkway, my thoughts struggled with what I had just found out. These big corporate drilling contractors were drilling over here with cheap labor. Why? We were working for an American oil company benefiting from cheap labor—nearly slave labor. *This is unreal.* Why didn't they negotiate for a fair price on labor? I was getting paid well, so why couldn't we give them a little more? It disgusted me, but I had a contract to fulfill and I guessed I shouldn't get involved with the political side of this. Accept it and say nothing. That seemed to be the norm, already, in society. I was in disbelief when I arrived at camp, wondering, didn't they have a union? This was where a union would be of benefit. I wouldn't let it go. They still seemed happy though. Why?

Then it hit me while having breakfast. *They had two to three hundred million people living in this country. What did they have for jobs? How did their education system work? Was there any government assistance for these people? Was the Western world taking advantage of these situations under the guise of help and creating jobs? Did they approach their governments with a plan that would benefit them for power and the almighty dollar? All these questions were in my mind. Sure, it created much-needed jobs, I thought, but at whose expense? It was at the ordinary people's expense. If they wanted food, they would get barely enough to buy it and have to work for this amount. They had no choice. What a society. Greed! Exploitation! We were pulled into this, all of us, and didn't realize it. We had well-paying jobs, and that was all that mattered. We thought of nothing more than self, and I had a contract with the rules laid out on it.*

I finished my breakfast of bacon and eggs and went to my room. I was young and foolish. Why was I thinking like that? Just go to bed and forget about it, get some sleep, and finish your hitch. You only have a week left, and you will be on days off. I convinced myself that it was okay, and this was just the way it was. I would finish my contract and maybe if I proved myself, I would get another. I wouldn't talk about it. I still had a long time on my first contract so why upset the applecart? I was hooked with dollars and a chance to get ahead. What could be so wrong with that?

I went to bed, exhausted from all the thinking I had done. I was more exhausted from thinking than I was from physical work and fell asleep immediately.

When I awoke, it was late, around five thirty. I had to be at the rig by six. I jumped out of bed and dressed quickly without taking a shower and left without supper. Proceeding down the walkway to the rig, I arrived ten minutes before I started my shift. Hap was sitting there waiting for me.

"Good afternoon," he said looking at me with concern on his face. "You must have slept in. You're always here at five thirty. Were you tired?"

"I must have been. I sure slept hard," I offered sheepishly.

"That's quite all right. Sometimes you need that," he said grinning. I knew what he meant. The climate and hard work was wearing me down, and I was probably getting bushed.

We poured a coffee and sat down, remaining silent for a few minutes. I had to get the cobwebs out of my head. It was hot and muggy, and I felt like I had been partying for three days, I had slept so hard.

We discussed the plan forward and chatted until about six thirty. He was going on days off in the morning and wanted to make sure we all were on the same page before he left. His relief would be here in the morning, and he wanted everything handed over smoothly. He was a good fellow, I thought to myself. He seemed to be fair, telling me once, "There is no such thing as can't. If you can't get it, you can't stay."

He was right. There was no such thing as can't. *You can do anything you want if you think positively. Can't is such a negative word. Remember when you were trying to leave Canada? Well, you're here, aren't you? You're doing your best, and it seems you're being accepted.* I was showing myself a lot of confidence and of course, a little pride. I was happy to be there. I had learned so much in the first hitch, I thought.

My thoughts drifted to home and Barb. How were they doing? I hadn't spoken to her for nearly three weeks. Was Tiffany all right? How was her mom doing? What about her dad? She and her dad were pretty close and had the same temperament. Then it was back to what I was hired to do, trying hard not to let home and work collide. I chose to do this, and Barb chose to accept it, so we lived by that rule for the time being.

We worked hard for the next week cleaning, painting, repairing leaks, and so on. The other rig manager came in and seemed to be happy with what was going on. He worked with us to keep things going and in the best repair we possibly could. We were short of parts but made do. That was what we got paid the big money for.

We were very careful not to hurt anyone. There were minor cuts and bruises, a black fingernail here and there, but all was going pretty well. We were in the jungle with a lot of humidity and could not afford to hurt anyone severely. Infections could set in very quickly here, and hospitals were few and far between. We had a medic who could repair us if small treatments were needed.

I suddenly realized I had worked here for nearly three weeks and didn't know where the hospital was. I guessed the chopper pilots would know if an emergency arose. We looked after the boys as best we could and were careful not to have an accident. We had a big responsibility to take care of, trying hard to accept and implement safety measures, and we were very serious about that responsibility.

This was my last night, and then I was free. I could go, feeling

I had done the best I could. I slacked off and let the boys do their thing, trusting them to do a good job. They did their jobs with pride, showing us they were responsible, given a chance. The rig ran smoothly, everybody busy tripping pipe to change the bit. This took up most of the twelve hours of my last night. I was anxious to get out of the jungle and back to Singapore. I needed a break. I packed my bag around five in the morning and was to leave at seven, weather permitting. It wasn't raining, so I figured I should be able to get out.

I was at the helicopter pad by six thirty, ready to go. The boys had just finished changing into their uptowners and were approaching the pad, smiling. They too were going on days off, happy to be homeward bound to see their families. There was a lot of chatter, laughter, and fun, teasing each other, some wrestling around, I observed. It was like a bunch of kids playing around, but these were grown men, just happy to have a break. They had worked hard and deserved it, I thought.

"Mr. Pat, you go to Singapore today?" one asked.

"Yes, I go today," I replied.

"You have madam in Singapore?" he said.

"No. My madam still in Canada," I replied.

"She need come soon or maybe you get new one," he teased.

"Oh! Maybe," I said jokingly. "My madam is coming to Singapore in one month maybe."

"Bagoose," he said smiling. "If you need madam, you come to my village. I find you one." He seemed to be the joker of the bunch. Everyone laughed.

They were genuine and fun, no different than we were. Maybe I could understand them better because of the way I had lived as a child, and they, sensing that, accepted me this first hitch. I was happy to be there, not raising my voice to intimidate anyone most of the hitch. There were a couple of times that I had to get firm, when they refused to do a task or request right away, but eventually, it would get done, and really there was no need to be disrespectful. After all, they only made sixty dollars a month. *How could they survive so cheap I wondered in bewilderment?* I still had a lot of thinking to do. I would learn, I thought.

The chopper came, picked us up, and flew back to the pad where I came in from. The same driver I had when I arrived drove me to the airport while the hands returned to their homes, and I was back in Singapore that same evening. I checked in to the hotel, put my bag down, showered, and then lay down, attempting to sleep. Sleep eluded me because I was overtired and hot, so I picked up the phone and dialed.

Chapter Five

"Hello?" It was Bill. He had another week off yet, so maybe we could get together for a couple of beers.

"Hello, Bill," I said. "How are you?"

"Okay. How are you?" he said.

"My first hitch went all right. Quite different than Canada," I said.

"Where you staying?" he asked.

"Here at the Flamingo," I replied.

"Why don't you come and stay here? Parker is talking about moving us to Australia, and there's no use you getting a place. It's pretty expensive here, and the guys are talking about going home if we don't get something sorted out. We can make just as much at home," he said.

"I will think about it. I'll come over tomorrow, and we can talk about it," I replied. "What is your address again?" I asked.

"I don't know. It's just off Orange Road in Bedok. Just tell the cab driver and they can find it," he replied.

"Okay. I'll see you tomorrow," I said.

"Why don't you come up tonight?" he asked.

"I just got in," I replied. "I'm tired and think I'll just go to bed."

"Okay. See you tomorrow. We'll have a couple beers. Bye."

I hung up the phone and tried to get some sleep. Thinking about home, I tried to call Barb and couldn't get through. The phone lines were terrible at times, and communication was difficult when going through the operator, because they had difficulty understanding us. Everything was Chinese, and most spoke little or no English. Whenever I called the operator, they would say, "Canada. Oh, I try for you. What number?" and then return saying, "There no connection to number," or the communication lines would be down. If you got through, the lines would crackle with delays of voice transmittal. Many times, we would be speaking at the same time, causing confusion. It was difficult, but we were in their country and had to deal with it. Eventually, we learned to wait a few seconds before speaking and would tell whomever we called to do the same thing. The system worked with patience, and we had to learn to use it properly.

I fell asleep and woke early the next morning feeling rested and ready to face the day. It was my first days off, and I wanted to explore Singapore, so I went to the office, picked up my check, and cashed it. Surprised at the size of their currency, I tried to fit it in my wallet, but I couldn't. It was a lot of cash, nearly double the face value of the U.S. dollar. I was rich!

The thousand-dollar bill was at least six inches wide and the length of a sheet of A4 paper. The five-hundred-dollar bill was three quarters that size, with the rest slightly larger than our money. It had to be folded a couple times to fit in our wallets, creating a bulge in our back pockets bigger than Dallas, but we were happy. We had fluse. That was what they called their money, pronounced like "floose."

I flagged a cab, gave him Bill's address, and he drove, weaving in and out of traffic like there was no tomorrow. We obeyed all traffic laws, going around cars stopped at a red light, and squeezed our way to the front of the line. Lined up five across at the lights on a two-lane road, obeying the divider lines that meant no parking, we waited for the light to change. When the light turned green, we were gone like a bat out of hell, steering in front of the cars that were five feet behind, not checking left or right and without any turn signals. The chrome mirrors added character to the vehicles and were there for decoration. You got more money for your car when it was traded in if it was decorated.

Just hang on. We'll get you there. Police waved at us a few times as we passed them, because we were doing everything legally. Man, those guys drove fast in that city, but we saw few accidents. Defensive driving was the norm, and everyone seemed to watch out for each other. Cars honked to let someone know they were there, taking their lane without hesitation, in a hurry to be at the front; people smiled as you cut them off. Everywhere there was honking continuously, like the jungle insects, humming and chirping.

I read a small piece in *Time* magazine once, saying a car had to be warranted for two million honks in China. They were getting their money's worth here. It was fun to see, and we soon got used to it. They were free and didn't worry about getting a ticket for every little infraction. The police did the same.

We arrived at Bill's in record time. Rolhani was sweeping off the front porch and smiling when I approached their place. She was a maid, who looked after Bill's place and others, at her leisure, it seemed. She would come in two or three times a week to clean, do laundry, and babysit when asked. She seemed to be happy having a job. She had a family of three or four kids. At times, she brought the younger ones to work with her. They had no daycare centers, but it seemed to work. Her children played with Bill's children, having fun. It was simple and cost nothing. She would ask if they were hungry and then make lunch for her children and Bill's, as they all played until she called them. Things seemed to work in harmony. She was respected for her work and who she was, without belittlement. When things were funny, we all laughed. Life was simple and good.

Bill came out smiling and stuck his hand out, "Hello. Good to see you."

"Good to see you too. Hello, Tammy. How are you doing?" I asked.

"Everything is going great," they both said. "How about you; how was your first shift?" They were laughing, interested, and enjoyed having me come over. It's always nice to see someone from back home, no matter where you are.

We spent the day sitting around telling jokes and having a few relaxing beers. We ate. We chatted. We laughed, having fun with our new adventures, saying things in the new language we had been learning. We had a long way to go to perfecting it, but we were learning. Rolhani would correct us without condemnation and then laugh when we pronounced things wrong, even when our words meant something else. All the kids were in the yard playing, and then all hell would break loose, with loud hollering and crying. We all turned our attention in the direction of the commotion, settled things down, and resumed what we were doing.

Rolhani finished cleaning and then went home. We loaded the kids up in a taxi and went out to a little restaurant and had supper. Bill and Tammy wanted to introduce me to some "good food," as he told me.

The restaurant, a dingy little place, looked dirty and unsanitary by our standards. Chitchats were running up and down walls, in the kitchen as well as the restaurant, chirping away as if to welcome us. The lights were low, so insects wouldn't get too plentiful, I assumed. Watching this with the greatest intensity, I observed a chitchat having his supper of insects without disturbance. The tables outside were made of rattan and wicker, the surface coloring worn-out from use, but no one seemed to mind. They were in there to eat, not to judge the place on appearance. The Chinese decor was noticeable, with paper fans spread out; electric lanterns of many different colors were strung throughout the open areas. A huge tarp with a hole in the center for ventilation, looking like an umbrella with wooden laths slanting outward braced to wooden poles on the outer edges, composed the roof, with open-air sides for our views. People didn't move or notice when we walked in and were seated at our table. If they did, it didn't show. They kept talking and eating their meals, some using chopsticks while others used forks and fingers. Each dish in the center of the table seemed to have one item on it, and people were passing the offerings to each other like they would in their own homes. There was none of the one plate per person with everything strewn on, like we have in Canada. They seemed to take pride in their service and presentation.

A waiter came to our table within seconds of us sitting down and brought us a menu. Not knowing what to order, I told Bill and Tammy they could do the honors. I reviewed the menu quietly, observing frog legs in oyster sauce or in soy sauce with ginger root; beef, chicken, and pork chow miens; sautéed vegetables with beef; ginger beef; ginger pork; hot peanut sauce; fried rice with ham; all of it looked good. Then I saw Bintang and Anker. "Let's order one of these," I suggested laughing. We got our beer and continued looking at the menu.

The waiter came back smiling and asked, "You weady to oda?" They had a hard time saying *r*, which made them that much more unique. I always smiled when I listened to them. They were so genuine.

Without hesitation, Bill requested a large order of frog legs and oyster sauce, while Tammy continued with the rest.

Bill said, "You've got to try the frog legs," motioning with fingers pressed together and brought to his mouth, making a kissing sound as he motioned away in an upwardly direction saying, "They're good." He didn't have the finesse I saw on television when watching Dean Martin.

"Whatever you like, Bill," I said laughing. "I'm for anything. I've tried the big green frog's legs at home, and they were good too. We fried them in butter though."

Tammy laughed the hardy laugh she always had when she really thought something was funny. I guess it was the way I said it, probably sounding like a hillbilly. We all had a good laugh.

We sipped our beer and chatted, while waiting for our meal. We were relaxed and sat back like we had it made. I was in awe of their lifestyle. I noticed the floor was dirt, no cement or tile, and people accepted that. They were just trying to make a living and having fun with it, I thought.

Waiters were running, nearly tripping over themselves, trying to please the public they were serving. All were smiling and joking around with customers. I don't know why, but *life is so simple* always crossed my mind.

Our meal served, we helped serve the kids and then helped ourselves. I took a frog leg and popped it in my mouth, curious to see if they tasted like the ones we tried at home. We were always told not to eat that kind of stuff, and I could never figure out why. I guess it was degrading to do that, I thought. I didn't know. We ate hungrily, enjoying every bite we took. The kids were always reaching for more and ate everything. They weren't fussy eaters from what I could see and sure looked healthy, for being there for three months already. I didn't see too much weight loss on Kimmy. When we were done, we had one more Anker and paid the bill. I couldn't believe we got all that for twenty-five dollars. What a deal. It was cheap to go out for a meal.

I stayed overnight at their place, drinking beer until the wee hours of the morning. Bill phoned the grocery store when we got back to his place and had another case of twenty-four brought over by the local grocer, just in case. We got up the next morning feeling a little hungover, but smiling. We had had a good time.

I asked Bill, "How do you make a phone call here? I seem to have trouble going through the operator."

He replied, knowing the problem, "You can use this phone. You just have to dial these numbers, your area code, and number. It will automatically go through. Be sure to wait a few seconds before you reply though, otherwise it gets all jumbled up."

I called Barb and was happy to hear her voice. We talked for a while, and I found out what I needed to know. I told her about living with Bill and Tammy and that we might move to Australia shortly if the deal Parker was trying to make went through. We hung up, and I had a lonely feeling for a while but ... it was my choice. I told myself that Barb would be coming up next time I came out of the jungle. Four more weeks and I would see my darling. Her mom had accepted us going overseas and was now fine Barb told me in our telephone conversation. I was happy. *Sometimes one doesn't realize how much pressure is put on others,* I thought.

"Bill! What do you say to these taxis to make them go slower?" I asked as I was leaving.

"Jappat," he said immediately.

My taxi arrived, and I hopped in, telling the driver to go to the Flamingo Hotel.

"Now *jappat,*" I said, confident I had requested we go slower.

He looked at me and smiled, so I thought we had it under control.

We pulled out from Bill's and headed to the Flamingo to pick up my belongings and check out.

We were hell bent on breaking the record of getting downtown the quickest, really flying when I said, *"Jappat, jappat!"*

"I am too much *jappat,*" the driver said laughing.

Realizing Bill had fooled me, I motioned with my hand to slow down, laughing.

When I arrived back at Bill's place, I told him about the trip downtown. He laughed the rest of the day. I agreed to pay half the expenses of living with them. They gave me a room to sleep in, and the house was as much mine as it was theirs, a good deal for both of us, as it was expensive to house yourself there. Rent was fifteen hundred U.S. a month, along with food, electricity, water, television, and so on. We had to have a license to have a television. It seemed odd, but actually it was the same as in Canada, with having to pay for cable. If they checked and you had no license, they would confiscate the television. They too had some Western values.

We spent the next couple of weeks hanging out, going back to the same place numerous times for a meal, drinking beer, and water-skiing. We went to the Big Splash with the kids where they had fun, along with us big kids, sliding down the waterslide. Time passed quickly, and then Bill had to leave for work. He was working in Balipappan, drilling on rig 190. I stayed for another week at their place, bumming around, not knowing what else to do. I went to the Jockey Club in the afternoon and came back early, usually before it got too dark, not trusting myself to know where I was going at night.

I worked my next hitch, moved the rig with helicopters, the time going by fast. I had Barb on my mind a lot of the time wondering, "Who was she flying with? What route would she take out of Canada?" I hadn't asked her. *How stupid,* I thought, but with all the excitement, I had forgotten. *I hope she brings her summer clothes. I told her how hot it was, didn't I?* I was questioning myself.

I started to laugh. It reminded me of my mother. "As long as you don't start answering yourself, it will be okay," she used to say. She was a good woman with a big heart.

Moving the rig by helicopter was pretty interesting. I had moved a diamond drill with an old Sikorsky once, but not a rig. I had to learn about hand signals, slinging loads, safety issues, and even to tie my hard hat on. It would blow off every time I would get under a load to sling it.

We were using what was called a sky crane that was supposed to haul eighteen-thousand-pound loads, making it easier to break the rig apart in larger sections and put it back together. Parker Drilling wanted to try and see if there were any cost savings. With the smaller choppers, it would take a month of labor-intensive work, breaking down the rig into four-thousand-pound loads with four helicopters hauling, and then rigging it all back up. They had a good idea, I thought, but we would see when the bills came in, as the sky crane was expensive to use and operate.

The chopper was an awkward-looking thing, resembling a huge steel beam with a bubble on the front, propeller and engine on top, and a rotor to keep it straight at the rear. It sounded like a jet engine when it started up. The propeller, probably a hundred feet across the top when it landed, looked like something from space. The pilot operated it from the cockpit, sitting forward, and held it from spinning out of control, while hovering above us, while another pilot, I guessed, sat in the bubble facing the rear, operating a winch to lift the load. It hovered about two hundred feet above the jungle, steady, when tying on to a load. The rear pilot would wait until given the signal, and then start winching the load upward on a cable, about an inch and a quarter thick. The downward wind at the tips of the rotor blades reached a hundred and twenty miles per hour; I was informed, finding out real fast when the load started to leave the ground. Cardboard, plywood, rags, you name it, came free, rising upward and blowing all around us. I tried to control some of the objects flying around but was blown to the ground instantly. I lay there until the load was winched up above the jungle canopy and the chopper moved forward, gaining altitude. I shielded my head with my arms, praying nothing would hit me. I hadn't seen anything like it, learning a good lesson to get out of harm's way quickly and stay back. I was unscathed. We scrambled putting stuff away before the pilots returned for the next load. They were serious at the safety meeting when they told us to make sure there was nothing that could end up flying around before starting the move. After each load, they returned, landing for fuel and taking on just enough for the round-trip to and from the new location, which allowed for bigger loads. When they returned, the pilots gave us supreme hell for that first load, ensuring we were prepared for the next one. They were right in doing so, but we didn't realize how much shrapnel would get up into the air. It could have blown high enough to get into the propeller and crash that thing, but all in all, we moved the rig in good time and rigged up.

On this particular move, we had more to contend with than just the rig. Some of the jungle people had moved in around the location while we drilled and built houses from the cardboard and wood pallets we discarded. Mothers nursing young babies, young fathers, children, aunts, and uncles were around the rig for the duration of the drilling the well. Some were given food and soap from the camp and had it pretty good. They were friendly and considerate of us all the time, but when the rig moved, we found we had a problem.

We blew down their houses with the helicopter, and they wanted compensation. The chiefs were adamant we pay for the structures they built with our discarded materials. We disagreed, but the local governing bodies filed a lawsuit for their homes and plantations of rubber trees.

Even though there were no plantations or rubber trees for miles around us, the company, I guessed, did something for them and calmed the situation.

I flew back to Singapore where I would have a couple of days by myself before Barb would arrive. She had told me she was flying Japan Airlines, staying overnight in Tokyo, and then flying to Singapore the next day. I was excited and happy she was finally going to get here, planning to pick her up at the airport and take her for Chinese food, if she wasn't too tired.

She arrived about four in the afternoon. I was waiting for her at Paya Libra Airport, excited and happy. I had missed them both and wanted to give Tiffany a big hug. She came through customs and looked like she'd had a long flight. We hugged and kissed, and then I gave my daughter a big hug and smothered her with kisses.

"Tiffany was quiet and good all the way," Barb offered, as if she would have told me otherwise. She was always with her and praised her in front of people, whether she was good or not. She had some problems with popping her ears when reaching altitude on takeoff and declining when landing, but most kids do. They don't seem to understand how to pop their ears, but sometimes, it's difficult for adults too.

"What would you like to do, honey?" I asked Barb.

"Could we just go to the house and relax?" she asked.

"I guess so," I replied, knowing what she meant.

I took them to Bedok, and we got settled in. I began telling them about the little lizards and all the other little encounters I'd had in Singapore, warning them, knowing Barb would have a difficult time off the start. At about nine o'clock that evening, after we had had something to eat, Barb wanted to go lie down. It was a long flight, and she hadn't gotten too much sleep. She had somehow gotten mixed up and took the wrong limousine, ending up at the wrong hotel. They got it sorted out, and the limousine took her to her own hotel, at no charge.

"The people in this part of the world are sure nice and try to accommodate you," I offered.

"Yes, they sure do," she said yawning.

We were crawling into bed when from nowhere; a chitchat appeared on the ceiling of the bedroom.

I told her, "Look!"

"Get rid of it. I'm not going to sleep with that in our room," she said smiling but nervous. I could see she wasn't real comfortable with it so I tried to make her feel better.

"They're all over the place here. They don't hurt you, honey," I said.

"Are you sure?" She doubted me already.

"I'm sure," I said. "Their tails come off if they feel threatened," I offered, trying to reassure her.

"Well, okay," she said as she watched that little creature for a while.

She put her pajamas on and crawled into bed. She was tired. Tiffany was already in bed sleeping.

We no sooner turned out the light and got into bed then, plop. Right between us landed this little chitchat on our pillow.

We jumped up, and she said, "I'm not staying here." She was frightened of that little creature. I was laughing but couldn't find it.

I tore the sheets off the bed and shook them out, but they moved so quickly, it was gone. Laughing, I said, "Honey, you'll get used to them."

She was laughing now and said, "I'm not so sure of that" and then went back to bed.

The next morning, we got up, made coffee, and sat around, chatting for most of the day. Barb slept whenever she had to, while Tiffany played with Blair and Kimmy, seemingly content. She didn't sleep at all the first evening, being excited and having fun. She sure gave Daddy a lot of hugs and kisses.

The next couple of weeks, we shopped, went to the Big Splash, and spent time swimming, water-skiing, and of course drinking beer, all the ordinary things one does in a day. We enjoyed each other's company and were glad to be together. That was all that really mattered. We were having fun, enjoying ourselves in our newfound home. We bought a camera and a stereo, took a lot of pictures, listened to music, and visited. We went to the markets and saw chickens hanging in the windows by the heads, which were still attached, plucked clean of feathers. They weren't refrigerated at most places, so some looked like they were fresh and some not so fresh. Down at the Jockey Club, we ate steak and kidney pie, a treat to some of us. We both were fascinated with the vegetation of big fan trees, palms, coconut trees, and all the tropical flowers. It was beautiful. For once, we could smell the roses and enjoy quality time. Not this rush, rush, rush, all the time, as we had in Canada. We didn't watch the news because we had better things to do.

It seemed we couldn't plan anything in Canada as we either were working or waiting for a call. Funny how those phones can take away a lot of one's time. We had a schedule now, most of the time getting our three weeks off without ever waiting for a call.

Bill and I went back to work at the same time. Parker had worked it out so we could spend our time off together, it seemed.

I got back, and Hap told me the rig was shutting down for repairs. I would be transferred to Medan in North Sumatra and would be working on a big diesel electric rig for Mobil Oil. He said he didn't think I would like it, but I knew I would. That was my background in Canada and the bigger, the better. I loved that equipment with big horse power but respected it at all times, and it was fun to operate. Boys and their toys, as the sayings go.

We racked the rig and came back to Singapore waiting to go to North Sumatra. I asked Bill if he knew where that was.

"It's in Indonesia," he said jokingly, laughing because he caught me off guard. We had a chuckle and then he said he wasn't sure what part of Indonesia it was in.

"Good answer," I told him chuckling.

Some of the guys and their families were already moving to Perth, Australia, by this time. It wouldn't be long and we would all be there. I couldn't wait. I had always dreamed of going there as a kid and recall looking at the encyclopedia books Dad had purchased for us to study and do our homework with, looking for information on Australia. I was fascinated with all the animals they had there; from what I read, most everything hopped.

We didn't do too much in Singapore this hitch. We tried to get back to normal living but went out a lot for suppers because it was cheaper than cooking for ourselves. We went to Newton's Circus and ate many fantastic meals.

It was a traffic circle filled with tables and little cookhouses strewn throughout the inside of it. You could get just about anything you wanted to eat there. The smell of cooking oils and food was rampant sometimes, making you gag, but the food was excellent, with many flavors, and there was good beer. People, thousands of them, gathered around tables, a steady hum of conversation everywhere. Everyone was bumping into each other. We couldn't tell who was working and who was not. When we ordered, they would go to all the different cookhouses, place an order with that particular cookhouse, and then gathering your meal sporadically throughout the night, they would bring it. It seemed they all worked together. The hustle of everyone was chaotic. The lights from traffic shone everywhere, steady streams of them lighting the atmosphere, and then darkness. There were the sounds of people crossing the streets, cars honking, kids playing, men and women talking, and the steady hum of voices of people playing and laughing, with some of the waiters speaking loudly so they could be heard. The toilets were crudely built and dirty, with Eastern-style commodes inside. Whenever you needed to use them, someone sitting at the entrance would collect whatever you offered. They were mostly janitors who cleaned them to earn a living. It seemed like everyone had a purpose, and no one looked down upon them. You would see them talking and laughing with the public, with their friends, who would stop by to see them.

The next day, we hired a boat, complete with driver, and went water-skiing. Traveling by boat about six miles out in the ocean, we came to what we nicknamed Coney Island.

The water was dirty because of the dumping of pig manure into the ocean from the pig farms within the city we had passed on our way to the dock. They smelled ripe, but no one seemed to complain. This was what we were buying in the meat markets and also the restaurants. We skied all day and had a really good time. We returned about five o'clock and had supper at the dock before going home. It was so different from what we did at home. It didn't appear that anyone got sick there. At least we didn't.

Chapter Six

Having been transferred to North Sumatra, I found working near Loc
Su Kon drilling on larger pads doing directional work was perfect for
me. Because we were trying not to interfere too much with the local
rice fields, we drilled up to twenty wells on a pad.

We flew commercial airlines to Medan, Indonesia, and then
chartered a small aircraft to Loc Su Kon, where we were picked up by
the Parker driver and taken to the camp.

While driving to the camp, I noticed the landscape was very different
from the jungle. Rice fields spread out, with small dikes built around
plots. People were in water up to their knees working their hearts out,
trying to make a living. Men, women, and children worked away,
hoeing, shoveling, and planting seedlings in the soil. What appeared to
be a handmade canal system fed water into these paddies from natural
sources and man-drilled water wells. Men were constantly digging
out the silt and dirt threatening to block off the flow of the much-
needed water with hoes. When it rained, it appeared to be much easier
to maintain, as there was plenty of water to grow rice. They tried to
drain off the excess water and flooded each other's paddies but worked
together to solve the problem, getting it under control within days. It
didn't appear to bother them when the water was a menace at times.

I had to take a course on well control to work there, so it was
arranged for me to go to these classes after my twelve-hour shift at no

cost to the company. They made sure we were trained, at our expense, even though we had finished our shift of twelve hours and were tired. Safety was a big issue at the forefront, pushed on all of us from their point of view, but it didn't matter if we got only four or six hours off between shifts, having to go to these courses. By the time we had our dinner and drove to the course, completed instruction, and drove back, it was midnight. We did this most of the week. We would go to bed many times without a shower, tired.

No one dared to complain because we were told we could leave our jobs if we felt it was too much. We were a human resource already, not human beings. Having no laws favoring us, we could be changed out any time the company felt, if deemed a hindrance. Corporate business worked like that already then, and many times, we were told, "You do as we say, not as we do."

We drilled well after well; some were more difficult than others, taking kicks and having many well control problems. Many times, we would work a full shift, just keeping the well under control. Mud weights were kept to a minimum because of differential sticking problems, and even then, sticking our pipe in the well was common.

We would hear about it and be accused of lack of supervision and not paying attention and all the other blame a corporate business could think of, many times being belittled for our stupidity. A lot of times when we would get into the pay zone, we were to leave the rotary table rotating, to make connections. We could get someone caught in the rotary, but if we stopped for twenty seconds, we would be stuck. This practice was unsafe, but we would be stuck if we didn't do it, so we did.

We had to rotate the kelly with an air spinner, snapping the connection together, pick out of the slips, and go to bottom quickly without torquing our pipe to the required manufacturer's specifications.

The pipe would fatigue at the joints and fail because of this, and we would get blamed when it twisted off or washed out causing a trip out or a fishing job. If we had an accident, like someone injuring his foot in the rotary table, we got blamed again. We were getting used to it but didn't like it. We were told to do this. Why would we get blamed?

Corporate business gets off the hook for repairs, downtime, and compensating injuries with this kind of behavior. Tell them to do something and then they lie, deny, and blame. Is this politics and Corporate irresponsibility? The one who gets hurt has to wait, hungry, until our courts decide who to blame, and whoever has the most money and time wins. That's what we have lawyers for, right? They too fill their pockets to the brim, if it takes longer to negotiate. This seemed to be how it all worked so enough of this for now.

When the rice was growing and appeared stable, they would maintain a water level about four inches deep until harvest was near, and then stop the water from entering their paddies, rerouting it with shovel and hoe, draining the land to let the crops ripen.

Harvest came and was amazing to watch, all done naturally, by hand. The rice and other crops would be picked by hand, laid out on a large canvass over a road or approach, and trampled on with their feet. The straw would be thrown to the side. Women, with round screens of woven wicker, would sift the harvested crop, dumping it from about five feet onto another canvass repeatedly, the wind removing the chaff until all of it was gone from the product. They would bag it and take it with horse, oxen, or car to the market, selling any excess they didn't need for their survival.

Cotton fields, which spread out over some of the areas, were also picked and bagged for market by hand.

I did not see any Western influence in the form of aircraft spraying for insects or any fertilizers being used. People let things grow naturally and seemed to have an abundance of food, clothing, and shelter, poor and disgraceful by our standards, but functional, I observed. It reminded me of my own childhood of fun, hard work, and satisfaction in what you did or had.

The only problem I saw was us producing the smoke and smog from the oil patch, and the people complained at times about it. Complain as they may, already their governments were sold on our ideals of greed and probably paid off through political deals to support our ways. Is this why we have all the terrorism in the world? Maybe they are fighting their governments and us so we don't force our so-called democracy on them. Maybe they see our lies and deceit and are angry at our corporate business, greed, and governments for pushing them around. Are we around the world being lied to by our corporate media and governments, telling us a bunch of propaganda and lies about them, to deflect what they are really trying to do? My mind already was geared to seeing things in a different way, things I had taken for granted and accepted at home.

I worked in North Sumatra for about three years for the drilling contractor and saw many things. In Loc Su Kon, ten Chinese people were killed because they owned businesses local people had deemed a threat or unfair, I was told. These businesses were burned to the ground and everything hushed up. We didn't hear about it in the Western world. Were we too busy trying to set ourselves up there to notice? Was it not our concern? Did they see the Chinese as a threat, or was it ethnic violence?

Once we had some problem with the workers, and they went on strike. We were told to cut costs and given a guideline where to cut them. One of the issues was soap. Yes, bar soap. We gave them our Western soap always, and they would take it home. Some of them would take as much as four bars a week home. They wanted lye soap though, as our soap wasn't good. It was needed to wash their clothes and such. When we cut back to one bar a week, a strike was called by a few of the leaders of the crew. Remember, a lot of the people were still tribal in those parts of the globe, so leaders were abundant sometimes. There was nothing we could do as they refused to work until the issue of soap was resolved. We were told to call in the government forces and get them back to work.

When the forces arrived, they wanted to know who the leaders were and who was responsible for the strike. It was illegal to strike against any government installation at that time, and I wonder if it has changed. We told the forces who we thought was responsible, and they went out, pointed their weapons at the crowd, and demanded they go back to work. The persons we named as responsible for the strike were loaded into a van and whisked off location.

About four days went by and I was concerned about these men, so I asked a couple of the crew what had happened to them. They told me "Kaput" gesturing with their finger sliding across their throat in a cutting motion. I couldn't and wouldn't believe what I had just been told, so I said, "Ah no. That's a joke."

They said, "No, Mr. Pat. True. This is what happened!"

A sick feeling came over me, and I was extremely saddened that we had called in the forces. What a price to pay for refusing to work! I made up my mind that I would never again call on the forces to solve a problem. This was shocking and truly uncalled for, if true. Thoughts went through my head. *Is mankind coming to this? Governments can already litigate you back to work and you have to go or be penalized. No, it can't happen in Canada. It's a free country, isn't it?* Doubts were about me as a chill ran up my spine.

A contract between the oil company and the contractor had been agreed on when the rig was contracted to Indonesia, and it was now coming to an end. I believed the oil company could purchase the rig for an agreed sum set out in the contract, and they were going to exercise this clause. I was asked to stay on a rig when the oil company took it over after the contract was fulfilled. I agreed and gave my notice to the drilling contractor.

When I went to the office to get my pay due me, I was told that I couldn't have it until I left Australia. I refused to leave, as the oil company said they would take over my bond, and I could rotate out of Perth.

I had to hire an international lawyer who wrote a letter to the contractor and threatened to seize their accounts if I didn't receive my pay. Within a week, I received a call from the lawyer and met him at his office. He handed me my pay, and we chatted for a while. I asked what I owed him.

He chuckled, saying, "You buy me a beer sometime. It would be enough as I didn't have to do a whole lot." I paid my dues and thought him to be one of the best people I had met. This is what it is all about, fairness. I still think of that man and hold him high on the charts of humanity. This is a true recipient of the Noble Prize and an asset to mankind.

Upon arriving back at the Arun field, now working for the oil company through a labor contract, I entered the rig manager's office and was going to do a handover with the contractor manager. To my surprise, he was angry that the rig had been taken over and his contract had expired. We couldn't get anything handed over, and they even burned all the parts manuals. We were going to have to start from scratch and get all the necessary parts manuals if we wanted to operate.

Some of us were called traitors and mocked for our decision to stay on and operate the rigs. Over time, we did get all the manuals and sorted everything out.

About six months into this contract, the Indonesian government wanted to nationalize the rigs. Fair enough, if they could do it, but this was an exceptionally hard field to work. Everyone had to be on top of things or many people could get hurt.

They started sending us people with no drilling background. We were to train them. It was difficult, but we tried hard and spent many sleepless nights, being woken up to give instruction and assist with problems. People were getting hurt, and many were frustrated, but we trudged along, sometimes at a snail's pace. Being young allowed us to be able to push ourselves for these corporate entities and still smile.

We were learning every day how to get along with people we felt were good but lacked experience and to tolerate people who were intelligent but had no sense of safety and lived with little experience of safety at home. Crude wiring, crude plumbing, and no driving skills or law enforcement as we knew it was observed throughout. Slip a cop five bucks and away you go. It was cheaper than our system, and people still survived, with very few accidents and disagreements. Police were friendly and not overbearing. Most were more than willing to help and would guide you if requested. Their system worked fine even though we found it chaotic.

If you're raised in this, it is normal ... for lack of better wording. By the way, what is normal? We think we are normal, and they think they are normal. A hundred and sixty million Indonesians can't be wrong, can they? Could forty million Canadians be wrong?

We completed the contract, and I refused another contract, due to stress, dealing with all the incidents, accidents, safety, and such being pushed on us with little support from the top guys. Investigate and blame was the norm. Talk the talk but see if they will walk the talk.

Chapter Seven

I left Indonesia and came back to Canada when I was around thirty years old. I had seen and learned a lot. I was thankful to God for letting me see other cultures so my mind would not judge people on what the media or other people said without any knowledge or common sense to understand we are all just trying to survive. We are all God's children. Thank God heaven will have all kinds of people there, and we will finally one day find true peace with each other, blessed with the biggest success of life imaginable. Only death will determine how successful we really are, no matter how much societies want us to believe that monetary things, positions, and money are measured as success.

I arrived back in Canada around Christmastime in 1984 or 1985 and was happy to be home. I was singing, "Rudolf the Red-Nosed Kangaroo" as I exited the plane at Vancouver, and people were laughing, finding this humorous. We had just arrived from Australia and were happy to be on Canadian soil again. I flew to Winnipeg from Vancouver and bought a car, a Lincoln Mark VI, used, but in good condition, allowing me to get around. Barb was still in Australia getting rid of our belongings, trying to be home for Christmas too. I felt lonely and was disappointed in myself for leaving her to do this alone, but I didn't have a job and I needed to start looking for one in Canada soon.

For a short time, I turned to alcohol and drugs, drowning my sorrows and ambitions in this horrible way of life. I despised it but stayed with it for some time, eventually pulling myself from the dooms of alcoholism back into reality and responsibility. I don't know why I let this take over for a time, but I thank God it was short-lived. To be honest, I believe, as I look back, that all of this was imminent as we did indulge ourselves quite a lot in Australia prior to coming back.

Many things happened while I was in this state. I was arrested for drunken driving, violence, etc. All this is part of it, but realization and admitting to yourself first and foremost that you have a problem is the biggest part of this self-induced disease. Accepting the problem is the beginning of its cure. Although I am lucky I didn't hurt anyone or lose my family, I feel remorse for what I have put some people through. To make it short, I was a rebel and probably still am, but I use rebellion differently. Thank God my wife supported me and helped me through all this with her understanding and kindness. I love her and owe her my life.

I tried to get on the rigs in Canada, but no one was hiring, as the patch was in a bit of a downslide and things were not looking good. I worked a week here and there shutting down rigs and racking a lot of junk. Some of this equipment I saw was not fit to work and was dangerous, but the boom that had been on had demanded it. Now most of the junk was being weeded out. A lot of oilfield workers were handing in their keys for trucks and homes they had bought on credit during the time of the boom. The patch has always been feast or famine, with many losses when the crunch hits.

I scored a job with Esso as a consultant in Rainbow Lake, and things were looking pretty good for a while, and then in the spring of 1986, I too was out of a job. The patch came to a standstill, and times were tough. Again, I jumped around for a time getting a week here and there ending wells and racking rigs.

We decided to go to Winnipeg and try our hand at construction. Winnipeg was booming with construction, and we found a job immediately. I was destined to become a drywall applicator and stay home. I wanted to learn a new skill so I wasn't so dependent on the rigs. The money wasn't as good, but I would be home every night and get to know my family.

Finances were tough, but we scratched through, as always, and the good Lord seemed to find a way to make things work out. That poem about footsteps in the sand really hits home, when one stops and realizes the hard times are very tiring, and one needs to be carried at times, so one can go on, but you learn, don't you?

It was Christmas of 1987, and we were broke. Barb's mom and dad were coming out for Christmas. We couldn't afford it, but we scratched and scraped making Christmas for what it was. With not a penny to our name, we opened our gifts and found that we had struck a jackpot. Grandma Nabe sent us a hundred dollars and we got fifty bucks from Barb's mom and dad. We survived, thanking God and family for these small tokens, which were greatly appreciated.

That night, we went to bed, holding each other close. I remember saying to Barb that God worked miracles. She whispered back everything always seemed to work out. We fell asleep and had a most needed rest. We were stressed out financially and appreciated the comfort that we could buy much-needed milk and food for our little daughter, Tiffany. I thank God for giving us the strength and courage to move forward every day and think back to this Christmas every time stress enters our lives and we feel we can't go on.

We worked at construction, remodeling Polo Park shopping mall, building Portage Place, and the TD tower on the corner of Portage and Main. Work was plentiful, and we were at the least, surviving. I didn't like the city way of life and was searching for a way out. After we had been in Winnipeg for about two years, the construction industry took a turn, and many people were getting laid off. I had taken on some weekend work and started with a small company doing just about everything from cement work to building garages.

I ended up getting hurt while unloading a tamping machine from the back of a pickup truck. The fellow I was working with had a bad back and dropped it. I took the full brunt of the machine, tearing up my back. I felt it but kept working, laying paving stones until quitting time at 4:30 in the afternoon. I was sore and could hardly stand when quitting time came around but managed to get myself home and lay on the couch. Barb was going to Roblin to see her folks that evening and asked if I would be all right. I told her to go, I should be okay. I tried to get up to use the washroom after she left and found I couldn't stand because of the pain. I crawled to the washroom, sweating profusely from pain and managed to get back on the couch thinking I would be okay in the morning. I was worse. I rolled off the couch, crawled to the bathroom, and pulled myself up using the sink for leverage. When I looked in the mirror, I could see my torso was shifted; my upper body was to the left and my lower body to the right. I was in so much pain, a tear ran down my face. Shuffling back to the couch, I lay back down to ease the pain. I did this for the weekend until Barb came back. She noticed I still had my work clothes on and hadn't showered all weekend.

Immediately, she helped me shower and clean up, wanting to take me to the hospital when she saw my torso was shifted. I said we would go in the morning if I felt somewhat better. I called my boss and told him I couldn't work and needed to go to the doctor. I told him I would probably need a week off. He was okay with it but cautioned me on drawing compensation.

We called and got an appointment with an orthopedic surgeon and were told I needed to go to physiotherapy. I tried that for a couple of weeks and wasn't showing any improvement. The next appointment, I told the surgeon that I wasn't any better and suggested I go to the chiropractor. He refused to let me go, saying they needed to operate on my back. I refused to let them operate and went to the chiropractor. Twenty treatments later, I was as good as new. I had pinched the sciatic nerve, which caused a lot of grief. When it came free, the heat sensation and relief I felt was immense. I could walk. I was sore and tense, but I was able. Ice packs on for ten minutes and off for ten minutes was his instruction, and by 9:00 PM the same evening, the swelling had dissipated and I took a Robaxecet and could walk pain free. Again, I thanked God for that gift of being able to walk. So far, I have not had that happen again. The twenty treatments helped to keep my back straight, and I was told I had a degenerated disc. No work for a while yet, I was told.

Six weeks passed and I was still waiting for a compensation check. We were broke and needed groceries so I called and was told it was still in the process. I called the MLA in St. James and told him my dilemma and asked him if he could intervene. He was reluctant until I told him that a 7-Eleven store was a block away and if I didn't have a check by that evening, I would have to rob the place and they would be responsible. It was Friday, and we needed to survive the weekend. Within two hours of calling the MLA, I received a call from the compensation board that I could pick up my check by four in the afternoon. In fact, when I got there, they had three checks for me totaling around twenty-seven hundred dollars. This again left a sour taste in me for government. Why is it you have to fight with government for everything? Why does one have to go through such extremes to survive? Because they are corrupt doesn't mean we all are, does it? They don't trust anyone. They seem to have to control and dictate. Are we free? They are, a lot of times, quite ignorant. Is this how they're trained and brainwashed? Isn't that why we pay for compensation so we have some kind of insurance when we get hurt working to pay our taxes?

I went back to work and continued to drywall without any more back problems. I was laid off, and work was grinding down. I applied for unemployment insurance and waited for the cards in the mail. The cards came; I filled out the necessary questionnaire and sent them in. Hunting season was about to begin, and the fellows I usually hunted with were getting ready to go to my father-in-law's farm, as we normally did for a week. I too got ready and made the four-and-a-half-hour drive to Roblin, Manitoba, so we could enjoy some fellowship and have a good time hunting for a few days. I left on Sunday and arrived for the hunt that same evening. We sat around and told stories, joked, and were having a good time joshing each other. On Wednesday night, around nine in the evening, I received a call from my wife in Winnipeg and was informed I was disqualified for my unemployment claim, as I wasn't available for work. The unemployment office had called around eight that evening and wanted to speak to me. My sister was at my place and answered the phone. She had no idea who it was, and when they asked for me, she told them I was hunting. That was what got me disqualified.

I was upset for having to leave immediately that night to be at the unemployment office first thing in the morning. I went to the office and inquired as to why I was disqualified and was told I wasn't available for work. I asked who wanted me to go to work at eight in the evening and was told nobody. They were just checking and assumed I was in a hunting camp out in the boonies. I said, "If no one wanted me, then why would you call?"

"We check on claims and call to see if people are available or just scamming the unemployment insurance" I was told.

I hit the roof. I told her I wanted her job and wanted to speak to a superior as the answer I got just didn't sit well. No job offer, no reason to disqualify me as I have the right to accept a position, and if I did, I had a certain amount of time to report for work. I was only four and a half hours away and could have gone to work when I arrived in Winnipeg that evening, but to be told they assumed I was in a camp so they disqualified me? I wasn't a steady customer, I guess, as I had not drawn any kind of government check. This really made me fume. When I talked to her superior, I was immediately reinstated but lost my hunting trip.

These are things I saw back in 1987–88. Government had to start doing better soon, I thought. Surely, we're better people than that. We are civilized and educated, aren't we?

During my stay in Winnipeg, I was trying to get my brother off alcohol and get him back on the straight and narrow. It was difficult knowing there was nothing wrong with him and he could work but got to know the system and enjoyed a life living off the taxpayers.

I went to the office on Broadway, introduced myself, and explained to them my desire for my brother to work rather than abuse the system. I told them there was nothing wrong with him, and they were responsible for his alcoholism. They were feeding him money, allowing him to drink all day and night, and supplying food, at the taxpayers' expense, when he could have been working and abstaining from alcohol, at least during working hours.

He was getting violent and had threatened me a couple of times. When I found out I couldn't intervene, I left it alone. Already, I had observed signs of his memory loss and lumps on his head, where he had been assaulted. He continued to live in this state of damnation. He had made his choice, or could he even choose already? Maybe if he would have had to pay his way, he wouldn't have done what he did.

Chapter Eight

The phone rang, and I picked it up.

"Hello!" I said half asleep. It was 5:30 AM.

"Allo," was the reply after a short delay. "Is this Pet?"

"Yes," I said somewhat annoyed, thinking it was some people my brother was hanging out with. I had to work at 7:00 and was really not in the mood to deal with his friends.

"Just one minute. Someone wants to talk to you."

"Listen," I said agitated, "I don't want to talk to some drunk right now," and hung up.

I rolled over and was nearly sleeping again when the phone rang again.

"Hello," I said in an unpleasant voice.

"Allo?" this person said.

I was fuming. This person was persistent. "Just leave me alone and don't bother me," I said and hung up again.

About fifteen minutes later, the phone rang again and I was about to give the intruder a blast, when "Hello?" this deep voice said. "Is this Patrick?"

"Yes," I said. "Who is this?"

"Ha, ha, ha," came this deep laugh. "This is Mike. How are you doing, Paddy? I was just about to give up on you hanging up on my secretary. This is Mike Cooper here."

Man, did I feel like shit. "Hey, Mike, I'm sorry, and please apologize to your secretary. I thought it was some of my brother's drunken friends. How are you?" I asked.

Talk about sticking your foot in your mouth, I thought. Mike and I had worked rigs all over Canada and the High Arctic and were pretty good friends. He was calling from the Middle East.

"I'm fine," he said. "What time is it in Winnipeg?" he asked chuckling.

"It's a quarter to six. Don't you sleep?" I asked.

"Sometimes," he said. "Listen, Paddy, I need you to come to Syria and help us out. I'm short a couple of people, and we need to get the rig straightened out. Are you interested?" he offered.

The Middle East! Syria? "What is it like over there?" I asked.

"I think it's pretty good," he replied. "We're paying sixty-two hundred a month on and off and 10 percent if you stay for a year."

"Gee, Mike, that sounds good, but I left the patch two years ago, and I don't even have any tickets. They're all expired," I said.

"All you need is your first line, Pat. Do you think you could get that in a couple of days and be on a plane? I'm really in a bind," he said.

"Holy shit, Mike," I replied. "In a couple of days; that's nearly impossible; maybe in a week. Do I need any shots for disease?" I asked.

"Yes, you'll probably need yellow fever and things like that. Try to be less than a week if you can. I'll work on your ticket, or when you're ready, you buy the ticket and we'll reimburse you. Let me know for sure in a couple days."

"I don't think we can do it in a couple of days. I need to drive to Edmonton and write my first line if I can even get in," I told Mike. "I also need to let these guys I'm working for know I'm leaving." I had gotten another job before unemployment kicked in. "I'll see what I can do but don't count on me."

"Paddy, you have to do this. I really need your help," Mike said. "Don't let me down."

"Mike, I'll do my best, but I can't commit to a couple of days. It takes time to set this all up, you know," I said. "I'll do my best."

"Okay! Thanks, Paddy. Don't back out now," Mike said.

We hung up, and I thought about this offer. It was good, but a couple of days? My head was racing. I was thankful for another opportunity to go overseas and somewhat excited.

"Who was that?" asked Barb. My bride was awake and wide-eyed listening to my conversation.

"Cooper. He wants me to go to the Middle East," I said. "I'll make some coffee," I offered.

Barb got up and asked, "What are you going to do?"

"I don't know. I sure wasn't expecting this. I thought it was some of Popeye's friends," I replied. That was what we had called my brother since he was a child.

"Well, what do you think you'll do?" Barb asked, badgering me.

"I guess I'll go. We can get ahead a bit faster, and it will be a good opportunity for us to see some other spots on our huge playground. I think it will be good," I said. "I'll tell Doug that I have this opportunity, then probably come home and see what I can do to get my shots and line up a class for pits to challenge my first line ticket."

"I'll try to get you in for your shots if you like," Barb offered.

"Okay. I better get ready for work," I said.

I got ready, grabbed my lunch, and headed out to the job. When I arrived, Doug came in.

"Good morning. How's Pat this morning?" Doug asked smiling.

"I'm great, Doug. How are you?" I asked.

"So what's up this morning?" Doug said making conversation.

"Well, I was woke up at 5:30 this morning and got a job offer in the Middle East," I told Doug. "They want me there in a couple days. Do you think that's possible? I hate leaving you in a bind, but the offer is too good to pass up, Doug," I said.

"When do they want you to go?" Doug asked.

"Today, if possible; they wanted me there yesterday," I told Doug referring to the urgency of Mike's request. "It seems when you get a call from the rigs, it's right now. I need to get started as I have to get my shots, go to Edmonton, write a test, and get on the plane as soon as possible, Doug. If I left now, would that leave you in a big bind?"

"Well, not really," Doug replied. "If you have to go, you have to go. We'll get by, and things are wrapping up on this job. You go ahead if you like."

Still doubtful, I said, "Are you sure?"

"Yes. We'll be okay," Doug replied. "You go ahead."

"Okay. Thanks. I really don't like doing this but ..." I said.

We shook hands and Doug offered, "Good luck. If it doesn't work out, give me a call."

I left the site by 9:00 in the morning and went home. Barb had made some calls. I could get my shots at 1:00 PM and was booked into PITS to challenge the first line course the next morning. It was at least fourteen hours to Edmonton. I packed some clothes for overnight, and Barb called her sister Debbie. We needed her car as Barb needed ours, and the truck wasn't really up to the trip to Edmonton.

Arrangements made, I was to pick up Debbie's car in Roblin, drop off our truck, and keep on going to Edmonton. By noon, we had arranged most everything and were busy getting ready to go. We sat down and had a coffee.

"Do those shots make you sick or drowsy?" I asked Barb like she was supposed to know.

"Gee, I don't know," Barb said.

"Ah! Why worry about it? I'm sure I'll be all right," I said talking to myself out loud. "I have been through worse, I'm sure. If I get tired, I'll stop and nap on the side of the road."

"Yes. But you be careful," Barb warned.

"I'll be okay. The good Lord has pulled us through before, and I'm sure he will help us now," I said relaxing with that thought.

I drank my coffee and then picked up my overnight bag. Barb was smiling, and we kissed good-bye. "See you tomorrow night if all goes well," I said smiling back at my bride. She was always so supportive of anything we do. *The best choice I ever made,* I thought as I was leaving.

I went to the Grace hospital where I got three needles for hepatitis, yellow fever, and something else. Leaving the hospital around two in the afternoon, I knew I had a long drive ahead so when I could see the outskirts of Winnipeg in my rearview mirror, I pushed the accelerator down on that old truck, and we were off. As I was cruising around one twenty to one thirty kilometers an hour my thoughts drifted off to my destination of employment.

They have some problems in the Middle East, don't they? What is it going to be like? Are they mad at the Western nations? Shit, I haven't done anything to them so they surely can't be mad at me, can they? I've never been there. My thoughts were calm, but I was somewhat apprehensive on going with all the news and media negativity about the place. *Ah! It's all propaganda. I have never met an Arab man so how can I be so naive as to judge him?*

I relaxed but started to think of actually leaving Barb at home again. Did I really want to do that? I was just getting used to being at home, and we had relearned to stay out of each other's space again. You would be surprised at how independent each of us get when we live a life apart. Over half of our married life was like this, and we would sometimes overstep our boundaries, having to discuss matters and set rules.

I got to Roblin around eight in the evening and had to be in Edmonton at nine the next morning to challenge the test. I would gain an hour going so it was no problem to get there, unless I had car problems. My arm was sore from the needles, and I was feeling a slight fever but had no time for self-pity. I picked up Debbie's car and was off within a half hour. I had no time to waste.

I was driving alone with only thoughts, and the road was long and quiet. I seldom listened to the radio, liking the silence. I let my thoughts drift away. It is such a peaceful way to meditate, with only the hum of the engine, the tires howling, and the whooshing sound of the wind as the car speeds down the highway, clipping along at one twenty. When I drive, I think a lot of the spiritual world and the many things God gave us that should be so easy and simple. Why are they so complicated? Many times, I thanked God for the small things we sometimes forget about, like our sight, touch, hearing, being able to walk, the sense of smell, the mind, and all the little gifts he gave us so we can live life as we choose. It is a blessing to have all of these things and to be able to use them to the best of our abilities, freely. Sometimes I say a little prayer and ask for guidance, especially when it comes to choices and flying. I really don't like flying but can tolerate it. A chill came over me just thinking about it.

I'm not sure how I got there with all my thoughts, but the sign said North Battleford. Did I go through Saskatoon already? I wasn't sure how I got through the city without remembering. I looked in my rearview mirror as if I was going to see Saskatoon and then chuckled at my stupidity. I stopped and fueled up. It was two in the morning. I yawned as I got out of the car to stretch. I hadn't stopped since I'd left Roblin six hours earlier. I was tired and needed a cup of coffee and a washroom. The gas attendant filled up the car while I went inside and did what I needed to and stretched.

Back on the road again with the engine humming, my thoughts drifted around and I said out loud, "If all goes well, I'll be able to have breakfast and study, if I can score a manual." It had been two years since I was on a rig, and I was having doubts about the test. Had things changed much since I left the patch? Again, out loud, I said, "Things couldn't have changed that much." *Hell!! I'm talking to myself,* I thought and chuckled.

To keep awake, I started to sing. I'm a title singer now as I forget the words to most songs we used to sing at bush parties. I repeat the chorus most times changing my voice, trying to sound like the artist, and then laugh at myself.

I pulled into Nisku, Alberta, around seven in the morning and drove to the truck stop for breakfast. I knew some of the waitresses as my sisters, Monique and Donalda, were employed there. Maybe I would have a coffee with them if they were working.

They weren't there, but another waitress, an older gal with blondish hair who recognized me, greeted me.

"Good morning," she said with a smile. "I haven't seen you in a while. Where have you been? What brings you here?"

"Good morning! How have you been keeping? I'm here to challenge a first line test and scored a job in the Middle East," I said. "I've been living in Winnipeg for the last two years."

"Yes! Donalda told me that. The Middle East! Are you crazy?" she said laughing. "According to the news and all, those guys are pretty radical, aren't they?"

"Oh! I don't think so. It's what you make of it, I guess. I haven't had any problems in other places, so this shouldn't be any different," I said smiling, remaining calm but feeling unsure.

"Better get to work or they'll fire me," she said laughing. "I don't know about you," she said as she left.

With all the media attention on certain areas, a person who doesn't know would think that way and be swayed to believe what is on the television, I thought. She was a pleasant lady, just making conversation.

I liked her because she always said "hi" and had time to stop and chat for a minute or two.

I left the restaurant about eight thirty and went to PITS to study for a half hour or so. Around nine, I wrote the first line test and failed it. I was too tired to think properly. They knew my situation and allowed me to repeat the test that afternoon so I slept in the car for an hour and rewrote the test around two in the afternoon, passing it the second time. With an hour of sleep behind me, I was able to think somewhat better.

Around four in the afternoon, Nisku was in my rearview mirror and I was headed back to Manitoba. Tired and worn-out, I trudged forward listening to the engine whine at one forty. I wanted to get back as quickly as possible and didn't want to waste any time. Listening to the disc player and singing to stay awake seemed to help my weary mind. I had done a lot of driving in a very short time, and my rear was getting sore so I stopped in Lloydminister for a break, had a stretch and coffee, and then left.

Time flew just as fast as I was driving. Soon, I was in Roblin, picking up my old truck, and then I was off again to Winnipeg. It was two thirty in the morning, and I had slept only about an hour in my vehicle since leaving Winnipeg. Three and a half more hours and then I could be in my bed, finally, I thought.

Cruising along by Portage la Prairie, I must have dozed off in my tired state. When I came to, a barricade jumped out in front of me. Swerving to miss the stupid thing, I lost control of the truck and was zigzagging down the two-lane highway. Thank God, it was quiet, and the highway was divided with two lanes. After getting the truck back under control, I stopped for a break right along the road and went for a walk. Still not sure about myself, I leaned back on the seat and fell asleep. It was five thirty by my watch, and I had been going for quite some time. I woke up at six, when a semi went by and shook the truck. Wiping the cobwebs out of my eyes and straightening my seat, I put the truck in gear and proceeded to get home. At around seven in the morning, I pulled into our apartment parking lot and met with my bride outside for a few minutes, just as she was going to work at Perth's dry cleaners. A smile, a peck on the cheek, and then she was off. I went up to the apartment, fell on the couch, and slept.

The phone rang.

"Hello!" I said in a sleepy voice.

"Paddy; How are you" Mike here?

"Tired," I replied.

"You getting old?" he asked laughing.

"I must be. I can't go like I used to when I was twenty," I said.

"How did you make out? Did you get to Edmonton?" Mike asked.

"Yes, I did and got my first line ticket. Think you're trying to kill me though." I laughed. "I was up two days getting this done. Hope you aren't canceling out on me now," I replied.

"Oh no, I need you here yesterday," was his reply.

Typical oil field, I thought. *They're always in a hurry.*

"Good. I will try to get an airline ticket sometime tomorrow and will call you when I'm ready to fly," I said yawning.

"Perfect. I will wait for your call," he replied. "Talk to you later."

"Okay! Bye!" It was two in the afternoon.

I fell back on the couch and must have fallen asleep. When I woke up, Barb was just getting home.

"Hi, honey," she said not knowing if I was awake yet.

"Hi, baby. How was your day?" I asked, yawning.

"Good," she said. "How was yours?"

I don't think she ever had a bad day.

"I must have been tired. I've slept the day away," I said.

"Mike call?" she asked.

"Yes! Told him I would check on a ticket tomorrow and call him back," I replied.

"Are you excited to go?" she asked.

"I think so. It will be different over there. A lot of negative news about the Middle East," I replied.

We had been watching the news too much since we were asked to go. I am not sure why, but I guess we had some concerns with a lot of propaganda I'm sure, on our television. The West seems to think that we don't have this and everything on television is true. Many people think that and are swayed by the anchors that deliver the news articles to our living rooms every hour.

We watched television while packing some things, getting ready to go to Syria. I would go to the travel agency in the morning and book a flight. We chatted about leaving and being apart and hugged and kissed a lot for the rest of the evening. We had to make sure we weren't deprived of this, making up for when we were away from each other. We laughed and giggled, but I had some concerns about leaving Barb alone again.

She said she would be all right, but leaving always made me feel kind of like I wasn't doing my part at home, raising our daughter. She was becoming a teenager at this time and was at a point where she needed more guidance. She had a little bit more of me in her than she did her mother and was rebellious at times but easy to talk out of things, when we sat down and explained them to her. Most times, she would listen, make up her own mind, and then let us know if she agreed. She was a pretty good kid, and we loved her dearly. It was getting late, and we had many things to do, so we went to bed, sleeping until Tiffany had to go to school.

"Breakfast time," I called to my daughter.

"Be right there, Dad," came her reply.

Barb was just about done cooking breakfast, and I was hungry. Tiffany came out looking pretty as a teenager always looks, with a little makeup highlighting her eyes and lips. She was definitely a pretty, attractive girl and quite unaware of it, down-to-earth and never prissy or high on herself. She had good values, and that made us proud. She sat down and began eating her breakfast.

I could tell she was thinking about something but never interfered with her thoughts. If she wanted to say something, she would find the right time. I watched as she dabbed her mouth, not to mess her makeup, and then she got up.

"Dad, are you going to be home when I get back from school?" she asked.

"Of course I'll be home. I don't know when I'm going, but it won't be today, sweetheart," I said smiling at her.

"Okay! I'll come straight home after school," she said kissing me. "Bye, Mom. See you tonight," she said, giving her mom a kiss, and then she left. She was going to Elmwood Elementary School at the time and was involved with a few friends. She had been moved around so much in her short life. She adjusted to different things quite easily, but we could see she was getting quite comfortable in this school. It was the first time, I believe, she had gone to the same school for more than two years.

After she left for school, Barb and I sat down and planned the day. Over a cup of coffee, we discussed many things, and the one major thing we discussed was moving back to Roblin. Barb wanted to be closer to her folks, and the school Tiffany was going to was getting quite a reputation for gang violence. It wasn't where we wanted our daughter learning all the negative things that, sometimes, were out of our control. Even though we would explain the different acts that took place at school and try to deter her from getting involved, we were noticing some changes in her attitude that concerned us.

After about an hour of discussion, I announced that I had better go get an airline ticket and get things rolling if I was to go work overseas.

I went to the travel agency and booked my flight to Damascus, Syria. I would be leaving in two days. The ticket was quite expensive as I wanted to go as soon as possible. I would fly to Toronto, then Frankfurt, Germany, and direct to Damascus arriving two days later with only twenty-four hours of flight time. How weird that was as we would be crossing the International Date Line again, and time would roll ahead. I always got a chuckle out of this and found it hard to adjust to. Sleep was disrupted as well as everything else your body was accustomed to, like going to the bathroom and eating.

I went home and dialed. Mike answered the phone, "Hello."

"Hello, Mike. How are you?" I said. "Did your secretary quit?"

"I'm fine. How did you make out?" he asked.

"Can't get a flight for two weeks," I joked.

"You're kidding me, aren't you?" he said somewhat concerned.

"Yeah, I am," I said laughing. "I'll be there Sunday night."

"You still tired?" he asked.

"I'm somewhat back to normal if you know what normal is," I said chuckling.

"Good. I'll pick you up at the airport myself on Sunday," he said. "Make sure you're there."

"Oh! I'll be there. You don't have to worry," I said. "See you Sunday."

"Okay! Thanks, Paddy. I really appreciate what you have done.

Only thing you will have to drill for a couple of weeks until I sort out this mess," Mike said.

"Well, what do you mean by that?" I asked.

"We need to make a lot of changes, and I think you can help me. I want you to push tools for me, but, like I said, we need to make some changes. I'll fill you in when you get here," he said. "Talk to you later."

"Okay! Bye for now, and see you Sunday," I said.

I didn't like what I was hearing but kept that to myself. I was wondering what kind of changes he was talking about. What was I getting into?

The two days flew by, and soon I was heading to the airport with my darling and our daughter. This was the moment I always dreaded. It seemed to be our last time together, and I hated it with a passion but always had to be strong. Most times, things were okay until I had to go through the security check.

Tiffany would hang her head and have a sad look on her face while Barb always had a tear to wipe away. She was so soft and concerned, she couldn't help it, even when I would attempt to laugh it off and tell her everything was all right.

Many times, I would hurry and go through the security check without looking back, as my own feelings would make me submit to tears. I hated to leave as much as she hated for me to leave, but we both knew it was for the best. It was going to be a long time before I would get home again, as we were scheduled for five weeks on and five weeks off, with this first hitch being a little longer, until we fell into a rotation, as we found more people to come over and work.

Chapter Nine

"This is your first call for your flight going to Toronto. All passengers please report to gate C. First call to Toronto; please proceed to Gate C," came over the intercom. I was sitting at the kiosk behind security. I finished my beer and then proceeded to the gate requested. I was nearly on my way and a bit nervous. The flight boarded, we took our assigned seats, and then the door closed. We were pushed back from the terminal and steered into the taxi run with the stewardesses giving the safety instructions and preparing for takeoff.

All the while, I was oblivious to what they were saying and thinking about whether or not I was doing the right thing. *It's too late now,* I thought. *I'm hooked, and there is nothing I can do unless I turn around in Toronto.*

We steered into the runway, the engines roared, and we were off. The flight was uneventful, landing in Toronto an hour and a half later. After getting off the plane, we had to get our bags and check in to the international terminal at Lufthansa. With my bags loaded onto the belts for the Lufthansa flight and my boarding pass in my hand, I checked my watch. We still had an hour and a half before leaving for Germany, so off to the kiosk I went for another beer. I finished my beer and then walked around looking at the different stores within the airport. Everything was geared to the tourist and quite expensive. Even the beer was double what it was at the local bars, so I didn't indulge in any more.

Soon, we boarded for Frankfurt and were off. Settling in, I found a seat to myself in the center of the Boeing 747, stretched out, and within minutes, I was sleeping and didn't get up until we were landing in Frankfurt. The stewardess was shaking me and asking me to put my seat belt on. It was 6:45 AM German time. The captain came on and again announced, "Fasten your seat belts. We are in our final approach." The plane glided downward and touched down, bouncing twice, then settled down to a cheer and noisy clapping. People were laughing and relieved; they had made it without incident.

The reverse thrusters were engaged with a loud roar as we slowed down when the captain came on the intercom and announced, "I guess we will have to let auto do this more often until he gets it right," he said to a laughing cabin.

I'm not sure if everyone understood what he meant, but I found it ironic, landing a plane on autopilot with a full load of passengers. Was this normal procedure? Anyway, we landed safely and proceeded to the terminal. We disembarked, and I proceeded to the arrival hall, looking for a restaurant that served bacon and eggs. Our baggage was checked to Damascus, so I didn't have to pick it up and recheck it. I was hungry, wanting breakfast and a cup of coffee.

Sitting in the restaurant watching all the people was fascinating. It was different, as I hadn't been to Germany. Everyone seemed to be completely organized in a sort of regimental style, everything having its place, appearing unused and tidy, even though it was well used.

People were sweeping the floors, mopping, wiping glass windows, serving drinks and food, looking at billboards and flight information, and the works. The airport was full. People were bumping into each other, running to their gates, dragging suitcases and children, reading the newspaper, looking around like they were lost. There was the steady hum of people talking, laughing, and getting directions. Buggies carried older and disabled people. There were police with machine guns and security police with pistols strapped to their hips, people holding up signs with names of people they were supposed to meet. Everyone was hustling and bustling, all kinds of people—Indians, Arabs, Pakistanis, German, French, Canadians, Americans, Englishmen, Scots, you name it—all speaking in different tongues. It was amazing; they all seemed to get where they were going and what they wanted, using sign language, motioning with their hands. Everybody seemed to understand each other.

I roamed around the Frankfurt airport looking at different shops for a few hours. We wouldn't leave until around four in the afternoon.

Soon, we were called to our gate and loaded for our trip to the Middle East. I sat in my assigned seat. A lady, about mid-forties, came and sat down beside me. I could see she was of Arab descent, but I didn't know where she was going. I smiled as she sat down and soon learned she spoke English quite fluently. I asked her where she was going, and she said to Amman, Jordan. We had to go to Amman, Jordan, first and let some passengers off and load some for Damascus.

As we struck up a conversation, she half whispered like no one was supposed to hear, "I am from Iraq. I cannot go there because Saddam Hussein will put me in jail," she offered.

"Why?" I asked. Then I felt it was none of my business.

"Because I left and never came back now for just about thirty years," she replied. "I don't like it in Iraq. There's too much problem for woman there. I live in Stockholm, Sweden."

"Then, why are you going to Jordan?" I asked.

"I will meet my family there. I have a brother living in Amman," she told me.

We conversed about many things—Stockholm, Iraq, her family—and had a few laughs about different things. She was a pleasant lady and had a very good perspective of the world, hoping that one day she would be able to return to Iraq to live in her country of birth. I felt sadness for her and understood the hardship she endured by not seeing her family as often as she wanted to. Those people were very family oriented, I came to find out.

We touched down in Amman, coming to a halt in front of the terminal. I was now sitting in the seat behind this lady as the plane was not too crowded. In a daze, tired and not paying too much attention to anything, I was taken aback when she got up, leaned over to me, and said, "Good-bye, my friend. I enjoyed talking to you. If we meet again, I hope you will remember me." Then laughing, she said, "You should stay in Jordan."

I smiled and said, "I hope we meet again. It's been good talking to you. Good luck to you and your family." As she left, I chuckled at her saying I should stay in Jordan.

The plane was back in the air and off to Damascus within an hour. It was only a half hour or so and I would be there. I had coffee and sat there thinking. *Is Mike going to be there? What if no one is there? Who do I look for? What is the name of this company?* I realized I had forgotten to ask Mike this very important question. *Ah! There will be someone with a sign out there.*

We landed, and all the chaos broke loose once we were inside the airport. People scrambled to the front of the line, pushing and shoving, trying to get through customs faster. Customs officers were running back and forth getting passports and taking them to the immigration check-in. People at the end of the line were getting frustrated while waiting patiently wondering what was going on.

Watching all this, I soon figured out that these people were bribing the customs people and getting special service. A small token was getting them stamped, while we waited. Chuckling, I thought, *I'll be smarter next time,* and waited patiently.

After about an hour and a half, I got through, picked up my belongings, and proceeded to customs. I had a green light and wasn't sure what I was supposed to do, so I threw my bag on the checking counter and was waved off. I got into the arrival hall where I was met with more chaos.

People were everywhere waiting for their passengers. Taxi drivers trying to lure you to their taxis were shouting above the crowd. Loud cheers would go up every so often when a loved one would appear through the arrival door. People were hugging and kissing—men were hugging and kissing—and children were wandering all over with moms trying to keep tabs on them. I observed police chatting off to the side, unconcerned and oblivious to all the noise. Some people were running back and forth peering through windows, looking for a glimpse of their relatives or friends still behind the customs door. It was complete chaos. Then I saw Mike laughing. He had probably been watching my expressions the whole time I was getting processed to get into the country. Holding out his hand, he said, "Welcome to the Middle East."

"Hello, Mike. Good to see you. Am I supposed to give you a kiss?"
I said laughing.

"Don't you dare," he replied.

"Is it always this crazy?" I asked.

"No, sometimes it's worse." He laughed.

"Holy shit; I didn't expect this! I think I am culture shocked again!"
I laughed.

"You'll get used to it. Pat, this is Abu Aimen, our driver." Mike
introduced the man with him.

Extending my hand, I said, "Pleased to meet you, Abu Aimen,"
looking him over.

He was a happy-looking fellow; he was smiling and round, with a
bald head, and weighed about 250 to 300 pounds. And he was loud.
He was comical to watch and somewhat hyper, but pleasant and had
many stories to tell.

"Pleased to meet you too, Mr. Pat," replied Abu Aimen. "Come,
let's go." Following him out, Mike and I chatted about home, the trip,
and family. We hadn't seen each other since we left the Arctic some
fifteen years earlier, so it was good to meet again. I was glad he was at
the airport.

We got in the car, a Mazda, and proceeded to the house where
the staff and Mike lived. I was in awe as we drove to the house. The
humidity and smell was repugnant, and I was sweating profusely. There
were no speed limit signs, I observed, as we rounded a few corners with
squealing tires on the hot pavement, weaving through traffic like there
was a schedule to meet.

When we arrived at the house, Mike invited me in for a drink and
to discuss what he had in mind. I met the rig manager, Al, and chatted
with him until Mike brought out our drinks. We chatted for a couple
of hours, and I was informed one of the rig managers had been killed
in a car accident. Then I went up to the staff house and crawled into
bed. It was about midnight. Sleep eluded me for a while, and I tossed
around before finally falling asleep.

I was awakened by this chanting about four in the morning, and at
first, I thought someone was partying too late. It went on for a while
and sounded like there was more than one singing. I went out to the
balcony to investigate and found it was the mosques all across the city,

singing their call for everyone to come and pray. I was told about it later that morning. I looked down on the street about six stories below and saw people everywhere, going to the mosque. This went on for about a half hour, and then it was silent, so I went back to bed but couldn't sleep. I had not been accustomed to such a thing before and was bewildered, thinking, *does this go on every night I must ask?*

A knock at the door about seven o'clock brought me to my feet. "Who is it?" I asked.

"Mike. Are you coming down for breakfast?"

"Be right there," I replied.

I went down to Mike's apartment and was greeted by his wife, Barb. "How are you? It's been a long time since we saw you. How are you?" she asked warmly. She was genuinely happy to see an old friend again, someone from Canada.

"I'm fine and happy to see you too," I replied.

"Did you bring any clamato juice?" she asked laughing.

I must have had a puzzled look on my face because she said, "Mike didn't tell you?"

"I'm afraid not," I replied.

"We can't have a decent Caesar here. They don't sell clamato juice anywhere, and I love Caesars," she said laughing. "Damned him anyway," she said still laughing. "He never tells people to do something for me."

"I'm sorry. Next time," I said laughing along with her. Mike was laughing and apologized for not telling me. "You're already in trouble." He laughed.

"Paddy! You need to come to the office and fill out your paperwork," Mike said. "Then you and Al can go to the rig and get settled in."

"Yep," I said. "Can do. When do we have to be out there?"

"You will meet the crew in Palmyra at one," Mike said.

"Palmyra," I said. "I've heard that name before."

"Probably in history," Al said while eating his bacon and eggs.

We chatted through our breakfast and then went to the office. Abu Aimen was there making coffee, grinning and saying with a wink, "Hello, Mr. Pat. Come meet Gazwa. She is our secretary and has your paperwork."

I followed Abu Aimen into Gazwa's office, and he introduced us.

She was a tall gal with a pleasant smile and had a pretty nice body. Abu Aimen was always drooling over her, and she would just play along, teasing him with her moves.

Extending my hand, I said, "Pleased to meet you, Gazwa."

Smiling, she said, "Welcome."

I filled out the paperwork and asked if there was anything else.

"You need go to see Zuhair," Gazwa said. "In the next office" she pointed.

I went in to Zuhair's office and introduced myself. He was a soft-spoken man with very good manners and presented himself with professionalism. We spoke for a while and got to know each other; then I filled out a few more papers for a work visa. I left him my passport so he could do whatever he needed to so they would allow me to work there, and then I went to see Mike.

"You all done?" he asked.

"I guess so," I replied.

"You keep an eye on Barber," Mike said. "And teach him how to push tools."

I could tell there had been some discussion previous to me entering the office and felt some tension in the room, but I said nothing.

We left the office and headed for the rig. It was quiet for a while, and then when we got to the outskirts of Damascus, Al said, "That fuckin' Cooper pisses me off sometimes."

"What do you mean?" I asked not knowing what to expect.

"Teach me how to push tools," he said sneering.

"Oh! I think he was just joking," I said.

"No fuckin' way," was the reply. "He's been on my ass for a while. Him and that fuckin' Jimmy Stevenson; they're both assholes," he said.

"Who's Jimmy Stevenson?" I asked somewhat bewildered.

"He's the electrician on the rig. He has his head stuck up Cooper's ass so far that he hasn't seen daylight for the last month," replied Al. "He's a fuckin' asshole I wanted to run off, but he's Cooper's buddy and you know how that goes."

"Well, I really don't want to go there," I replied.

"Are you Cooper's buddy too?" he asked sarcastically.

"Well, I've known Cooper for quite a few years," I replied wondering what I had gotten myself into. "He and I worked the High Arctic for a few years together."

"Well, I guess you and I will have to work things out," he said, again sarcastically.

"Hey, listen! I didn't come here to disrupt anything. If you have a problem with those guys, don't take it out on me. I'm not going to get in the middle of this, and I sure as hell won't put up with bullshit," I said laughing at his anger, matter-of-factly and with some authority. I wasn't going to be drawn into a fiasco I knew nothing about. "If you're going to carry a chip on your shoulder because of this, then you best get it straight with those guys. Is that why you were quiet last night?" I asked calmly.

"I don't fuckin' know," was all he could say.

What the hell is going on? I guess we will see. I really don't need this shit, but I'm here now and I hope everything works out, I thought.

For the next two hours, it was quiet. We didn't talk. He had a scowl on his face, and I knew something was bothering him. I couldn't quite figure it all out but had a pretty good idea of what Mike meant by his comment before I left Canada. His words, "We need to straighten out this mess," went through my mind over and over. What did he really mean?

When we approached Palmyra after driving through nothing but desert sand and cactus with small spindly shrubs, I was somewhat impressed at what I saw. A small oasis appeared with palms greeting us as we pulled in to the Cham Palace Palmyra Hotel and parked under a crudely shaded area made of poles with palm leaves over the top two-by-fours. Ruins, from the days of Queen Zenobea, stood out, a couple hundred yards away. The pillars, some thirty feet tall, were still intact. Some of the pillars had fallen over and lay in ruins, piled up in areas four to six feet high with trails throughout where local people and tourists had been walking. A saddled camel, with its owner sitting by on a piece of ruin, waited for tourists vacationing there to ride through the ruins and enjoy the scenery.

We entered the hotel and were greeted by marble floors, columns of cement pillars carved and shaped by local craftsmen, I presumed, and a bar where one could sit and listen to Arabic music while sipping on a cocktail or beer. Shops lined the south end of the hotel selling trinkets, which, while appearing old, had actually recently been made by local craftsmen trying to make a living on the tourist industry.

Across the road in front of the hotel was a sulfuric stream running through rock below the surface and accessible by a stairway, called an Afka. It is a site known to many tourists who dip or bath in the water, believing it to have some type of healing power, keeping you young.

Sipping beers, we waited for a short while until the crew going out arrived from the rig. This was our meeting point, saving the drivers from driving too far in one day. The crew entered the hotel where I was introduced to them. Brian and Tom spoke of what was happening at the rig and laughed at a few jokes. They seemed happy to be going on days off. A half hour later, we were off to the rig with Maher at the wheel.

Prior to leaving the city, I looked around and saw an old amphitheater I assumed was used in those days probably by gladiators and for speaking to the people. Many of the ruins were in pretty good condition, and one could draw a picture in one's mind of what it might have looked like back in the days of old. History claims this city was a huge trading center for silks passing through to Europe, and from what I saw, there certainly was a lot of history.

While driving through Palmyra and looking intently at the surroundings, I was in awe observing, for the first time, that cars and donkeys shared the same streets. A man with a donkey pulling a cart loaded with propane bottles trotted along the main corridor exiting town. People, selling figs and dates that had just been harvested, were along the street shouting in Arabic, announcing their wares. We stopped and bought some, wanting to experience the taste of the fresh commodity with no chemicals, and found them good.

Exiting town, Maher put the pedal down and was cruising at one forty. Volvo buses carrying people and sheep passed us like we were standing still, swerving around us, weaving, trying to maintain control as they reentered the proper lane. Police checkpoints were about a hundred miles apart, with two policemen or customs agents manning the building, a small mud and plaster hut with a couple of beds and a fire pit outside. An old Toyota Land Cruiser sat outside each station, seeming not to be used much. Sometimes they would walk out to the center of the road, their arm extended waving up and down to stop us and ask us for *moya* (meaning water). We would give them a bottle or two, gladly.

Al was sleeping in the front seat as we drove. With nobody speaking, it was nice. I was just looking around and observing the culture.

We arrived in Deir ez-Zor. I noticed the activity around this small city as people crossed the street everywhere, with barely enough room for one to drive, as you crept through the crowd, careful not to injure anyone. Cars, Lorries and donkeys were everywhere. Carts, loaded with propane and other goods as high as one could reach and tied down with twine, were common throughout the city. People were shouting out their wares; many others were pushing, shoving, and pressing through to each stand set up along the street in front of other shops to buy vegetables, meat, fruit, clothing, and shoes. I'm sure all had permits and licenses to operate their businesses, especially by codes and standards forced upon us in the West. No one seemed to mind and tolerated each other. Three-wheeled tricycles with a box, three feet by maybe five feet, putt-putted along with cows and calves tied in, the rider struggling to control the thing so it would go straight. Many times, we slowed down and waited until one would get to the right side of the road, and then we would pass. Light poles had wires strung crudely across them and over them; some had bare wires going to small shanty shacks so one could have a light or electricity for whatever they needed. Some were leaning as much as ten degrees. It appeared chaotic and disorganized, but everybody was doing what was necessary to make their way of life work.

Finally making our way through town, we proceeded to the rig, about a forty-five-minute drive, passing many people walking or traveling on carts being pulled by donkeys, lorries, and old buses loaded with goods, sheep, and children. It appeared they were content with the way of life they were living. They had enough fresh vegetables, meat, and other commodities, untouched by chemicals, growth serums, chlorine, and polymers, for all. Their food appeared to be good, wholesome, and natural.

I did not see anyone spraying for insects, putting down fertilizers, or spraying for broad leaf plants. I saw people working their fields mostly by hand, with hoes and shovels, trenching water to their plots of land, allowing enough water to make food grow. Some of the dikes and trenches had been destroyed by some force, probably over years of fighting for power, which made it more difficult for everyone. Everybody worked. Men, women, and children were in the fields. The odd small tractor with a three-point hitch and plow, probably owned by the whole community, was working and utilized by all. They were good, hard-working people, trying to make a living with what they had, not wanting anything more than food or shelter, as I found out.

Arriving at the rig, I was dropped off at the camp and given a room. A young fellow, who was introduced as Mohamed, guided me to my room smiling, trying to make conversation in his broken English. He checked to make sure I had towels and soap and made sure my bed was clean and made up. He was happy and smiled the whole time he was around me. When he left, I thanked him, and he replied, "Welcome, Mr. Pat."

I unpacked my bags, put my belongings away, and then went into the mess hall and poured myself a coffee. When I walked into the mess, all eyes turned toward me and everyone smiled and said, "Welcome." Some were inquisitive and wanted to know where I was from and if I had a family. After a lot of small talk and questions, I was allowed to drink my coffee. I felt no negativity coming from them toward myself, and everyone appeared happy.

The cook was busy cooking supper while some of the staff were cleaning dishes. The mess hall was relatively clean but could have used some fine-tuning in the corners and such. As I sat there drinking my coffee, I realized why the corners were not so clean. Thinking to myself; m*ost probably have dirt floors* clued me into their way of life of cleanliness. *Dirt floors would not show any un-cleanliness,* I thought and smiled to myself. They were doing the best they knew how.

I had to go to work to relieve the driller, who had been on shift since early morning, so I got up and thanked the fellows and then left for the rig. It was arranged that I would drill until midnight and then come in and be back out at eight, starting our twelve-hour shifts and two weeks of daylights.

Arriving at the rig, I went into the rig manager's office and discussed the plan forward and then went to the rig floor and met the relief driller. We chatted for a little while, and then he handed over the tour book and left.

The assistant driller came to the rig floor and introduced himself as Carlos Yap. He was a Filipino man, about five feet five and quite heavyset. He smiled the whole time he talked. He appeared somewhat tired and nervous at first but soon calmed down and settled into a conversation.

"Mr. Pat. We have too much problem out here," he said.

Not knowing what to expect, I asked, "What kind of problem, Carlos?"

"All people here too much yap yap and no too much work," he said in broken but pretty clear English, motioning with his hand and thumb opening and closing.

"About what" I was curious?

"Everything; These people no like work, so yap yap," he said again motioning with his hand and thumb.

"Oh! We get them to work. We just need to treat them good," I said to Carlos. "Maybe they are frustrated with not understanding English?"

"Maybe," Carlos replied. "But you see. They not understand the job." He left grinning.

We were drilling, so my first shift made it easier to get back into the swing of it. It was time to make a connection, so I blew the horn. The men came up, some smiling. Some came over and shook my hand, while a few sort of sneered, taking their positions for the connection. I pulled off bottom slowly and worked the pipe a couple of times, getting a feel for the controls. The phone rang. I chained the brake handle down and answered it. Al said, "You don't need to work the pipe," sort of gruffly.

"Oh! Is the procedure different here?" I asked.

"Just follow instruction," he said trying to show authority.

I laughed and told him, "I am following instruction. Where I learned to drill, you always worked the pipe to clean the bottom of the hole so you wouldn't get stuck in the cuttings."

He swore at me and then said, "You don't need to work the fuckin' pipe," and hung up.

At that point, I knew there was going to be some head-butting or I would leave. I wasn't going to tolerate being talked to like that.

I finished the connection, ran the pipe back to bottom, and started drilling. I told Carlos to watch the brake handle for me while I went to the office. I was going to discuss this and get things straightened out immediately.

I walked into the office, and Al was sitting with his feet on the desk, showing me who the authority was.

I calmly said, "What was that all about?"

He replied, "You work for me. If I tell you to do something, you just do it. Do what I say and not what I do."

I lost it on him. "Who do you think you really are?" I asked, changing the tone of my voice. "I don't work for you. I work with you."

"I'm your fucking tool pusher," was his reply.

"You're not my tool pusher. I have respect for the ones I've worked with. Maybe this is why Mike said he needs to make some changes out here." I glared at him. "Don't you ever talk to me or anyone like that or you'll be drilling if this happens again. Like I said to you on the way up, if you have a problem with some people, don't take it out on me." I walked out before he could reply thinking; *my first hitch and first day on the job. What did I get into?* I was angry and frustrated already, having only worked for about an hour. Maybe that was what Carlos had tried to tell me. This wasn't going to be easy, I thought.

Back on the rig floor, I asked Carlos what Al was like.

"You have problem already, Mr. Pat?" he asked. He must have seen the expression on my face, even though I tried to mask it.

"Not really," I replied, lying.

"Mr. Pat, sometime Al get too angry all the time and come up here *fuck, cocksucker, sand nigger,* and make too many people angry," he told me excitedly, with a lot of expression.

I left it like that and asked no more questions, understanding why we had some problems. The rig was running normally, but the place was a mess and disorganized. It looked like nobody had cleaned or painted for quite some time. Tools were lying around and crossover subs were everywhere. Drill pipe was piled in the desert with no organization, and thread protectors were missing on quite a lot of them. Drill collars of all sizes and Hevi-Wate drill pipe were mixed together, making it hard to know what we had on location. It appeared nobody was actually leading these guys. *Why?* I asked myself in my mind.

Ross, the company man, came up and introduced himself at around five thirty. He was going for supper and asked if I wanted anything. Since I didn't, he turned to leave and then came back and said, "Pat, finally someone worked that pipe before making a connection."

I was dumbfounded. I asked him, "Do you want me to work every connection?"

"I would appreciate it," he said. "Just don't work it too fast."

He was the boss. We worked for him, so I continued to work the pipe for the rest of the shift.

Ross was a tall Australian fellow with a good knowledge of the rigs. He and I hit it off right away, so when he came back from supper, he came to the rig floor and chatted for an hour or so. He was around fifty with graying temples. He seemed jolly and positive. He was about to leave when this smaller, red-eyed man came to the rig floor and started into the conversation, abruptly.

"Pat. This is Malcolm. He's your night pusher," Ross offered smiling. "You get any sleep, Malcolm?"

I stuck out my hand. "I'm Pat; pleased to meet you".

Ross left and went back to his office. Malcolm asked if I wanted to go for a smoke, so I accepted and walked around the pipe area looking at the equipment we had.

Things went pretty smoothly for the rest of the night. I observed the hands, checking on them from time to time to see what they were doing, trying to help them where I could. Some accepted me right away while others were doing their best to either avoid me or say something to see if I would retaliate. They were testing me out.

As the days went by, more of the men were talking and joking around, but a few were adamant about causing problems. They didn't like us there, but there was nothing they could do about it. After about six days, this one fellow, who told us to fuck off whenever we asked him to do something, caused a problem so I stood up and fired him. I guess he did this to everyone and nobody would do anything about it. I didn't know their labor laws and wasn't about to let this fellow disrupt the other hands. He threatened me for a minute, so I walked right up to him, putting my face close to his, and glared at him. He soon cowered, left the rig, and went to camp, cussing as he left. The next day, he was back on the rig and ready to work as if nothing had happened. I walked over to him and told him to go home. I meant what I had said the day before and wasn't backing down. He left. This set a precedent for the rest of the fellows who were troublemakers, I thought.

I went on night shift with a new crew. Some of them knew what had transpired a few days ago and were timid at first. After a few nights, I caught one of the derrick men sleeping inside the de-sander trough. He had turned off the de-sander, made a bed in the trough of old sacks and paper, and was fast asleep when he was supposed to be keeping the mud in good condition.

Startled when I woke him up, he immediately told me he wasn't sleeping. I laughed and told him I had to shake him and knew he was sleeping, but he was adamant he wasn't. I then told him to get the de-sander running and clean the pump house. He thought I was punishing him for sleeping, got really mad, threatened me, and then took a swing at me. I immediately fired him. He was one of the troublemakers the crew was happy to see go. I found out later that night from Carlos that they didn't like to lose face and would really put up a fight, even if they were in the wrong.

We had quite a crew: a Filipino truck driver named Victor, Filipino medic called Mandy, a warehouse man named John, and assistant drillers, Carlos Yap, Ding, and another fellow from the Philippines, but I can't remember his name. Jimmy the electrician and Neil our mechanic were from Scotland and England respectively. Andrew Stevenson and the other mechanic whom I can't remember were their relief. They were a good bunch of guys, but the Europeans were as high-strung as us and seemed to have to work by special departments, which was something we didn't do in Canada. The rig in Canada was controlled by the rig manager and didn't have a maintenance department, so we did have some conflict there at times, but it was nothing we couldn't iron out.

Everything was working, and the rig was taking shape, but we had a long way to go. I had a few days left on my first tour, and then it would be over. Al was still being an asshole once in a while, but he mellowed out quite a lot. I think he was afraid I was going to take his job and seemed to bring that up once in a while. Malcolm was Malcolm. He liked his weed and was pretty well not with it most times. He put in time and did some of the small stuff, but he wasn't pushing material.

All in all, the hitch went pretty well, and we were going on days off. I didn't have to stay extra time. We drove to Damascus and met up with Mike. Laughing, he asked, "So what do you think?"

"I guess it's all right," I said smiling. I was tired after thirty-five days.

"Come on. Let's go have a drink and something to eat," Mike said.

"Sounds good to me," I replied.

"Yes! That would be good for a change. A decent meal," Al said.

Mike and I looked at him and shook our heads. He was not happy with the food or the people on the rig. I found it to be adequate, although it wasn't what we were used to. The steak was cooked as best they could, and the vegetables were different from what we got at home. A lot of leeks and squash were cooked, but that was what you could get in town. We had corn and other vegetables from time to time, along with a lot of rice—their staple.

We went out for dinner, and then Al left saying he was going out on the town and would catch up to us later.

We drove back to the apartment where Mike lived.

"Come in, Paddy," he said. "Let's have a nightcap. I want to talk to you."

"Okay," I replied.

He poured us a Caesar and came and sat down across from me.

"Tell me how it really went," Mike said.

"Really, it went pretty good, Mike," I said. "Al was a little difficult at first, but I think it will be okay."

"He can be an asshole at times," Mike said. "I should just beat him up."

I laughed and said, "You can't just beat him up."

"Oh yes, I can," Mike said. "I've wanted to before, but I would hurt him too bad. Did he do a good job? What did you think of the rig?"

"The rig is in pretty rough shape, Mike. It looks like nobody is leading and there's no organization. The hands seemed to do as they pleased the first few days. I had to run a few guys off, you know," I said.

"Yes, I know," he said. "That's what we need out there. It seems like those other guys are afraid of the Arabs. Just be careful how you do it.

We could get into trouble with the labor laws here if we don't write three letters."

"Someone told me that, and we are trying to adhere to the laws, but some of those guys are so pissed off at the way they are treated by the expats, they will attack you," I said. "They tell me that they are being sworn and cussed at all the time. I also saw it a couple of times, and when I said anything, I was told to look after my own job. You can't treat people like that and expect them to work for you."

"I know. That's why I want you to push tools for me. I think you can sort things out. You are strong in nature, and I think they will respect you. Al has already lost that respect. I think it's too late for him to regain that, but we are going to give him a chance for a while."

"By all means, Mike. He's earned that."

"I have to let Brian go though, Paddy. I have a lot of complaints from the company men about his drinking. Even though I have warned him, he still continues to do it. He won't come back after next hitch, so be ready to push. You may have to stay longer next hitch," Mike said.

"Well, with all due respect to Malcolm, maybe you should give him a chance first. He's probably earned it being here longer than myself," I said.

"No way; he has a big problem with drugs, and I don't need that headache. He'll never push for me," Mike said.

"Well, I'll think about it and talk to Barb about staying longer next hitch. I sure don't want to upset the applecart," I said.

"Paddy, you won't. If they get upset, then I will deal with it when it comes. Malcolm is next on my list," Mike said. "We need to get this straightened out or we might lose the contract."

"Okay! I don't mind pushing if everybody is for it. I don't like it when I have to argue with the older hands to get shit done," I said. "I'll see. I'm going to bed."

I finished my drink, grabbed my passport, and headed to the staff house. I was exhausted. Five weeks was a long time, working every day, twelve hours a day, without a break.

The bed felt good when I lay down, but I was excited about getting home and seeing Barb and Tiffany. We were still living in Winnipeg and were anxious to get moved back to Roblin, but we hadn't told Tiffany yet. Tiffany was still in school, so we had to decide if it was better for her to be moved or stay in Winnipeg. That poor kid had moved so much with my work taking me to every end of the globe.

We flew back at six thirty in the morning through Frankfurt and then Toronto to Winnipeg where my bride picked me up, of course, with my daughter, Tiffany. We chatted on the short ride home and had a few laughs, happy to see one another.

We settled into the apartment, put on some coffee, and discussed moving back to Roblin with Tiffany. She was against moving to Roblin as her friends were in Winnipeg and she was tired of moving all the time. She pouted for the evening, crying a little, while we tried to convince her. The school was getting to be too much for us to handle, due to some of the violence.

Some of the kids, Tiffany included, were supposed to meet, and a fight was to ensue. We stopped Tiffany from going, and sure enough, a problem did arise. We received a letter from the school attesting to this making our decision easier. Like it or not, we were moving.

We got up the next morning and drove the four and a half hours to Roblin to see what was available to rent, so Tiffany could start school there in the fall. We found a trailer house and decided to rent that for the time being and then visited with the folks before leaving to go back to the city.

When we got home, packing started immediately. Tiffany was nearly finished with school, and we had a few weeks to pack so we were taking our time. The phone rang.

"Hello," I said.

"Hello, Paddy. Mike here; how are you" came over the phone?

"I'm doing fine, enjoying days off. What's up" I asked?

"Do you think you can come back a week early? I'm trying to set up a schedule so you can push in Brian's place," Mike said. "You'll work three weeks then have three weeks off, falling into a five-week rotation with Al. You will drill for three weeks then come back as a rig manager."

"I guess I can do that," I said. "What about the rest of the guys. Maybe Tom will push tools. Did you ask him?" I replied. "And what about Paul Black? He's been there for quite a while," I replied.

"No! I want you to push. That's why we hired you," Mike replied.

"Well, okay. I'll be there," I said.

125

"So you are coming a week early?" Mike repeated.

"I'll be there," I said.

"Okay, Paddy. Thanks and I'll see you in a week or so."

"Okay. Will they change my ticket here, Mike?" I asked.

"They should. If they don't, just get a one-way ticket and we'll reimburse you," he said.

"That will work," I said. "Okay. Bye."

We hung up, and Barb looked at me. "What was that all about?" she asked.

"I've got to go a week early to get on schedule. I'll be pushing tools after this stint. I'll be gone for only three weeks this time so that's okay," I said.

"We have to move," she said. "We'll be okay. We can work it out. I'll just call Tony," she said. "Isn't that what brother-in-laws are for?" She laughed. She was always positive about these kinds of things. She would get it one way or another.

We were still packing when I had to catch the plane. The flight back was already routine and uneventful. I arrived back in Damascus and was picked up by Abu Aimen. We joked around and had some fun on the way to the staff house when he informed me that Mike was not there and Dale was relieving him for a few weeks. He dropped me off and left. I didn't see Dale that night, so I went to the staff house and lay around for the evening. I didn't know where to go in Damascus for a beer.

The next morning, Abu Aimen picked me up and drove to Palmyra for crew change. Another driller was coming in on days off, and I was to replace him for the three weeks to get on schedule.

We crew changed in Palmyra, handed over the shift, and then proceeded to the rig. I changed clothes and went to relieve the driller on tour. We chatted a while, and then he went to camp and slept until midnight. I was glad to see him arrive as I was tired from the long trip to work.

I had gotten into the rotation and things were going fine when the phone rang in the doghouse. Al called me down to speak to Dale. He asked me what I was going to do and informed me that someone else had been chosen to push tools. I said that was okay but was somewhat bewildered by that. I went back to the floor and wondered what was going on. The reason I came in early in the first place was to get on rotation so I could push. *I'll just wait until Mike gets back,* I thought. *Something must be crossed up.*

When Mike arrived, about a week later, he came out to the rig. I was called into the office and asked why I had declined the pushing job. Somewhat surprised, I told him I hadn't declined anything. I was informed that a decision was made to give the job to someone else.

"Who told you that?" Mike asked.

"Well … Dale phoned out here the day after I got back and informed me. I thought you and he must have discussed this, deciding to give it to Paul or Malcolm," I said. "That's okay," I said referring back to our conversation when I had gone on days off.

"Fuck!" He cussed a minute and then said, "I didn't say anything to Dale. In fact, I told him you were going to push. What the fuck is going on?"

"I don't know," I said.

"Those bastards are playing games. Dale was upset when Attiga sent me here instead of him," Mike said. "What did Barber say?" he asked.

"Nothing; He went outside when I talked to Dale, and I didn't say anything to him," I said.

"They are all in this. They all said that Paul should get the job, except for Jimmy," Mike offered.

"Well, maybe you should consider that because I can foresee a few problems," I said.

"There won't be any problems. If there is, we'll run them off," he said stressing *we* and chuckling. "Paddy, you are going to push, and that's all there is to it. Let's have a coffee. Fuckin' Barber can look after the floor for another hour. You and I are going to visit."

I was having doubts about this as it was already causing problems. I wasn't afraid of these kinds of things, but I wasn't sure if I wanted this at this time.

We had our coffee and chatted about our families and things; then I announced I should go back to the floor and left.

"What took so long?" Al asked sarcastically.

"We had a visit. Were you scared up here by yourself?" I asked jokingly.

"No. Did he ask about me and you?" Barber said.

"Why would he ask about us? He wanted to know if I was pushing tools or not," I replied.

"Well?" he said questioning me.

"I don't know," I said. "Appears there is some confusion on who is supposed to push," I said.

"Dale said Paul was going to push," Al said and then wanted to swallow his words. He had let the cat out of the bag, so to speak. He had known all along what was going on.

I smiled and said, "You better go down and have a coffee with Mike. He looks lonely."

Mike was peering out the window. He would move away and then reappear, holding his coffee. He was a little taken aback on what had transpired, and so was I. *What is it going to be like? Will they work for me, or will I have to send one of them home to make a statement?* My thoughts were spinning around in my head. Choices! Sometimes you are forced to make a choice you really don't want to.

Al left the floor and went to the office. He was concerned somewhat and didn't know how to react or what to expect. He would have to get used to things and pick up the pace. He needed to manage the rig and his people so that a team could be formed and things would get done so we wouldn't lose the contract. He was aware of this and saw progress on the rig. Equipment was getting organized, the men were showing signs of improvement, the cussing had stopped somewhat, and people were smiling.

It was a good three-week hitch, uneventful except for the confusion. A lot of progress was made. Everyone was busy trying to organize the pipe bins and sub box and clean the rig. A few local hands were weeded out and calmness amongst the crews was observed and appreciated, not only by the expatriates but also by the locals who wanted to work. I went home for three weeks while a new driller relieved me.

Merrill, the bomber, was hired. He came with a full load of experience in the drilling industry and had been rig manager in Canada for a drilling contractor. He was keen and experienced in drilling wells but hadn't experienced the overseas operations, where everything is done by the rig crews. He had to learn about fishing, coring, and running power tongs, but he had been around the patch long enough to assist service hands in these areas, so it wasn't going to be a problem.

I arrived back as the rig manager.

Mike told me when I arrived at his place. "You will be the senior rig manager out there."

"What?" I asked in disbelief.

"The senior rig manager," he said again. "I see some big changes out there, and Al Furat is happy with the way things are going."

"Everyone is doing a good job, Mike," I said. "Everybody is trying real hard to get things better."

"I know. Since you went out there, everyone doesn't know what to expect," he said. "I like that."

"Oh come on. Those guys know what has to be done. I told them we all wouldn't have a job if we didn't improve," I said.

"Whatever," Mike said. "It seems that things have done a one-eighty. See if you can pull everyone together as a team."

"Well, I can't take the credit for their work. It was just getting them organized and asking them to do the jobs they were hired for. I gave them some insight to their positions and explained their responsibilities to them. Once they knew what was expected, they did most everything on their own," I said.

"That's why I want you as the senior push," Mike said. "Al is a good guy, but he needs to learn how to do things, like organize and explain rather than cuss and cause confusion. You can help him."

"He's doing a lot better and has been here a lot longer than me. Give him the senior push job, and I will help him as much as I can," I said.

Mike was stubborn when he had it in for someone and was relentless, not hearing anything I said. "No! You lead those guys," he said.

It was no use talking any more about it. I shook my head and changed the subject. "Where is Barb?" I asked.

"I'm batching for the next couple of weeks or a month maybe. She went home to see her mom," he said. "You hungry?" he asked.

"Kind of," I replied.

"Let's go to the Sheraton. They have a good little outside restaurant that serves a pretty good pizza. We can have a beer and enjoy the atmosphere," he said, grabbing his jacket. We had a couple beers and a pizza and then went back to the apartment. After some chitchat, I went to bed.

I couldn't fall asleep. The thought of being promoted above the whole bunch of the workers didn't fit well with me. What the hell was it going to be like? I knew I was in for one of the biggest tests of my life. I knew Al wouldn't like it, but he was working opposite me. I would crew change in Palmyra, and he would be going home so that wasn't a big concern. What about Paul and Malcolm, though?

The next morning, I had breakfast and left for the rig. I handed over with Al, making small talk, not letting on about Mike's plans. He was happy to be going home, and Mike would inform him of his plans, if he wanted to. I wasn't going to say a word that would cause disgruntlement.

I had the driver stop at the museum in Palmyra before we went to the rig and browsed around there for about an hour. There were many things to see from ancient times. We came across a glass display, holding the remains of two mummies, dried up and discolored but in pretty good condition, a man and a woman, about five feet tall, preserved, but exposed to the elements under a sealed glass for everyone to see. Thoughts of, *Rest in peace,* ran through my head. *How can they when they are dug up and displayed?* I wondered if, in two thousand years, someone would be digging us up and displaying us. What a thought, but true, isn't it? I chuckled at my thoughts.

Arriving at the rig, I noticed more changes. The rig was definitely cleaner and more in order. I entered the office, threw my bags down, and read the handover notes Al had left. He had done a lot, leaving the rig organized and in good condition. A list of what was completed, started, and actioned was attached to my notes. I smiled, went into the back room, put my things away, and changed into my work clothes. This was going to be a good shift, I thought.

Everything had been put away, but the sub bin was a pet peeve of mine. Even though it was clean and all the subs were in it, I wanted something to make it a little more organized, allowing us to see at a glance what we had. We had to protect the threads on the crossover subs, as costs were escalating for re-cutting threads, and our costs had to stay within budgets, Mike informed me.

I walked over to the welder's bench and greeted Rudy, our Filipino welder. He was smiling, and we struck up a conversation, which lasted for a few minutes; then I asked him what he could do with that bin to make it more organized. We walked over to the bin and discussed what we would do and then agreed on installing pins welded to the floor of the bin, standing the subs upright, and numbering them by row. *Just what we needed,* I thought.

We were drilling surface hole while the men were getting the BOPs (blowout preventers) ready, banging up bolts on the flanges in preparation of installing them on the wellhead. We would start nippling up whatever we could while drilling surface hole, cutting our nipple-up time in half.

Rudy went to the welding area and started cutting pipe for the bins while I went to the office to draw a plan on how we would number them. I called Ding, the assistant driller, in and informed him of what we wanted to do. He laughed and said, "That won't work, Mr. Pat."

"Why won't it work?" I asked.

"Everybody will just throw them in and break the pins. You will see. Nobody cares," he said.

"I have a plan for that," I said chuckling.

"What you do Mr. Pat?"

"I will check the bin every day. If I find one sub out of place, whoever is the assistant driller on tour will have to empty the whole bin, clean all the threads, and put them back, organized as planned. I don't care who is responsible for messing the bin," I said laughing.

"Look at these guys. They just stand by and wait for me to do the work. They don't understand," Ding said.

Ding was always trying hard but was pessimistic about a lot of things. He laughed, realizing what I had just said then, "You mean all the subs. Even the ones not messed up?"

"Yes, all of them," I replied. "Maybe if you have to do it two or three times, all assistant drillers will pay more attention. Discuss this with your cross-shift," I said. "I'm going to make the assistant drillers responsible."

Laughing, he said, "Mr. Pat, you're crazy," making a circular motion with his hand around his ear.

I told him to sit down and have a coffee while I listened to some of his stories. He was a fun guy, also the slowest-moving person on location, but he knew what was expected. Finishing his coffee, he said, "I go empty the bin and get it ready for Rudy to weld. This is my first time," he said, laughing as he left.

Things went pretty well for some time, hitch after hitch. With the rig organized, everything was working pretty smoothly except for the normal problems associated with drilling oil wells. After about the third hitch pushing tools, we installed moving gear on the rig that allowed us to move in one piece with the derrick standing, full of pipe, if we didn't have to move too far, saving us a lot of rig-up time.

The men were getting the BOPs ready when Ding came into the office upset. He was having one of those days. He was lonely and thinking of home, I guessed, having been in about four months now. The Filipinos worked for twelve months and then had one month off.

When I was informed of this, I was astounded. I hadn't taken the time to observe this and wondered who could focus when away from home that long. I wanted to work on that and see what I could do.

"I will see what I can do for you guys," I told him. "Leave that with me."

"What you gonna do, Mr. Pat?" he asked.

"I'll talk to Mike," I said. "What would be fair? What kind of contract did you sign?" I asked.

"Everybody contract the same. All Filipinos work like that," he said.

"Maybe we can work three months and one month off," he said. "One year is a long time not being able to see your family."

At that point, I knew what was wrong and felt sorry for them but knew I would have to convince Mike.

"These guys all lazy, and we work too much," Ding said.

"I know they just stand around and let you do all the work. There are only three stupid people on this rig, and they are all assistant drillers," I said making him laugh. "Just go out there and do the best you can." This was my chance to explain what they were doing wrong, and I had to let them know. They worked too hard and needed some guidance on their positions as assistant drillers. They always tried to accommodate us when we asked them to do something and didn't utilize their crews. I said nothing yet.

Turning around, he asked, "Why you say all the assistant drillers are stupid, Mr. Pat?"

"When you change shift tonight with Carlos and Naoum, I need to see all of you. Tell them to come by the office before they go to work. I will explain then," I said.

Sure enough, all approached the office at six that evening with Ding in the lead. He was in better spirits now and was laughing. I could see he was telling the other assistant drillers what I had said.

They all came in, so I offered them a cup of coffee, and we sat around the office. Ding was laughing, Carlos was smiling, but Naoum was more serious. He was a bit more timid than the Filipinos, but the nicest man anyone could meet. He was our only Arab assistant driller.

After some small talk, Ding spoke up. "Mr. Pat, you tell us why we are stupid," he said laughing foolishly.

"I don't think you're stupid. I think you work stupid," I corrected what I had said.

"Why?" Carlos said grinning.

"I see all the assistant drillers are tired at the end of their twelve-hour shift. All the floor hands and roustabouts are not. The assistant drillers are in bed by eight o'clock, tired, and the others are still up laughing and talking until midnight. I think they are smart, and the assistant drillers are not. They get paid for doing nothing, and you do all the work, so you tell me who is stupid. I see this every day and was hoping you would do something about it." I wasn't going to lie about it.

Hanging his head down for a second and then laughing, Ding said, "What we going to do?"

"Let me explain," I said. "Assistant drillers are supposed to walk around and look the rig over. If there is anything to fix, he gets a roustabout or floor hand and tells him what to do, then walks away and finds something else to do. When everybody is working, he goes around and checks to see if they have a problem, then assists them. When everything is getting done, he finds a little job for himself, works for half an hour, then checks on the hands again. Your job is easy, but you make it hard for yourself when you're afraid to instruct someone to help you," I explained.

"Mr. Pat, they don't understand," Ding said again.

"Of course they don't understand. If you do all the work, how will they learn?" I asked. "I want all of you to try this for a week, then let me know if it works. I'm sure you'll see a big difference."

"Okay. We try," said Naoum. He was laughing along with us now and understood. They left and went to work, laughing.

After about a week, Carlos came in. I saw the changes in their attitudes, and they appeared to be a bit more relieved.

"Mr. Pat, you busy?" Carlos asked.

"No! Come in," I replied.

He was grinning from ear to ear. "I guess you're right. We were stupid," Carlos said getting himself a coffee.

Laughing, I said, "You know, Carlos, there are no stupid people. It's just some people have more experience than others. Everybody can learn. We might know how to drill, but we know nothing about many other things. We too can learn every day if we watch and want to. I think these hands have taught me some things too," I said.

"Really Mr. Pat; what did they teach you?" asked Carlos, chuckling, not believing me.

"I watch them catch pipe with a rope when running in the hole. I never saw anyone do that before. They don't get thrown around like we used to when I was a floor hand. I think that is a good idea and wonder why I didn't think of that before," I replied. "Some of us used to get thrown around, many losing their fingers by getting them squashed between the pipe and the stump. When we stop learning, we will be dead."

"I never think like that before," Carlos replied.

We still had some disgruntlement with a couple of the expatriate hands who thought they should have gotten the position Mike had put me in, so we weeded out the ones that were the problem, and operations ran smoothly. Al was still somewhat annoying at times, but we could put up with that, seeing he was doing well, taking responsibility for the leadership role he was in.

It was November 1991. We were drilling a well right along the Iraqi-Syrian border. Things were heating up over the invasion of Kuwait by Iraq. George Bush Sr. was preparing to liberate Kuwait with military action, and we were preparing for the worst, planning our escape if problems arose. We were to drive to the Turkish border if we were not captured and kept the Nissan Patrol full of fuel, along with four full jerry cans strapped to it.

Everyone had to register with their embassies as a precautionary measure, so we could be accounted for if we were unfortunate enough to be taken hostage. Syria and Turkey were part of the coalition, so tension was high amongst the Arabs. Some agreed, and many didn't, especially the Palestinian Arabs. They seemed more adamant about fighting along with Iraq, some taunting us at times. I recall one Palestinian from Jordan telling us we were going to get our asses kicked and Saddam was going to control the world. Knowing better than to get involved, I changed the subject and attempted to get him to do his job. At first, it seemed to distract him. He would get on the forklift and get whatever we required.

I came home for Christmas around the twentieth of December, and everybody in our little town was curious about what was going on over in the Middle East. Inquisitively, they asked if I knew or saw anything. Of course, I wasn't involved, so I really couldn't help them with their questions. The news blared out constantly, with the invasion imminent, near to start. Warships and machines were being deployed to the gulf with a showdown of power about to begin. Coffee shops were buzzing with curiosity; some patrons with maps questioned me when I walked in for coffee. Spreading their maps out in front of me, they wanted to know where I worked and what this war was all about. Are they fighting for oil? Are those people crazy? Many unknowingly blamed the States for the problems. Many blamed the Arabs.

I replied, "Sometimes, I think we watch too much television." I wasn't choosing sides as I had my own personal feelings for those people. I had been working there for a year by now and found them to be no different than we. Some were a bit more aggressive than others, but we had the same problem here. I really didn't understand what was going on anyway, so how could I give them answers?

I believe it was around January 15, 1991, I was still home and the news broke that coalition forces had started to liberate Kuwait. The war had begun. I went to town to get the mail, and people were buzzing with gossip about the war. Many people were adamant it was the right thing to do; some were very opinionated. Self-righteousness was rampant throughout the country. Many asked if I was going back.

Many thought I was crazy when I said I was. They really had no idea what they were talking about. Brainwashed as they were by the media and such, no one sat down to think about what they were saying.

Oil was a big topic. Some accused the Bush government of that. I still wasn't picking sides but did say to one gentleman that I didn't believe it was all about oil. "A country was invaded. Its women and children were being raped and tortured, thrown out of their homes, bank accounts seized, cars stolen, etc. Do you think that's okay?" I asked, trying to make him think about people rather than oil, still trying to avoid picking sides and remembering what Issam told me at camp. "It's too bad we haven't learned to use our power of speech properly," I offered.

"What do you mean by that?" he asked.

"I think this has been going on for a lot longer than a year. We have had a lot of time to work with these people through diplomacy but we have failed. We propped them up with arms when they were fighting the Iranians. Governments all over the world seem do the self-righteous, then sway you through the media that they are doing this for the betterment of man and country, under the guise of help and safety making everyone feel pity for their actions. They sway many within their borders to believe they are just, and really, they are doing it for power, sponsored by corporate business," I said without giving him a chance to speak. I hated this kind of mentality especially when one hadn't been more than two hundred miles from his hometown and had seen nothing of how these people were. *Brainwashed by the negativity of the media and swayed to support the killing of people through wars,* I thought.

He picked up his map and found another table. I saw he was thinking about what I had said and felt he knew I was perturbed by his initial remarks. More people need to travel and see for themselves that people can get along. *It is governments who can't and draw us into their schemes,* I thought.

I left the coffee shop and drove home, thinking about the time when Regan sent aircraft into Libya and attempted to get Gaddafi. That was big news at that time also. They missed Gaddafi but killed his seven-year-old daughter. How sad this was, that not many gave it a thought. A poor innocent little girl lost her life because her dad as head of Libya and Regan of the USA couldn't work things out through speech and diplomacy. We are now in the same class as we condemned. Terrorist! We killed an innocent child and never thought about what we did. My mind was racing.

When I arrived home, I phoned Tom in Athabaska, Alberta.

"Hello," his wife answered.

"Hello, this is Pat. Pat Carriere. Is Tom home?" I asked.

"Yes, he is. Are you going back?" she asked.

"Yeah, I think so, unless we get a call not to," I replied.

"No way Tom is going. We already talked about that, and he's not going back," she said matter-of-factly. "Here's Tom."

Laughing, he said, "Hello, Pat. I guess you know, huh?" he said.

"I guess so," I said. "You're not going back?" I asked.

"No. That's asking for a divorce," he said. "Are you?"

"Oh yes. I don't feel we will be in any danger," I said.

"I don't care. I'm not taking that chance," he said.

"I don't blame you," I said. "How was days off?"

"Kind of just stuck around home and got the honey-do list nearly done," he replied.

"That sure keeps us busy," I said laughing. "Most people wouldn't understand that because they are home every night and weekend to do the odds and ends around the house."

"Yes, I guess so. I've never thought of that, though. Anyways, could you tell Mike I won't be coming back? I tried to phone him, but I'm having a hard time to get through," he said.

"I'll tell him, but you keep trying to get hold of him," I said.

"I'll try. You have to leave day after tomorrow, and I don't know if I will be able to contact him," he said.

"I'll let him know, Tom. Bye for now, and keep in touch," I said.

"Yes, you keep in touch too. Bye for now," he said and hung up.

He must have gotten hold of Mike because that evening, Mike called.

Chapter Ten

I answered, "Hello."

"Paddy, Mike here. How are you?"

"I'm fine. How are you? Are things heating up out there?" I asked.

"It's pretty quiet. You know, I don't think we have a lot to worry about," he said.

"I kind of feel the same way. I think the Syrians are pretty good and reasonable," I said. "What's the atmosphere like?" I asked.

"A lot of people are talking and don't agree with the USA, but they're staying pretty calm. You coming back?" he asked with concern in his voice.

"If I'm not fired," I said jokingly.

"Tom called tonight, and he's not coming back. I tried to talk to him but his wife gave him the ultimatum. I think he would come back if his wife wasn't threatening him with divorce," Mike said.

"Well, I guess family comes first in these kinds of situations. Some people can handle it and some can't. I am concerned but not afraid. Maybe you and I are just plain crazy and don't care," I said.

"You're probably right. I have been working here for quite a few years and never had a problem. When Libya got bombed, it got somewhat scary at first until Gaddafi made a statement, telling his people not to bother the expats in the oilfield. After that, everything calmed down," he offered.

"A man gotta do what a man gotta do," I replied. "See you in a couple days."

"Make sure now. Don't leave me in a bind," Mike said laughing. "We're shorthanded a couple of guys now. Bye for now." We hung up.

"Was that Mike?" Barb asked.

"Yes! He was concerned I wasn't coming back," I replied.

"Are you going back?" she asked, not interfering with my decision.

"I'm going to go back," I said. "You know television always shows you the worst of the worst. It's too bad they sway a lot of people and scare the hell out of everyone. I believe we should do whatever it takes to stop this kind of activity and keep our noses out of other people's business. The problem is that everybody likes to run the States down, but who do they call whenever there is a problem? I have mixed feelings for what is going on especially when Issam told me he lost everything fleeing Kuwait. You know, those guys have been fighting for centuries now and haven't solved anything. Power, self-righteousness, and suppression are the only excuses for why war is fought. Why does one think they have to control someone or something? Corporate business," I said.

The next couple of days were spent getting ready to go back to the Middle East—packing, checking my passport, getting cash in case of a problem, wondering what was going to transpire. Many thoughts were going through my mind. "Am I doing the right thing?" I said out loud.

"Honey, you have to just forget about everything and go with what your heart tells you," Barb said. "I think you have made many right decisions but … you also made many foolish ones." She laughed.

"You're right," I said. "At least we agree on that."

We were off to the airport in the morning. It was cold and clear. As we approached the airport, we could see steam coming off the aircraft engines as they fired up. Workers were deicing planes, busy trying to keep up and make these things fly, regardless of temperature. The airport was buzzing with travelers going to Toronto, Minneapolis, and Montréal. Airport staff announced flights in preparation for departure to destinations within Canada and the U.S. Walking over to the check-in, ticket in hand, I placed my bags on the scales. I was going.

"You're going to Syria?" the check-in agent asked. I could tell she was wondering what I was going there for with the Gulf War going on.

"Yes! Gotta go," I said in my bravest voice without hesitation.

"You with Desert Storm?" she asked.

"No. I work in the oil patch," I said.

"Are you close to the action there?" she said inquisitively trying to make small conversation.

"We're right on the Iraq border. About a mile or so inside of Syria," I said.

She smiled and said no more, handing me my boarding pass and throwing my luggage on the belts.

"Good luck," she said as I was about to walk away.

"Thanks," I said and left.

Barb had gone up and found a coffee shop. We had a couple hours to kill so we sat around and chatted and then looked around at the shops that were open, finding me a couple of magazines to read on the plane. I liked *Time* or *Newsweek* because they had some stories that made sense at times. Some of the reading was quite political, and I wanted to know more about the way all this crap worked. *Can't learn enough,* I thought.

We said our good-byes, boarded the aircraft, and were off to the Middle East. Barb had to drive back to Roblin but wanted to shop for a few things in Winnipeg. She loved to spend time in the shops, usually buying only what she needed.

Sometimes I would joke around and tease her about buying tops. She was forever buying a new top or shoes, even though she had a closet full of clothes. I would call her Imelda and laugh. I didn't mind at all, because she earned everything just putting up with me. There were times I would mention that we couldn't afford it, causing a disagreement, but it never lasted too long.

My dad was showing signs he was sick and would be irritated because of it. We were taking them to Regina and Winnipeg, trying to find out what was wrong. Many times, round-trips were made in a single day. Barb would continue this whenever I wasn't home knowing we needed to help out where we could. My home was always open to family when they would come home for visits or to help out. We were preparing a meal, cleaning house, or washing laundry, all trying our best to make life enjoyable for Dad. It was the focal point for everyone to help, wherever they could. We enjoyed these special times to visit, help out, and get caught up on what each of us was doing in our lives.

Arriving in Syria a day or so later, I found the airport chaotic. People were leaving Iraq and going to Syria, Jordan, and wherever they could escape the throes of war. I had learned to put a five-dollar note in my passport, giving it to the customs agents, and was able to pass through quite quickly. They were there as soon as we arrived asking for our passports, knowing a little token awaited them. Upon getting through customs, I found the arrival hall full of people, shouting names, chaos everywhere. People were pushing and shoving to get to the front of the line to greet their loved ones, friends, or acquaintances. Taxi drivers were looking for fares, and personal drivers, standing around with company logo signs, waited for workers to take them to their hotel rooms.

"Hello, Mr. Pat," I heard. Abu Aimen was standing off to the side and spotted me as I came through.

"Hello, Abu Aimen. How are you?" I asked.

"Good. Let's go. It's crazy here now with all the people trying to get away from the war," he said. "Maybe we have problem in Syria because they fight with the U.S.," he said.

"Oh, I don't think so," I said knowing full well what he meant.

"Many people don't like the war," he offered. "Everybody's crazy now."

I left it at that as we proceeded to the car in silence. As he was taking me to the staff house, a police car went speeding by us.

"Too much police now," he said. "Everywhere they stop people and check."

"Why?" I asked.

"Many are ... maybe not from Iraq and make big problem for Syria. Before, we had a big problem in Hamas with Abu Nidal and some of his people. Many people died because of that problem," he said.

I had read a book on Abu Nidal and found it interesting he would speak about that. I also listened to another man, Mayad, tell me the story of how the army went in to Hamas, destroying houses, killing many, looking for this man. He mentioned somewhere upward of twenty-five thousand people died.

Nidal, apparently, was asked to leave Syria, and from what I understood, didn't in the time frame he was given, causing a bit of a problem for the government of Syria. A lot of pressure was put on some of these countries to locate this man, who had been branded a terrorist. I am not schooled on this but was informed, by chance, *Time* magazine, the news, and the book. It appeared these people wanted the outside world to understand their strife, but with them being branded, no one was interested.

Upon my arrival at the staff house, Mike greeted me and invited me in for a nightcap. I was tired from the flight and after having one drink, went to bed.

The next morning, I went to the rig with Abu Aimen and crew changed in Palmyra as usual. People seemed pretty calm and appeared like nothing was happening. Some fellow came up to me and asked if he could have a few words with me. I agreed so he hopped into our Nissan. Abu Aimen was standing outside and waited for me.

Once inside the Nissan, he introduced himself to me as a reporter/journalist for some European newspaper. He asked if I was comfortable in Syria, and I replied I was. He then asked me if I had seen anything unusual in Syria, to which I said no. He told me, rumor had it, some people were trying to overthrow Hafas Assad, the president, and it was planned from Deir ez-Zor. "Have you seen or heard anything?" he asked to which I replied I hadn't. I was somewhat bewildered by this man, and I told him it wasn't my place to get involved with this, excused myself from him, and got out of the car. He was an Arab man, well presented, and I, not wanting to get involved with politics, especially when the neighboring country was at war with the West, left. Sometimes you don't know whom you are talking to.

While I was walking toward Abu Aimen, he asked, "What does that man want?"

"I don't know. He said he was a reporter for some paper and heard there was some problem," I said.

"What problem" asked Abu Aimen?

"Something to do with people maybe trying to overthrow Assad," I replied.

"Oh! Many people talk like that and all bullshit," he said. "That man might work for the police and wants to see if you're involved with anything in Syria. Sometimes they do this sneakily."

I thought about this for a few minutes and was glad I didn't know anything.

Back at the rig, everything appeared normal. The hands were talking about the war and were concerned about what was happening. The forklift driver approached me sneering and said, "See, Mr. Pat, Saddam is going to control the world."

I wasn't in a mood to be sneered at and intimidated. I said, "Really. What makes you so sure?"

"He make promise on television that he will fight to end and will win," he said.

"Let's just do our jobs and forget this is going on. We have work to do, so let's go to work," I said attempting to persuade him to concentrate on work rather than on the war.

"You see!" he said as he left.

The first week went by somewhat normally. The hands were listening to the news constantly and keeping up with what was going on. Desert Storm was making huge progress liberating Kuwait. They were ready to move into Iraq. They had captured some of the soldiers and had free reign of the skies, patrolling the south of Iraq and setting up a no-fly zone. Many sorties were coming overhead from Turkey, up to twenty-five aircraft, flying low enough so the payload was visible. Saddam had warned of blowing up the Kuwait oil fields and people were concerned. The Iraqi army was retreating and blowing up some wellheads; some were already on fire.

One night, I was standing out in front of the rig office having a smoke, and the hands approached me. They were smiling and wanted to visit. We talked for about ten minutes and then the driller sounded the horn. It was connection time. One of the fellows stayed behind; he spoke pretty good English. Out of the blue, he said to me, "Mr. Pat, who is the terrorist, me or you?"

Somewhat taken aback, I replied, "Let's not talk about that. I don't want to get involved with government issues."

This fellow was always kind to us and liked us, so I was surprised when he asked that.

"No! No Mr. Pat. Me and you *sideek*," he said, meaning friends. "Tell me."

"I don't know," I said chuckling. "You tell me." I didn't want to get caught up in this subject, but he appeared to have something to say and who was I to deny him that?

"Okay! I think you are the terrorist," he said smiling.

"Why?" I asked curious to see what he wanted to say.

"Mr. Pat. The West makes all the bombs. They make all the airplanes to carry the bomb. They make guns, tanks, missiles, and train their people to kill others. They sell to countries that don't like us, bombs and aircraft, and bomb our houses and families. They make all the chemicals, and then they are used on us if we don't agree. Who made the big bomb that killed many people in Japan? They even train other people to use this. We don't do this to you. This why the people are angry at the West," he rattled off.

I saw an expression on that man's face as he spoke that made my heart drop. I wasn't sure what to say, because even though I looked at things that way sometimes, I was set up in my comfort zone. I was seasoned to the Western propaganda, and my views sometimes swayed to the Western values that were different, but I knew in my heart he was right. I wasn't up to speed on history and knew it. I would have to study a bit more so I could understand it better. Remaining neutral, all I could say was, "I'm sorry. I'll think about that." He went back to the rig. I had this guilty feeling of denial, not fully realizing this and accepting it.

Some nights, we would see Scud missiles take off from the desert on the Iraqi side of the border going to Israel. We even saw one get struck by a Patriot missile. As it flew toward Israel, the light grew dimmer, distancing itself from our view, and then a flash lit up the sky in the distance, as it was struck by something. Whenever they would see a Scud, the hands would shout and cheer, *"Yahudi,"* meaning Israelis. I did ask why they were so against the Israelis, and everyone told me, "My father doesn't like, my grandfather doesn't like, so I no like."

Can you believe that? They learned to hate because of their upbringing and didn't know why. Not one had a better explanation. They too were born with a clean heart and learned this from others; whether it was schools of hate or from parents, this is how they were educated. History tells them to hate and teaches them how. We definitely have a problem around the world with education systems.

I hated history in school because it taught us the negative things, like wars, and kept us in this mindset we have today. It seems to idolize certain people who invaded or suppressed different cultures through choices used wrongly, inflicting pain and scars throughout nations, for no other cause than power, control, and greed. Living in the past seems to keep segregation going, fueling hatred and reminding cultures around the world of the atrocities inflicted on man. It needs to go away. Good history is near extinct.

We were just finishing a well, laying down drill pipe, when I noticed the forklift driver getting more aggressive. He was picking the forks up as high as they would go and then dumping the drill pipe from that level, damaging a lot of our pipe string. I walked over to him and asked, "What are you doing?"

He swore, grinned, and then dug into the pile of pipe doing it again, followed with an attempt to injure me with the machine. He was testing me to my limits now, so I relieved him of his duties. He was angry at the way Desert Storm was going, knowing what the outcome was going to be. They had already liberated Kuwait and were talking about going right to Baghdad, but Saddam retreated and the war was over in six weeks. About twenty minutes after the episode, he came over to the office and apologized crying. He said, "He promised us. He promised us."

I felt sorry but knew he needed some type of help to stabilize himself. He was going to hurt someone with that kind of mentality, and I couldn't take that chance, even though I did ponder the idea of letting him stay.

Kuwait was on fire and talk of getting the wells under control was in the works. Many companies were working on ways to extinguish these fires. Thank God for that.

When I think about those fires, I find it hard to believe that no down-hole shutoffs were used in those wells. This disaster could have been somewhat less if the oil companies would have used these valves, which are regulated by flow and shut the well off in these types of situations. Everyone around the world knew the turmoil, how volatile it was in this part of the world, and took no initiative to protect the wells and the people. Again, governments and corporate business need to take some responsibility for this, even though they blame Saddam, who was part of the cause. The cost of this would have been minimal compared to what they experienced, not to mention the damage it did.

We felt the scope of the problem when it rained in Syria. We had just cleaned the rig, and I noticed, when walking around the rig, the air tank, which had been white before the rain, was black with sticky oil fallout. *What a disgusting problem,* I thought. *How many people are going to be affected by this? How many health problems will these people have? Are they not concerned about the people? Why do governments around the world vie for power at the expense of people?*

Rig move started, and it was a tough move. A sandstorm, the first I had seen in Syria, was in progress. Sand was blowing so hard it was penetrating under the seals of our safety glasses, causing our eyes to turn red and sore. Dust masks couldn't keep the dirt from our lungs, and our skin was pelted with small, sharp bits of sand, causing welts and small abrasions. Trucks were jockeying around trying to load and unload to get off location and go home.

The turnkey office, controlled by whomever, was responsible for the trucks, and each driver was given a number. If we didn't load them by their number, many arguments erupted between the drivers to the point guns were drawn and a few shots fired. They didn't understand the process of the rig move, causing some of the larger trucks we tried to save and load with appropriate loads to be loaded lightly. The drivers were getting angry and displaying their number, given to them by the turnkey people, to us. When we tried to explain, they wouldn't hear of it. Their number was that, and we would load them or there would be a big problem. They surrounded the cranes and trucks being loaded and created a chaotic scene. The rig move was shut down until calmness was restored. We had to call in the police and army at times to restore order, and then it was our fault. We commenced work until the trucks were finally released. The rig was being rigged up, and things were going pretty well. The hands were doing the best they could, and we couldn't ask for anything more. No one got hurt.

It was one of our more trying hitches, and I was glad when it was over. I had stayed for a couple of extra weeks due to them being shorthanded. I was stressed out and exhausted, unable to function properly, it seemed. Now I knew what the Filipinos felt like, working a year at a time. *I can't do it,* I thought.

I arrived in Damascus around four in the afternoon and went to the office. I discussed the rig with Mike and had the driver pick us up some chicken from Popeye's Fried Chicken, just around the corner from the office. We ate, and then I asked about the progress on the Filipinos' schedule. Mike reached into the folder on his deck and pulled out a piece of paper and handed it to me.

"That's great, Mike," I said. "Those guys are going to appreciate that." We had gotten approval for a three-month-on-and-one-month-off schedule. This was a lot better than one year and one month. "Did you implement it yet?"

"No. Not yet. I just got it the other day, Paddy. I think I'll wait until you come back," Mike said.

"Why? Let's do it now," I said.

"Well, you're the one who initiated this, Paddy. I think its right for you to give them the news."

"Hell! Just start it rolling. Carlos is about ready to go now. Let him go on field break now. There are three assistant drillers out there, and we only need two. Naoum is trained up good enough to allow that. He drilled before, Mike," I offered.

"I didn't know that," he said. "Can he handle it?"

"Of course he can! He's as good as the Filipinos and better than some of the Canadians I've worked with," I said to Mike trying to convince him. "Just do it. I don't need to be here. I don't need the recognition. They just want a fair deal, Mike."

"You got a soft spot for Carlos, don't you?" Mike accused. He wasn't onboard for the new schedule and once told me, "They signed a contract," which kind of made me angry. I didn't like that mentality and wanted to tell him slavery was extinct but kept my mouth shut, because he was African-Canadian and may have taken offense. His dad was white, and his mom was African-Canadian. I had met his mom and found her to be very down-to-earth, good people.

"Maybe; I think I have a spot for all those guys. They work hard every day and never complain too much except when they miss their families or phone them. Have you ever left your family for that long, Mike?" I asked.

"No," he said.

"Well! Neither have I. I would be damned if someone would entice me to sign a contract that has that clause. Those guys are exploited because there are so many of them with not enough jobs or poor-paying jobs in their countries," I said defending them.

Sometimes, Mike would get under my skin when he would be inconsiderate to the other nationalities. I could see the changes in him as he strived to be at the top with the company. He seemed not to care much for the people who tried to do right by others. He would make statements to justify his actions. I was beginning to see many things, and it strained our relationship as friends, but he couldn't send me home because he knew with the turmoil going on, it would be hard to get people to go to the Middle East.

I went on days off. The war in Iraq was over, and people were working better with not so much talk about the war.

Many people were curious when I got home, asking questions I couldn't answer. I tried to tell them I saw nothing. They were thirsty for firsthand news from there about the action that had transpired, with no one really knowing why. They were curious and relieved it was over. Many blamed oil. Many blamed power. Many didn't understand and never will. It was typical small-town talk and gossip. They were educating each other, and stretching the stories to suit their imaginations in coffee shops, amongst people who probably understood very little of what governments did.

Many were opinionated though most had never left the outskirts of Manitoba, passing judgment from what they heard on television. They were judging based on what the elected leaders were telling them through the media, learning from gossip and not using their power to think and understand what the real problem was. It seemed they were not looking at the whole picture of what had happened to those people throughout history and the suppression perpetrated by the rich on the poor.

Many did not understand the killing going on in many parts of the world for oil, diamonds, plutonium, and other minerals greedy businessmen wanted at any cost. Blood money is what it's called. Many didn't understand the diamonds they wore may have come from Africa, where a lot of blood was shed over the smuggling of them through the ruthlessness of big corporations, greedily enticing those people with big dollars, so they too might one day live in peace with jobs to support themselves, knowing full well it would last only a short time. It wasn't understood that the sanctions put on these people after the smuggling and killing got out of control were starving the innocent, depriving them of medicines and food, because of the greedy, leaving them to go it alone after they got what they wanted. They did not understand the suppression of the black communities through apartheid. They were controlled by some foreign leadership, who took their country over in years passed, through war and barbarian tactics, killing many who opposed their leadership. They blamed the so-called terrorists without understanding the political field and how it worked under the power of big business. We need proper education for all, so everyone who wants to gossip knows the truth.

As time passed, the hype slowed, and it was now 1994. Days off flew by, and I went back to rig move again, and then back to drilling for the rest of the hitch. As soon as we commenced drilling, a sandstorm started brewing; the wind was picking up when the hands came into the office.

"Mr. Pat, come look!" one of them said with excitement in his voice. "For sure, we will have too much *ajug*." This meant dust.

I walked outside, and to my amazement, a huge wall was moving toward us about a mile away and just as high. It was as wide as your eyes would see from side to side, a massive rolling cloud at ground level. Standing there watching it come toward us, I wasn't sure what to do. When it was about a quarter of a mile away, I went inside the office and called the rig floor. Ralph picked up the phone and I told him to keep drilling, while we monitored the dust storm to make decisions later. Then it hit.

For the first few minutes, it was a beige color with sand swirling around, pounding on the walls of the office. It sounded like rain, but no water was falling. We couldn't see the rig now, although it was about three hundred feet away from the office. The wind was loud but not frightening, as dust came through every hole in the walls, between the roof and walls, the windows, the air conditioner, the holes for piping through the floor, everywhere. Stuffing rags and paper in the cracks did nothing so we put on dust masks. It was getting so thick inside the buildings, the countertops and desks were covered in a fine dust. Ralph called down after about five minutes and informed me he couldn't see the brake handle, which was right in front of him, and he couldn't see the gauges to control the pull on the pipe. We shut the operation down and circulated.

It was 1:00 PM, and the sky was turning black. By 1:30 PM, it was so dark it looked as though night had fallen. So much dust had accumulated in the air it blocked the sun out completely. It was like someone had turned the lights out. A sense of eeriness crept over the location, no one knowing where they were or where to go to escape the choking dust. No lights were visible on the rig, so speaking to the driller from the office phone was all the communication we had. No one dared to leave their protective cover as it would have meant being lost and at risk of getting hurt. I instructed Ralph to let the crews know they needed to stay where they were and to get some indication of a head count. I was concerned that someone was caught outside in that dust storm. It was the worst thing I had ever experienced. In the Arctic when you had a whiteout, the daylight was visible and you could still see. Here, you couldn't see a thing, except the inside of your room, with the lights on. Dust was floating everywhere, piling up on everything.

At about 3:00 PM, it started to rain. Drops of mud as big as dimes started falling out of the sky, and then it increased to a downpour of mud and rain that lasted for around two hours. By 5:00 PM, the sky had turned a bright orange, a cross between the color of blood and a pumpkin color. Finally, I was able to see shapes and shadows appearing. The rig was now visible, a black silhouette against the orange sky, the derrick lights still dim from the mud on them, and then things in the desert started to appear. Clumps of desert grass and shrubs were becoming visible as black silhouettes, as far as the eye could see. Hills and small valleys looked like rivers with blood flowing through them the water was so red from the reflection created by a mixture of red mud and the color of the sky. You could see silhouettes of a few small, crudely made dwellings the local people lived in. It was still raining, but we were able to commence operations. Dust was a half inch deep on our desks and throughout the office. It was fruitless trying to clean it while the storm was in progress.

At 6:00 PM, it was still raining but lightly now. I decided to go and check on the camp and have supper at the same time. Water was running in the ditches, flooding the road everywhere. It looked like the desert was a huge lake with islands protruding all over with so much rain in such a short time. Everything was flooded. When I arrived at camp, all the camp staff was busy cleaning up the mess hall and equipment in the kitchen. With dust and dirt everywhere, they couldn't cook a meal for the crews.

"What we do, Mr. Pat?" they asked grinning, everyone trying to speak at once.

"Whatever you can," I said laughing with them knowing there was nothing I could do trying to make the situation lighter. "Make soup and sandwiches."

"Maybe this take two hours," I was informed.

"No problem. Do the best you can. We'll have to work around it," I said scanning the area for damage.

"Enchalla," the cook said, meaning, "God willing."

"Maybe Allah angry," said another worker, concerned but smiling.

"Maybe," I said. "We need to work late tonight and clean up."

"For sure," the camp boss said. "Mr. Pat, I no see this before."

"Me neither," I said.

This storm, compounded by the fallout from the Kuwait oil fires, was enough to keep us busy for the rest of the five-week hitch. We cleaned and cleaned whenever we weren't repairing or pulling pipe.

Martin, the new company man, came into my office the morning after the storm and complained the rig boy hadn't done his job. I went into his office to see what the problem was. He complained the cleaning boy had knocked his pencil box over and said I needed to discipline him. I looked at the room, and it appeared cleaned pretty well, but his pencil box was lying on its side with a few pens out of the box. It would have taken him all of two seconds to upright his pencil box and put his pencils back, but he made a scene. When he finished his little rampage, I looked at him and asked somewhat sarcastically, "Did he steal your coloring book?" trying to make him understand it wasn't a big deal. He flipped out on me and swore. I just laughed and walked out shaking my head. He instructed me to let the boy know he wasn't to touch his desk anymore, which I did.

About a week later, we had a small storm, and again, dust was throughout the cabins. When the boy came and cleaned, I reminded him not to touch Martin's desk. He smiled, made a circular motion around his ear, and promised he wouldn't touch the desk. After he left, Martin came to my office, complaining the boy didn't clean the dust off his desk. I laughed and told Martin he was following his orders and to make up his mind. Either the boy cleaned the desk or not. I said, "The boy is confused enough, and you need to make up your mind." He angrily left, and no more was said.

One morning, about a week after the storm, the Egyptian mud engineer came to the office complaining the locals had stolen his pallets from under his bags of mud.

"You need do something, Mr. Pat," he said.

"What can I do?" I asked. "Move your mud pallets beside your shack."

"I no sleep with forklift coming for mud all the time," he said.

Laughing, I said, "Well, figure something out. If I needed wood to cook with and I saw those pallets, I would take them too. They have nothing to cook with."

He was upset I would say that and took it that I though it was okay. Complaining to the company man proved futile, and he cleaned up his mud, putting it on more pallets.

He came back in and asked, "Can we have one man watch tonight?"

"They all watch. Maybe the wood is going to their homes," I said jokingly.

"You no care about my mud!" he said.

"Yes! I care, but I am not a babysitter," I said. "You get paid to look after your mud so do what you have to and don't blame anyone."

I had a few days left and was looking forward to going home. I was tired of the complaining, blame, and everything else. I wondered where these grown men learned to think like this. What was wrong with them?

Back home, it was spring. Barb picked me up at the airport, and we checked into the hotel room. Once inside, Barb said, "Did you hear about Popeye?"

"Now what happened?" I said.

"He's in jail," she said. "He killed Claire." Claire was the woman he had lived with. She was quite a bit older than he and looked after him well. She cleaned his clothes and apartment and cooked for them. She too had a major problem with alcohol and substance abuse.

Hanging my head, I replied, "That doesn't surprise me for some reason. I knew he would eventually harm someone. He pulled a knife on me and others before."

"I'm so sorry. I didn't think his problem was serious. I knew he was dangerous at times but didn't expect this. Your mom and dad are really upset," she said.

"Has he been charged?" I asked.

"I don't know. His trial is in a couple of weeks. I think a lot of your family is coming out to support Mom and Dad," she said.

"Damned him; Dad is not well, and Mom isn't either. They needed this right now, didn't they? They always blame themselves for his problems as any mother and father will. It's not fair to them," I said. "I need to talk to them and make them understand that they had fifteen kids and only one went astray. We need to make them feel that he is responsible for his own actions as an adult. He is nearly forty-one years old."

"I know, honey," Barb said. "What can we do?"

"I don't know," I said, my mind racing for answers. "Are you hungry?"

"Let's order a pizza and just stay in the room," she said.

"Okay; how are you?" I asked giving her a peck on the lips, realizing I hadn't shown any joy in seeing her.

"I'm okay. Missed you though," she said smiling.

"I missed you too," I said.

Not being able to let go of the situation, I said, "Well, maybe some jail time will make him realize his problems and set him straight. If he gets ten years, then he should have some control on what he does from there on. He's been in jail before, and it didn't help. He definitely needs to change his attitude and friends."

Barb just let me vent for a while and sat there listening intently, not saying a word. I was angry at what he had done to another human being and frustrated at the system. I had tried to get him off social assistance, but he seemed to know what to do to get reinstated and they fell for it every time. They once said, "He's entitled to it. There's nothing we can do," which made me furious. I hate negative words like *can't* and *nothing*. Those words are an escape for what can be done and excuses, so to speak. There are two can'ts in my vocabulary. If you can't get it, you can't stay. I live by that motto still. There was a knock at the door.

Barb dug in her purse and paid for the pizza. We chatted, forgetting what was going on for a while. Eating our pizza, we talked about maybe building a house and selling the trailer we lived in. We wanted to set our roots down, and Roblin was a good place to do that.

Unable to let go, I said, "Something good has got to come out of all this. At least we'll know where he's at, and he'll have a place to stay. We won't have to worry about him freezing outside anymore," I said, chuckling but remorseful for the family of the victim. "What a waste."

We went to bed. Sleep eluded me for hours. My mind raced to find answers, not excuses, for his demeanor. *Why was he like that? What was he thinking? Does he really remember? How could he do this not only to himself and his common-law wife but to his family, especially Mom and Dad?* "Was he drunk?" I said out loud.

"I don't know for sure, but Diane said he was," Barb replied sleepily.

"I'm sorry, honey. That just came out. You get some sleep," I said.

I don't know what time it was, but I finally succumbed to sleep. I was tired but restless. The change in countries had an effect on everything, making my body function to odd hours when at home. I awoke at 4:30 and needed to go to the bathroom.

Jumping out of bed anxiously, I went to the loo and sat there for a while half asleep. Again, my mind started to react to the situation with my brother, but I convinced myself there was nothing I could do at the present time and went back to bed, sleeping until seven fifteen in the morning.

I got up and showered. Barb woke up and had a shower while I made coffee. We sat around and chatted for a while and then packed our belongings and drove home. It was a four-hour drive that seemed like one hour with all we discussed. Tiffany was doing well and had accepted Roblin as her home. Her attitude was changing, and she was happy again.

Arriving in Roblin, I went over to my folks' place immediately and talked for a while about Popeye. As hard as I tried to convince them it wasn't their fault, they held doubt. Finally, I said as softly and comfortingly as I could, "Look, he's an adult and is responsible for his own actions. We can't go on blaming ourselves for his problems. You had fifteen kids, and he's the only one who is like this. I think you have done well, treating us all the same. No matter how you look at it, he has a choice and the power to change. How can you blame yourselves?"

They finally accepted it somewhat, but I could tell it wasn't from deep within them. They weren't convinced but felt somewhat relieved they had our support.

Dad said, "He was always the weak one. Maybe we could have done something different."

"Like what?" I said trying not to be forceful.

"I don't know," he said. "Maybe something happened at birth. You know, we nearly lost Mom and him when he was born. He was premature and weak."

"We don't have control over these types of things," I found myself saying. "These things are up to the Big Guy. He's the one who makes those kinds of decisions."

"I know but maybe ..." he said, trying to let it go. He never did finish what was on his mind.

We were learning a lot about dealing with a crisis. We had to be strong and positive about what was going on. There had to be a reason things were done to certain families. We weren't the only ones, so what was it? I was thinking in spiritual terms and wondered what this was all about. We had to forgive and move forward. We couldn't get engulfed in self-pity and dwell on this. He screwed up and had to pay the piper. He needed to learn about God and accept the truth, instead of hiding behind this wall of manliness, disoriented by booze and self-pity, and get himself off this pile of living death. He needed to pull himself out of the doom of hell. He needed to believe in himself and quit blaming all his faults on someone else. He needed to take ownership and responsibility for his actions, look in the mirror and see who did that to him.

He was remanded in custody. His trial would not be until after I went back. My other brother Joe and Dad were working on getting a lawyer and posting bail. They felt they needed to do this as a family, and I guess, rightly so. We didn't know what had happened as Popeye couldn't remember, so he said. He claimed he was drunk at the time.

I returned to the Middle East and commenced work on the rig. I left everything involving home at home, as always, and concentrated on work. I always seemed to have the ability to do this throughout my career. It was dangerous work, and we needed to be on top of the game all the time. There was no room for error usually, because when we had a problem, usually, it was serious and costly.

I relieved Mike many times. I had to stay for my five weeks off this time, so Barb came up to Damascus to be with me. It was her first time to the Middle East, and she was excited when she arrived but culture shocked at first, observing many things we took for granted at home, somewhat remorseful for having so much. She visited museums and ruins and then went to Sydnaya, Mallula, and many other places with religious history, seeing many things that stick in our minds like old churches, mosques that were once Christian churches, places holding myths about John the Baptist, and much, much more. We went out for supper many times enjoying the Arab dishes served to us, watching a belly dancer once, with Attiga, our general manager, from Libya.

We went to the rig and visited with the men, checking on the operation, and then decided to load up with fuel, food, and water and head back to Damascus. This time, we were going to some ruins just outside Deir ez-Zor, and then we were going across the desert to Palmyra, wanting to see something different. Our driver, Maher, thought we were crazy and tried to deter us.

"Too much problem in desert," he said.

"What do you mean 'too much problem'?" I asked.

"No have road and maybe get lost for too much days," he replied.

"Ah! We watch the sun and we can cross," I said. "Maybe four hours, and we'll be in Palmyra."

"Too much Bedouin and maybe no like us in desert," he pleaded.

"It will be okay. You have gun," I told him laughing. He was just scared because he hadn't done anything like this before and wasn't sure of himself.

As we crossed the desert, watching the sun, Maher did well following what I had told him. A herd of about seventy-five camels crossed our path, with Bedouins following, keeping an eye on them. We came across a ravine, got twisted around, and were heading into the sun instead of keeping it to the right of us. I let him go for a few minutes and then asked him where he was going. Barb was laughing and enjoying herself.

After straightening him out, we came across some Bedouins herding their flock of sheep and goats. They came over and asked Maher if he was lost, grinning from ear to ear, and then Maher told them we were crazy and it was our idea to cross the desert. To make sure we weren't lost, Maher asked them which direction Palmyra was. They pointed us in the direction we were going, so he looked at me saying, *"Fi mook,"* meaning I had a brain. I laughed.

It was about three hours into our journey when we came upon a little settlement in the desert. A guard came out, brandishing an old army rifle. Barb cringed as Maher pulled up to him. I watched as Maher's hand slid down to his weapon, holstered on his hip. A conversation took place, and he explained what we were doing. The guard lowered his gun and leaned on it for a few more minutes, smiling, and then waved us on. We made it to Palmyra around five in the evening, Maher breathing a sigh of relief when we found pavement had lunch and carried on to Damascus.

Arriving back in Damascus, we had to shop for groceries so Maher took us to the market. We bought meat, rice, and fruit. Most of all, we enjoyed the fresh fruit and vegetables. We ate red plums that were so juicy it would run down your chin when you bit into them. The taste still lingers when I think of them. What a difference between the fruit you get there and that you get in Canada. Most of it in Canada is preserved, dry, or pulpy, with no flavor, even when you let it ripen for a few days on the counter. We waste a lot of our hard-earned money buying this kind of fruit and throwing it out because it isn't good and doesn't taste the same. We think we have it good.

Mike came back, Barb went home, and I returned to the field for another five weeks, without days off.

Work went fairly well. Rig move, drilling, the routine was pretty much the same. Very few problems were encountered on a day-to-day basis, but the locals complained the smoke from the refinery plant and emissions over their villages were making them sick.

We were in safety meetings every month discussing problems and given time frames for actions on certain items. One particular meeting, I recall, was a little disturbing to me, and I spoke up. The oil company would find many concerns with the contractors to complain about and let you know in no uncertain terms. This went on for the duration of my existence in the Middle East, and I was getting a little upset with all the complaining. We were working hard to keep our men safe and keep them out of harm's way as best we could, but some of the contractors had some accidents that may have been preventable. You cannot control every situation without incident, try as you may. Attitudes of people cannot be controlled.

We were held responsible for all the service contractors that came on location. We were to inspect their equipment and make sure it was safe to work with. The oil company was distancing itself from its obligation and putting the brunt of the problems on us, a contractor providing a service just like the ones they wanted us to control. "It's your location," we were told as if we had decided to drill these wells ourselves and were the ones who had the say in spending their money.

I was disturbed by this and spoke up. "Why are we being held responsible for the service contractors when they work directly for you and are contracted to you, not us?" I said.

"You are the main contractor as the drilling contractor," I was told. "You are held responsible for everyone on location."

I knew this was coming up so I had looked into our contract to see what was signed by the general manager. "Our contract with you does not say we are responsible for other contractors," I said. "We don't know enough about the service contractors that bid and got these contracts from you to determine if they are safe," I replied. We were going to take this to another level. "We don't have time to babysit every contractor and do our own jobs."

"Well, you will just have to make time," they dictated.

I lost it. Again, we were being pushed into something so they wouldn't have to accept responsibility and blame. "Do we have to be responsible for all the smoke and emissions bellowing out of your plant causing my men to complain? I think if you're going to talk safety, you need to walk the talk. You need to lead by example not by dictation," I said.

The safety man from The Hague stood up furious at me and made a sneering remark about my attitude, trying to intimidate me and justify their action. He didn't like the truth. An argument ensued, and I reached across the table and got hold of him. Everyone in the meeting stood up and separated us.

"Meeting adjourned for a break," Tom said laughing at what had just transpired. He was the drilling manager for the oil company.

I was vibrating with anger. The other contractors were behind me but didn't say anything and took me outside. I lit a smoke while we stood around discussing the meeting. We all started to laugh and calmed down.

Tom came up to me and asked if he could have a word with me. He was chuckling and agreed with my comments but told me I couldn't react like that, especially to the senior safety man from The Hague. I told him that this man needed to know he wasn't God and he wasn't beyond responsibility. "He was the one who set things off with his remark," I said. "If we don't stand up to these types of leaders, we are doomed to forever being blamed, and I'm not going to have this," I said. "The oil company need to assume responsibility and control of their own business, treating us contractors the same and equal to the other contractors they signed up to drill and complete these wells." I was still somewhat furious but had calmed down enough to accept responsibility for my action and apologized for grabbing the safety man. *Rebel,* I thought and laughed.

I was going home soon and didn't really care if I was coming back. I didn't want to work in this kind of atmosphere. I expected to be released when I left the rig and took my gear home with me. My mind was shaping up to the world of corporate dictatorship, and I didn't like it. *Surely, it's not like this at home yet.* I hadn't been around the oil patch much in Canada lately and wasn't sure how things operated there. I arrived in Damascus and went into the office.

"Hello, Paddy. How was your hitch?" Mike asked.

"I guess you probably know what happened. You tell me," I said grinning.

"What happened? I want to hear it from you. The company wanted you released, but I told them I wouldn't do that. What would I do if you don't relieve me once in a while?" he said making a joke of it and laughing.

I told him what happened, and he agreed with me. He didn't agree with grabbing that safety man but said he probably would have done the same.

"Me and you go back a long way, and you know I would have done the same thing," he said chuckling. "I'll smooth things out, and you make sure you don't quit on me."

"Mike, I don't want any favoritism. I will not work here under this kind of pressure. We are not babysitters for others, and they need to know that. The atmosphere out there is deteriorating and needs to be corrected. How can we do that with them dictating and not taking responsibility? Their safety operations meetings are nothing more than ridicule, and the drilling contractor, being run by Schlumberger try to make us buy into their safety equipment and ideas, with no idea they are the ones having the most problems. You can put up all the barriers you want, but if you don't train and supervise, they're all futile. I'm getting tired of all this crap," I said.

"I'll have a meeting with Issam and sort this out. Paddy! Don't take any of this personal. Sometimes I feel you take responsibility too personal," Mike said.

"We work hard out there and take pride in what we do. We try hard to get things done safely and efficiently, but these oil companies are ruthless. These people need to come out there for a month and see for themselves it is not an easy task, pushing twentieth-century technology on people who have no education and are suppressed, with no future. Take a look around Deir ez-Zor and see the electrical cables hanging from the poles with bare wires, the streets, jaywalking, the homes, businesses, hygiene, and the likes. These people have no concept of safety, and it takes time to teach them. They will learn eventually but not tomorrow," I said. "The oil company and the people from The Hague need to understand this. Everything takes more time when you are trying to educate people who don't understand our language. That is one of the biggest problems throughout the world today. Misunderstanding! I believe that along with trying not to lose face, language is the biggest hurdle we have throughout all of mankind. We all speak in foreign tongues, self-righteously. The one thing I do know is, they try hard to please us."

We left it at that, and I went to the staff house. Mike wanted to finish up some paperwork so he stayed behind. I went upstairs and flopped on the bed, falling asleep immediately. I awoke to the call of the towers at about nine that evening. People were flocking to the mosque for prayer. Rubbing my eyes, I looked outside and then down at the sidewalk below the apartment staff house, which was swarming with people.

I went down to Mike's place and found he wasn't home, so I walked about two blocks to a little pizza joint, sat down, and had a beer with pizza. It was humid, but people were enjoying lunch, dinner, and whatever, talking and laughing.

People were being served in a friendly manner. They were looking after me splendidly. It seemed they couldn't do enough for the expatriate people in their country. Sitting there and listening to their music, I enjoyed myself, relaxed and content to enjoy their culture, observing mothers and fathers hugging their children, teaching them to be quiet, awesome! I hadn't been out that much in Damascus, as we would come in and leave within twelve hours. Of course we knew where the bars were and how to get a drink whenever we wanted to, but tonight, I was content to observe them in their own environment without much influence from outside. I was the only foreigner there.

I had relieved Mike a few times when he would go for a break but didn't go too many places by myself. Most times, I would go back to the apartment and hang out. The electricity in Damascus was sporadic. We had power from 7:00 AM until about noon and then no power until evening, around six or seven at night. I would go back to the office and work until midnight without the phone or interruption and get a lot done. At midnight, I would go to the Café Noir, have a few beers, and watch the show.

It was mostly cultural dancing, with girls from Romania, Russia, Poland, and other countries doing cultural dances. Sometimes when a belly dancer came in and danced the crowd would go crazy because of her movements. It was fun to watch. I believe some of the girls were prostitutes, but I didn't really care. Most were friendly, but you had to be careful because they would come and sit at your table and chat, convincing you to buy them a drink, and then you would be charged a horrendous price, just because they accompanied you.

It was a scheme of the owners, I found out the hard way, when I paid about a hundred and fifty dollars for what I thought was about eight drinks we had between Al, I and a lady from Romania, who made herself welcome at our table. She told us about the scheme, but we let her stay and paid the bill. She was friendly, talking a lot about her family and home, telling us she was on a contract and didn't like it but was forced to stay nonetheless.

I finished my pizza and went back to the staff house. I sat outside on the balcony and enjoyed the beautiful evening. I went to bed around midnight and woke up the next morning to the doorbell ringing.

Shit! Abu Aimen was here to take me to the airport. I let him in, had a quick shower, and left. Thank God my bags were ready to go or I probably would have missed my flight. It was foggy, and the trip to the airport was a little hectic, but we made it. As we approached the airport, Abu Aimen pointed out where the president's son had been killed in a car accident about a week before. Apparently, he was going too fast, trying to catch his flight and had a horrendous crash, killing himself and the driver.

I flew home and wondered whether I wanted to come back. I knew I wasn't released, but I was getting a sour taste in my mouth working under the conditions I had just experienced. I was getting frustrated with corporate business and wasn't about to take a back seat and obey everything they wanted. I knew in my mind there were a lot of things that weren't right, but I needed a job if we were going to build our house. Did I want it bad enough to allow myself to be dictated to and knowingly work for this kind of company? Maybe I was just getting tired and needed a good rest. Fifteen weeks was a long time. Maybe I needed more time off. I was doing a lot of extra time relieving Mike and getting only a couple of weeks off here and there.

I returned back to work finding things had changed quite drastically for me. The oil company had brought in new people who were difficult to please. Even the Syrian company men had changed and were getting difficult. I am sure they were instructed to give me a hard time to make me quit, because I hadn't been released. I put up with this and did the best I could. They were getting under my skin, but I plugged away and it appeared to get better. It was nearly back to normal when in May of 1995, disaster struck.

Chapter Eleven

We were drilling outside the Omar field and ran into numerous problems with a particular well. The oil company had purchased a number of bits of substandard quality and then attempted to drill a well with a lot of volcanic sands. They were abrasive and difficult to penetrate with the bits they supplied, with no gauge protection, as evidenced by the problems we had trying to get back to bottom. We had to change the bit without making a new hole. We would ream to bottom and then have to pull out to change the bit. Every time we pulled out, the bit was so under gauge, we would have to ream from the beginning. This caused a lot of trips out of the hole, creating a problem with worn casing. Their policy was to pressure test casing every twenty-eight days or run a casing wear log to determine the strength of the casing.

We drilled a pilot hole and had many problems. We spent time fishing for twisted-off pipe, pulling damaged bits, etc. Many times, we would get into disagreements with them because they were abusing our pipe, trying to drill faster and faster. Harmonics on our string were causing fatigue, but they didn't want to hear that and knew what they were doing, supposedly. I complained to Mike about the problem, and he in turn tried to convince them harmonics was causing this.

We had a brand-new string of pipe in the yard, but the hard banding was aggressive and made of tungsten carbide. At first, they were reluctant to use it, so we ordered more drill pipe. Eventually, they requested this pipe, so we brought it out to the site and had the Al Nassar group come out and machine the hard band off, flush with the box/pin of the connection ends. They approved it for use. They had been warned of the hard band and accepted the pipe anyway.

We changed out the string of pipe on trips, noticing a lot of wear on the tool joints, as they were called. The collars had black spots indicating we had encountered some H_2S gas or other chemical in the well. Monitors were set up, and nothing appeared to be out of normal. We never did smell the gas, but the indication on our pipe told us something was wrong. What was it if they believed it wasn't H_2S?

Finally finishing the pilot hole, we pulled out and plugged back. We were going to cut a window and attempt to drill a horizontal well. Many of us had not drilled this kind of well but were keen to learn. This appeared to be the thing of the future. We were waiting on cement when I went on days off and Al relieved me. Mike wanted to stay around to see how things were going to work out.

In the pre-spud meeting I attended, I was told there was a pinnacle on the seismograph charts that indicated a fault about three hundred meters from where we had set the rig up. We were to drill into this to see if there was a good zone to produce from.

I packed up and went home on days off. It was the end of April when I left, and I was expecting to start building my house in a couple of months. I had a plan in place and had just sold my trailer but was allowed to stay in it until the house was ready as part of the deal when we sold it. I finished my plans and started looking around for someone to build it. We hired a contractor, but he wasn't sure what we needed to do when he got it to lock-up stage. I assured them I would be home from time to time and Barb could contact me anytime if required.

About May 10, 1995, I received a call from Mike.

"Hello," I said.

"Hello, Paddy. It's Mike here."

"What's up?" I asked.

"We're in a bind, Paddy. I need you to come back," he said.

"Yeah right," I said. "I've got to get my plans completed for my house, Mike. I'm not coming back early this time."

"No Paddy. Really! I need you to come back right away. We have a blowout."

"Mike, don't give me that shit," I said. "You just want to go to Cypress or something. No, I'm not coming back." Mike had pulled this on me a number of times, and I wasn't falling for it this time. He was good at fibs and many times, would laugh when we fell for it."

"Paddy, you have to come back," he pleaded, but I refused. He hung up on me, and I could tell he was pissed off.

"Was that Mike?" Barb asked.

"Yes! He's trying to get me to come back right away. I think he wants to take some time off, and I am not going to go this time. We have a lot of planning to do for our house, and I need time off too," I said to Barb.

"To hell with him," Barb said.

"You're damn right to hell with him," I repeated.

We screened our calls for a couple of days. He called a number of times, but I wasn't going to fall for this. I finally answered about three or four days later.

"Paddy, I'm not kidding. We have a major blowout, and I need you to come back right away," he said.

Still not believing him, I said, "What happened?"

"I don't have time to explain. Here ask John," he said giving the phone to John.

"Hello, Patrick," John said in his mild voice. "How are you?"

"I'm okay, but what's going on?" I asked.

"Oh! Mr. Mike is not lying, Pat. The rig has a big problem," John said, and I was convinced that there was a problem.

Laughing, Mike said, "Well, do you believe me?"

"I'm not sure," I said. "You've pulled so much shit on me I don't know what to believe."

"No, seriously, we have a blowout. Boots and Coots are here, and I need you to come back. We're pulling the rig off location already, except for the BOPs, and they are investigating what happened. I want you to come back and be part of the investigating team with us. They are trying to blame us for the problem, so we need to go over the contract." He was convincing.

"I'll leave right away, Mike. If you're pulling my leg, I'm coming straight back," I said. "I don't care if I have to buy a one-way ticket back."

It was May 20, 1995 by now, and I left for Damascus. Arriving back, I soon found out we had a problem. Everyone was working frantically trying to get all the paperwork in order. I stayed in Damascus and immediately started going through the contract.

After about an hour or so, we stopped for coffee. Mike looked worn-out and tired. He had been in meetings trying to defend ADWOC from the oil company but was up against a bunch of people who wouldn't accept their involvement in the problem.

"Mike, what the hell went wrong?" I asked.

"I think they wore a hole in the casing. They lost circulation, and Zuhair pumped all the drilling fluid away. Fuckin' Barber let him, and now we have this problem. It kicked, and they held it for a while, then the pressure dropped on the casing side. For some reason, they pumped diesel fuel, water, and just about everything they had on location down the well and couldn't figure out the hydrostatic pressure. When the pressure dropped, they thought they were getting the well under control and were waiting on the mud being mixed when one of the hands noticed that gas was coming out behind the rig. Barber looked at it and got everybody out of there. By this time, it was blowing as high as the crown, so they shut down the engines. When they were leaving the rig location for safer territory, they tell me it was like a Steven Spielberg movie. The ground around the rig was cracking everywhere as they left. They got everybody out, and no one got hurt. I don't really know what happened, but they're investigating right now, trying to hang us," he told me.

"Did they do a casing wear test?" I asked.

Mike looked at me with concern and replied, "I don't know."

"They are supposed to pressure test or run a casing log every twenty-eight days. It was time to do that when I left" I said. "It's their policy".

"They are trying to blame the pipe," Mike said.

"How the hell can they blame the pipe? They requested it and were adamant about not using it," I said.

"We have nothing signed," Mike said. "I didn't get them to sign a waiver."

"Shit! There's Goddamn paperwork for everything. Got to have everything signed or they take no responsibility," I said disgusted. "If it goes to court, I will attest to their request."

"We don't have a leg to stand on without that signature," Mike said. "We need to go through the contract and see if they can actually hold us responsible. I looked at it, and it appears we are all responsible. I fucked up and actually forgot to get them to sign. Also, Al's second line ticket expired so they are all over us for that."

"Does Zuhair have his level-two Shell ticket yet?" I asked. "He was having a hard time with the exam and didn't pass it the last I heard, but they still let him operate as senior company man," I said. "We need to find out."

"I'm glad you came back, Paddy. I didn't know anything about this," Mike said.

"Let's phone Barber and ask if they checked the casing. Maybe we'll be lucky and at least have an argument if they are responsible by contract to do this" I said searching for a way to defend ourselves. I was getting angry they would attempt to distance themselves and try to blame us for the problem. I was willing to take some of the responsibility, but when someone uses deceit for their benefit and tries to justify it by lying, self-righteousness, and pleading ignorance, this was too much. I would make sure we did everything possible to make them understand.

"We have people from The Hague and Germany, and I don't know who else," Mike offered. "They all have a share in this well."

"Sounds interesting" I laughed trying to lighten things up. "I guess they're all the brains, and we are stupid."

Laughing, Mike replied, "That's about right."

"Looks like we have our work cut out for us," I said getting up. "We've got to get at it."

I went back to my desk and flipped through the contract, reading what Mike had highlighted. For two days, I read and reread the contract; finding out it was pretty gray in most areas. It seemed to contradict itself at times, the more I read it. Many times, it was hard to decipher because it was written by some lawyer with many clauses of hereto, forthwith, and garbage I couldn't really grasp. What the hell did all this mean, and who the hell would use this old Caesar language? Only governments used this when explaining laws so the average person couldn't understand what it meant.

After I finished highlighting what was necessary and after two days of true grit, I finally went to the rig with Mike to assess the problem. I wanted to know firsthand what had transpired.

I found out the same as Mike had told me and more. Some of the IADC reports were taken away by Al Furat, and no one, except they, had a copy. "Why did you give them all the copies?" I asked Al.

"I didn't. They ripped them out when they were investigating and never gave them back to us. They said there was evidence of deficiencies and claimed them for the investigation," Al said.

I couldn't believe this. I called Mike and informed him of the missing reports. He was going to look into it and get us a copy. We needed them for our investigation.

After talking briefly to Al, I went outside and talked to some of the hands. Many were worn-out and tired with red eyes and skin irritations from working in the blowout zone, removing the rig. They smiled slightly and didn't say much. Most didn't understand what had happened and asked, "Big problem, Mr. Pat?"

Nodding my head, I said, "Yes, *big* problem," stressing *big*.

The hands were cleaning and repairing what was damaged on the rig. Many would turn around and gaze at the gusher coming out of the earth. Nothing like this had ever happened in the whole time I had been in the patch. Nothing!

I looked at the site, amazed at the scope and size of our problem. Oil was shooting out of a crater about forty feet wide by approximately a hundred feet long, blowing about thirty feet in the air. I was told about forty thousand barrels of oil with four hundred million cubic feet of gas per day was blowing out of the earth, but I don't know how accurate that figure was. I know it was a lot from looking at it gush out of the ground. The blowout preventers were closed around the pipe with the drill string still in the well, and a manifold in the shape of a cross protruded above the BOP, connected to the string in the well. It was a sight to see with the cross in the horizon about two thousand yards from the camp.

A burm, approximately a mile or so square, was built around the well to contain the fluid coming from it. There was a lot of excitement,

I observed, and people going in and out of the area, with very little precaution taking pictures from in close, too close for my comfort. The well could catch fire from the camera flash or any kind of spark, I thought. There wasn't a command center yet; everything was being handled from the field office. They were working at setting up a command post, preparing to directional drill into the problem well with three rigs to establish communication with the bore, allowing us to bring it under control. Sites were prepared for the three rigs, with movement of equipment into position imminent. I continued to investigate, sometimes getting into discussions with the company people to say what was on my mind. I found they didn't like it and were uncomfortable at times, telling their superiors what I had said. I really didn't give a damn and was sure they were just as responsible as we were.

Shawn was there, so we discussed many things. We told him if he didn't think it was safe, he could pull our men out of the danger any time he felt it was necessary. He was a good hand, quite intelligent for a young fellow. He was around twenty-six or so at this time.

Many different men were occupying our camp. Boots and Coots had just finished in Kuwait, putting out some of the fires, and came directly to Syria to help us with this problem.

Martin seemed to be the leader with Joe and Danny as his assistants. They were big, burly boys, powerful, smart, and professional. They were all about six feet six and larger. They were very spiritual, saying a grace every meal before joining us in conversation and joking around with laughter. They worked hard trying to contain the flow of oil and were busy trying to install a separator on the end of the relief line they put out there to relieve the pressure on the crater. It was supposed to help to slow the crater from getting too large. This was requested by the oil company.

The oil company was having problems with their plant in Omar accumulating too much sand hauled in with the vacuum trucks sucking fluid from inside the burm, trying to keep up to the flow of the crater.

When they opened the valve to the separator, it resembled a huge steamship bellowing steam, oil spewing everywhere in the middle of the desert. It was too small as pointed out by the Boots and Coots boys, but the oil company wanted it rigged up.

On Sunday morning, Carlos came in and asked if he could use the truck to go to town, but we were under strict rules not to allow our vehicles out to anyone. It had started quite some time before the blowout, as a result of too many vehicles being wrecked because of speed and carelessness. I think we had bought three vehicles since I arrived in Syria, not counting the ones bought for town. I had no choice but to say no.

He looked at me and said, "I want to go to church. You never know what could happen here with this problem." He was working with the Boots and Coots guys whenever they needed assistance, which was nearly every day. He would be covered in oil from head to toe and never complained. I was under strict rules and told Carlos I couldn't do that.

"Okay, Mr. Pat," was all he said as he walked out. This was a decision I have regretted, and it haunts me to this day.

On Monday, while I was sitting at the table for breakfast with Joe, Martin, and Danny, Martin told me he was having problems with his truck. The oil company had given them a small Chevy crew cab truck to do their work, but it was giving them problems, running rough and backfiring. Martin was concerned about going to the wellhead with it, because with the amount of oil and gas from the crater in the air, it could ignite.

"Why don't you request another truck" I asked?

"We did, but they said they don't have one," Martin replied.

"They don't have one," I said questioning him?

"That's what they told us," he replied.

"Then refuse to go in until they give you one," I said.

"We tried that, and they told us they would get someone else in here if we didn't want to go in. With all the little firefighting companies that started up in Kuwait, we don't have a choice anymore," he said.

I was shocked to hear they used this type of threat to get these boys to work in unsafe conditions. I couldn't believe what I had just heard. This was corporate business, dictating safety and not adhering to their policies!

"They said they will look at our truck today, so we'll see what happens later," Martin said concerned but smiling.

"Good luck," I said as they left.

We worked and investigated until June 11, at which time Mike asked if I would come in and assist with some paperwork. The rigs drilling the relief wells were set up, and drilling had commenced. Mike was getting overloaded and tired. There was nothing we could do in the field, and Shawn had everything under control, so things were going as well as they could.

Mike and I left around ten in the morning and got to Damascus around two forty-five. Abu Aimen made coffee and brought us a cup. We hadn't sat down yet when the phone rang. John answered, and I heard him say, "Pat and Mike just walked in. Who do you want to talk to?" Then he handed me the phone.

"Hello" I said into the mouthpiece of the phone.

"Paddy, she just blew up," Shawn said, his voice trembling.

"What?" I said shocked, not wanting to hear that. I knew the possibilities were extremely high for this type of accident but didn't want to believe it. I wasn't prepared for what I was hearing.

"Yes, Paddy; She's on fire," he said.

"Is anybody trapped?" I asked, my voice trembling, not ready for what I was about to hear.

"There are five of them trapped in the fire. Three of the Boots and Coots guys, Carlos, and a crane operator," he said.

"We'll be right out there," I said and hung up.

My heart sank. I had never felt so helpless. A tear rolled down my face as I tried hard to control my emotions. I put my head in my hand and turned away, my thoughts drifting from anger to fear and then sorrow for the men who had lost their lives and their families now having to deal with their loss.

John was staring at me when I raised my head. He asked, "It's on fire?"

I replied, "Yes," and turned to Mike, who was sitting a few feet away. "We gotta go now."

I paced the floor waiting. Mike wanted to finish his coffee and call the oil company. I knew we had to wait, but it was difficult.

After Mike hung up, he turned to me and said, "Paddy, there is nothing we can do. Let's have another coffee, and then we'll go."

I knew that we couldn't do anything so I agreed to have another coffee before leaving. We finished our coffee and left without changing our clothes. We picked up some chicken and headed out to Deir ez-Zor, stopping for fuel in Palmyra. We had Abu Aimen with us so he could drive. We were tired and needed to rest, having our work cut out for us and many questions needing answers. The investigation just got bigger.

I was sitting in the back. A tear rolled down my cheek from time to time. I was devastated by this and angry, but determined to find out the truth, so help me God. We were about thirty miles from Deir ez-Zor and could see the sky glowing orange where the location was. It was about seventy miles from where we were to the fire. I knew it was big but didn't expect to see it from that far away. "Mike! Look! This is a big fire," I said not realizing he was napping.

He rubbed his eyes and said, "Where are we?"

"About seventy miles from the rig," I said.

"Looks pretty big," he said with concern on his face. Mike didn't show any other emotion.

It was quiet the rest of the way. When we arrived at the site, people were about the location, and there was a lot of chaos. Shawn approached us and stuck out his hand. "Good to see you guys," he said. "I think we need some help out here. The crane operator's brother tried to go into the fire to rescue him, but the police shot his tires out then restrained him. It was a friggin' nightmare out here," Shawn said.

"Do you know what happened?" I asked.

"Not really, Paddy," Shawn said. "I talked to the boys on NKV. They told me they saw a flash come from around the little truck Boots and Coots were using. That's all I know."

Mike was talking to Issam and a few of the Arab men around the camp. Our men were acting responsibly, and no one was moving. All eyes were fixed on the fire. They were staring straight ahead with wonder on their faces. Then I saw Naoum.

As I walked toward him, I noticed he had been crying. He was wiping his eyes as I approached. Ding and Saleh were standing with him. Looking straight into his eyes, I extended my hand and said, "Hello, Naoum. How are you?"

He grabbed my hand and shook it, bursting into tears and sobbing violently. "My *sideek*! My *sideek*! Carlos was my *sideek*!" he said. I put my arm around his shoulders. The other assistant drillers joined in, hanging our heads in a prayer for the boys, and then everyone broke down and cried. Naoum kept repeating, "My friend; my friend!"

I was torn up, my mind racing, and all I could think of was the past Sunday. He knew. Carlos knew he was going to die, but I didn't pick up on it. *Damned rules,* I thought. *I'll never forgive myself for this. I'll live with that decision for the rest of my life. I will never forget Carlos. Never!* I was already haunted by it. Try as I might, it wouldn't go away that night. I would nearly be asleep, and then I'd be wiping away tears. *Damn these corporate rules! Damned this job!* I was angry. *Did this really have to happen? What could I have done better to prevent it? Why? Why? Why?*

I blamed myself and took responsibility for this problem. I was haunted by the worst decision I had ever made. I could have bent the rules, but I didn't. I thought I was strong by enforcing the rules but found I was weak, not using my power and authority properly, not making the right decision, the right choice, to let him go and pray. I would regret that decision forever. I learned. I would never do that again. I don't know how many times I have asked for forgiveness, and although I sometimes forget about it for a while, it always comes back. It is embedded deeply into my heart and mind, and is a constant reminder of weakness. How weak we humans really are.

The next morning, I was up early and ready to investigate what had caused the fire. I suspected the little truck immediately and was quite sure this would be evidenced as the cause. I asked a lot of questions. I drove to the burm around the wellhead and searched for clues. I wanted answers. The men were still trapped inside the fire zone even though the fire had burned itself out, with only the crater now on fire.

Why were those men trying to install a separator in a dangerous zone? Was it economics, or was there really a problem at the plant? The burm didn't appear to be leaking or overflowing when we left prior to the fire. It didn't appear to be out of control and full. There was no evidence of the oil building up to dangerously high levels inside the containment walls. I believed it was economics. I believed it was dollars and corporate greed. I felt they didn't want to clean the sand out of the oil if they could find a solution.

The separator had never worked and was being disconnected at the time of the fire. Drilling of relief wells had already commenced, and vacuum trucks appeared to be keeping up with the oil. Why were these men inside the danger zone when everything appeared to be contained? There was no logical reason in my mind, and I wanted to ask these questions. Ironically, they were doing their own investigation, and we weren't allowed into their business unless we were being drilled about our failure to perform. They were blaming us and wanted no responsibility.

Boots was called to come in and help with the problem. The command center was up and running but was not very well organized. People were talking, and I observed many disagreements as to what needed to be done. They were making some kind of plan, but nobody seemed to know what to do yet. Who was the master?

They were calling in pumping equipment and arranging for it to be in Syria to coincide when the rigs finished drilling the relief wells. They needed to be here and rigged up, ready to pump, when communication with the problem well was achieved.

Arrangements and testing were being done on cement and gunk plugs that needed to be pumped to control the problem well. The task was immense, but everybody, despite the disagreements, was working hard to get this under control now.

Inside the command center, in full view behind the staff manning it, was a sign; "Our martyr," depicting only the Arab man who was a crane operator that died in the tragedy. The other men who had lost their lives were not acknowledged. I was appalled at the disrespect of this and mentioned it to some of the superiors only to be told not to upset things in Syria.

Boots arrived on the scene about four days after the crater ignited and was pretty upset about losing his men. I couldn't fault him for being angry and was hoping he would be able to help us with understanding what had happened and how this fire had started. He couldn't give us any answers until he went in and rescued the bodies of his men, which were still in the area around the wellhead. I could tell he was angry and heard him say, "They will pay dearly for this."

Immediately, he requested a Cat and some tin to make a shielded vehicle to go inside the fire area to rescue the men. We worked, building a shield around the driver of the Cat, extending it to beyond the front of the blade. We put up a steel framework from the blade upward and then connected it to the frame of the Cat, supporting the tin walls that were tied with wire and screwed to the framework. He requested the fire truck from the oil company so we could have a water shield, to spray cold water over the tin to keep it cool so it wouldn't disintegrate and burn whoever went in. We built a small platform on the blade frame to support a body, in case we were successful in retrieving the fatally injured.

We could see two bodies inside the area close to the wellhead. By this time, the fire was upward of fifty to seventy feet high above the crater and with the crosswind, stretched to about a hundred feet long, horizontally.

We needed to get some of the blowout prevention equipment out of the way so we could have a clear view and access to the bodies.

"Does anybody have some trucks and equipment to move that accumulator?" Boots asked.

"Yes," Mike answered. "We have a 953 sow and a C500 Kenworth."

"Do they have winches and anchors?" Boots asked.

"They have winches but no anchors," Mike said looking at me for support.

"Why do we need anchors, Boots?" I asked.

"That fire was so hot the skids are probably melted into the sand. Without anchors, we probably can't move the building unless we can get close enough to lift it to break it free. I don't think, with a fire that big and the wind blowing, we can get close enough. We don't need anyone else hurt," he said. "We might have to wait out the wind."

"Paddy, do you want to drive one of the trucks? If you do and I drive the other, at least we won't put anyone but ourselves at risk," Mike asked.

Without hesitation, I answered, "I'm in. Let's do it." I wanted more than anything to retrieve those men and at least have some closure for their loved ones. Not once did I think of getting hurt. I felt responsible for this disaster as one of the senior supervisors, and nothing could have stopped me, no matter how dangerous.

"Where are the trucks?" Boots asked.

"At the camp," I blurted out. "We'll go get them."

"You bring them here, and we'll have a meeting before we attempt this," Boots said.

We got the trucks and parked them just outside of the area we were working in. We held a safety meeting and checked the trucks, winches, cables, and whatever else we needed to.

"Now you all pay attention to my commands and signals," Boots announced. "There is only one of us going to give signals and commands, and that's me."

"Got it," we all said. There was another engineer with Boots who was calculating everything out to see if we could accomplish our tasks.

"If I say stop, you stop," Boots said.

We had agreed to tie the two trucks together and use the winches, holding the brakes full on. We got into position and were told to stay inside the trucks. They would hook up for us. The fire was blowing just above us and wasn't more than twenty feet above the cab of the trucks. I was sweating from the intense heat as I waited for the signals.

I watched in my mirror and then saw Boots give us the thumbs-up, so I moved forward, tightening up the cable from my truck that was tied to the one Mike was driving. I was signaled to move ahead slightly more as Mike tightened up the cable hooked to the accumulator. Our full concentration was on Boots at all times while he signaled us to start winching.

With brakes full on, on both trucks, we started our winches slowly. We were skidding backward toward the fire; the heat was becoming more intense. My skin was leaking sweat from my arms and every pore on my body. We winched for what seemed a long time, and I heard, "Stop."

I kicked the winch out and held the brake but was still going backward toward the fire. I then saw Boots running toward the truck Mike was driving. He was yelling at Mike. "Stop, you son of a bitch! When I said stop, I meant stop!"

I turned around to see what was going on and noticed we had stopped. Boots was on the running board, chewing Mike out severely. He was really mad, cussing and shouting at Mike.

Mike had turned around while winching to check his cable on the drum just when Boots told us to stop and didn't hear him, which upset Boots. We disconnected and left the zone, congregating around the safe area for another meeting. Boots was still mad but apologized to Mike for cussing him out, warning, "I told you to pay attention and watch me," shaking his head.

He was a firm man but very professional and dedicated to what he was doing. He had no tolerance for shortcomings from anyone and would let us know immediately. We worked with him diligently for a few days.

We could not get the accumulator out of the way, so we went back to the burm wall and assessed the situation again. Every time we went to the burm, I would look at that little truck and think; *this was the cause of the fire.* We had tried three or four times now to move the equipment, and finally, Boots said, "We got to get in there. Let's have a meeting and make a plan."

We went to the makeshift safe area, poured a coffee, and discussed a plan. We sat on the end gate of the truck as we didn't have a shack. Why? I don't know.

The fire truck and ambulance were about two hundred feet from where we were, so Boots went to get the fire truck and let the driver know what he was supposed to do. The driver point-blank refused, saying, "The oil company won't allow the fire truck close to the fire. This is as far as it can go. We don't have enough hose."

Shaking his head, Boots came back and asked, "I need someone to come in with me. Who's going to come? This is fuckin' bullshit," he said referring to the fire truck.

Immediately, without thinking or any fear, I said, "I'll go."

"Okay. We go in slowly, staying to the left as far as we can go, then come around the first body swinging to the right. This places the shield between the fire and us. It's going to be hot, so if something goes wrong, swing early and move out. If it's too hot, I'll give you a signal," he said motioning to the Cat operator with his thumb downward. "Don't panic, and what you're going to see will not be very nice," he warned.

"Where do we position ourselves on the Cat?" I asked wanting to make no mistakes.

"We don't. We walk inside the shield, so keep up with the movement of the Cat. Watch your feet at all times. When we get to the body, we will stop just long enough to put it on the platform here on the blade frame and move out immediately. We'll come out and cool down for a half hour and do it again."

"You okay with that, Paddy?" Mike asked concerned.

"Yes, we gotta do what we gotta do," I said.

"You ready to go?" asked Boots.

"Let's do it," I said.

We buttoned up our fire-retardant coveralls and proceeded into the area, going left and past the body far enough for the Cat to swing around without hitting it, and then turned right. Sweat was leaking out of me like a fountain. It was hot. My skin tingled from the heat and felt like it was blistering. My adrenaline was running so high I felt no pain. The hair on the back of my neck felt as though it was singed, but we needed to move on, no matter what. Boots looked over at me to see how I was coping and yelled, "You okay?" making sure I heard him over the roar of the fire.

"Yes! I'm okay!" I hollered back.

The Cat stopped. Boots and I loaded a body on the blade frame and immediately started out of the area. It seemed like it took a long time, but it was only minutes. We got out to the safe area and stopped the Cat. The operator, who was the Boots and Coots engineer, jumped down and helped us lay the body on the ground.

"This is Danny," Boots said bowing his head. I could tell he was saying a silent prayer.

How he knew it was Danny is beyond me. He was burned so badly it was hard to tell. His hair and scalp were burned to charcoal, and we could see inside his skull. It was black and looked like a piece of volcanic rock used on a barbecue. His arms were burned off at the elbows, his legs missing from the knees down. When we rolled him into a body bag, I could see yellow sinew or muscle protruding from his blackened shoulder blades. We loaded him into the ambulance. At least we had a body for the family to put to eternal rest, so they could have some closure.

When we picked him up inside the fire area, it appeared he had tried to run from the position his body lay in. His one arm was outstretched, and one leg was bent in front of him, as a runner, while his other arm and leg appeared to be straight. With the force of the explosion that had happened, I could only imagine a whoosh, and all the oxygen would have been consumed by the fire. The oxygen in his lungs would have been sucked out of him, collapsing them.

We rested for a while and remained silent, collecting our thoughts. My skin was starting to feel normal again, and although I was red, I wasn't burned. We had successfully accomplished part of the task we had planned for. We had to get the others.

We reviewed our plan while drinking our coffee.

Boots announced, "You ready?"

"Let's go!" I said, buttoning my coveralls. I was ready.

This time, we were going to get a lot closer to the fire as the body we could see lay about fifteen feet from the little truck. The little truck was close to the wellhead. Again, we were to stay left as long as we could and make a sharper right turn as the distance between the truck and body was limited. Walking along silently within the confines of the serrated metal of the shield, we did as planned and stopped at the body. We were looking for other bodies too, but hadn't seen any. This one was burned badly too. We had some difficulty picking it up but managed to get it loaded on the platform then, proceeded out of harm's way. I again observed the little truck as we approached, and this time, I noticed something I hadn't before. The hood was blown back over the cab. I was thinking of this while we exited the danger zone until we stopped at the safe area. Immediately realizing the task at hand, I shook my thoughts clean and focused on the task at hand. We unloaded the body, and again, Boots identified the body, this time as Joe. Joe was a big man, and this was definitely Joe, I observed, but he was badly burned also with limbs missing and his skull burned to charcoal. We put him in a body bag and loaded him into the ambulance.

We quit for the day as we hadn't seen any more bodies. We had to try, somehow, to move some equipment out of the way for a better view of the area, but we had no means of doing so. It was about four in the afternoon now, and Boots wanted to go to the clinic to see what they had done with the bodies. He wanted to make sure they were respected and sent home as soon as possible.

My thoughts drifted. *Where the hell is Carlos? What was he doing when this thing went up?* It was sketchy at best, and no one really knew. I asked the fellows on NKV and was told he was on top of the wellhead doing something, the last they remembered. They were about a half a mile away and had a pretty good view of the whole area that was burned. If he was on top of the wellhead, he could have been blown right into the crater, I thought. He could have fallen down beside the wellhead and would never be found. *Please, God, let us find him,* I thought.

We went in to camp and cleaned up for supper. Mike was sitting at the table with a long face and in deep thought. I sat down and quietly ordered my supper, eating silently. I had not thought about what we had done that day and really didn't care to think about it. It wasn't my most pleasant day in the oil patch.

"How are you doing Paddy?" Mike asked as he lit a smoke.

"I'm okay," I said. "You know, I noticed something out there today that might interest you."

"Really" Mike said. "I am just about worn-out from all of this."

"Yes, I am too. You know that little truck that was backfiring I told you about?" I said.

"Yes. What about it?" Mike asked.

"When we went in the second time for Joe, I noticed the hood on the little truck was blown back over the cab."

"Yes. What about it?" Mike asked inquisitively.

"Well … maybe the explosion was caused by the truck, Mike. I'm not an expert but believe that's where it started. How else would the hood be like that if it was latched down?"

"Boy, I wouldn't say that to too many people right now. Let's let them finish their investigation and see what they come up with," he said.

"What are they saying caused it then?" I asked.

"They're not sure, but I've heard them mention static electricity," he said.

"Right," I said. "That would clear them of responsibility."

Mike said no more, but I could tell he was thinking about it. He didn't want to get too involved with this and upset anybody. He agreed with a lot of what they were telling him, and when he would fill me in on some of the details, I would let him know that I had a different perspective. When you look at something, sometimes it doesn't take rocket science to figure it out. I was getting somewhat agitated, because they were avoiding me and my thoughts in this investigation. Whatever I told Mike, they would find an excuse for their reasoning to be better.

I was called back as an outside resource to help, and maybe they didn't want to hear another possibility—the truth, I suspected.

I got up and went to bed. I was tired and content to put things out of my mind for the night and get some sleep.

Boots came in the next morning and said we would not go back in the fire until it was extinguished. It would be another month or so, but there was nothing we could do. There didn't appear to be anything else that resembled a body from our view of the zone. Mike decided we should go back to Damascus, get caught up on our paperwork, and start ordering some well control equipment. I agreed.

It was the end of June by now, and I hadn't been home for about six weeks. I had talked to Barb many times throughout this ordeal as she was looking after building our house. I called, and she was having problems with the staircase, not understanding the plan. The contractor put the opening in, but she didn't think it was supposed to look like he had it. I asked if there was something else they could work on for a few days, knowing I would be flying into Houston, Texas, to look at some equipment and I would be able to meet her there for a day or so to look at the drawings.

"Do you think you will be home for a few days?" she asked on the phone.

"I don't think so," I said. "We are up to our asses in alligators right now."

"How are you holding out?" she asked.

"It's been very trying," I replied.

"How are things going?" she asked.

"She's still on fire, and we did recover two bodies," I replied referring to the blowout. "Not the best six weeks I have worked, but you do what you do. I guess it's the price you pay for industry." I was trying to downplay the situation.

"I think you should come home for a few days and look at the stairs. I don't think they're putting them in right," she said explaining how they would look as best she could.

"Honey, I'll see what happens. We're really flat out right now getting things ready to go back drilling. We have a lot to do," I said.

I was to leave for Houston in a couple of days, and my goal was to find blowout preventers and related well control equipment. I left

Damascus and flew to Holland. Having a few hours layover, I went downtown and checked out the city of Amsterdam. It was funny when I asked for a menu at the Hard Rock Café. They brought me one with little pouches of every different kind of pot you could imagine. Marijuana was legal, and you could have your pick of whatever you wanted. I was tired but laughed when I saw this.

Calling the waiter back, I asked, "Could I have a food menu?" He obliged. I thought of smoking a big reefer in the restaurant, in public, and chuckled to myself. *These people are pretty open-minded,* I thought.

My breakfast came, and I gobbled it up hungrily, as I hadn't eaten much on the aircraft. Aircraft food wasn't the best most times. With the price of a ticket, one would think they would give you a decent meal but … I guess they needed to make more money.

I left the restaurant and walked the central station area for a couple hours taking pictures and just being a tourist, enjoying the architecture there. At about one in the afternoon, I caught the train back to the airport and waited around until we were supposed to board. Soon, our flight on Northwest Airlines was called, and we were supposed to check in.

I headed to the security area and was in the line waiting to get through when I noticed something different. Podiums were set up, and passengers were going to the podium, one by one, before proceeding to the gate. I wondered what was going on.

My turn came, and a young lady of about twenty-five or so, looking stern, asked me for my documents. She was looking through my passport and noticed I was traveling through the Middle East quite a lot.

"Where are you coming from" she asked?

"Syria," I said calmly and quietly.

"Where are you going" she inquired?

"Houston, then Canada for a few days" I replied.

"What's your purpose in Houston" she asked?

"I have to look at some equipment our company may purchase," I said.

"So you'll be working in the United States" she asked?

"Not really. I am just looking," I replied.

"If you're looking for equipment, that's classified as work," she said with authority.

"Well, if you don't want me to go through the States, I won't," I said somewhat irritated.

"Are you involved in any terrorist activity" she asked?

Laughing at the question, I replied, "No. What kind of a question is that? Who would say yes to that question" I asked?

Looking directly at me, she replied, "They are watching you on camera. They check your reaction," she said waving me through.

Shaking my head, I left the podium. I guessed they were okay with my behavior. I was chuckling about this and thinking how stupid this question was as I went through the check-in and had my carry-on x-rayed.

Flying to the United States was uneventful, so I slept most of the way. I was exhausted from all the pressure of the oil patch, and the rest was much appreciated. I had a busy couple of days ahead of me in Houston.

Arriving there, I was picked up and taken to the hotel room by the people from Varco. They assured me they would come fetch me in the morning and would start showing me their plant and the required equipment.

I went to bed and slept until seven in the morning. I must have been tired as I had slept most of the way on the flight and then slept all night in my room. I showered and went down for breakfast. The waitress came, and I ordered my usual, bacon and eggs with rye toast. I read the paper and ate my breakfast, not realizing how much time I had spent there. I was content to relax for a while. It was around nine thirty when I went back up to my room and called Varco. They informed me someone was on the way and should be at the hotel in a few minutes. I set the phone down and waited, lying on the bed watching the news on CNN.

It was all negative as usual—there was fighting somewhere in the world, the Israelis and Arabs were still in conflict, someone was killed in an accident and headhunters were trying to find out who to blame. There was gang violence, and all the crap the media thrived on. I wondered what the world would be like if legislation was passed so the media would have to show 90 percent positive news and only

10 percent negative. *I bet we would have a more upbeat population,* I thought. They pass all kinds of legislation to control people, but certain groups are protected by protection laws, and then there's the choice of freedom of the press. These people educated the population in a negative sense, creating a lot of problems in societies. My mind was kicking back into gear.

The phone rang; the fellow from Varco was downstairs. We left, driving for a long time before we arrived at their office. Houston was a huge city, spread out over many miles. At times, it appeared we were in the country, and then buildings were everywhere. The driver and I chatted about what we needed, the code specifications for sour gas applications, and such. He had a control stack and was just in the process of rebuilding it and an accumulator to new condition.

The shop was immense with a lot of activity going on, from cutting and welding to machining out steel, making equipment for the oil patch. There were robot welders and machines run by computers with very few people around in some of the areas. It was incredible to watch as I learned how the equipment was made from a ball of steel to the finished product, which was then tested and approved for the patch.

"We need a test pump," I told the salesman.

"Come over here and I'll show you some," he said.

We walked to another part of the plant and looked at some test equipment.

"You see anything that will suit your needs?" the salesman asked.

"I see a bunch that will work, but they take a lot of time to test with. Do you have any that are electric over air?" I asked.

He looked at me somewhat puzzled at first and then said, "We can probably build one. We have never been asked for something like that. What are you looking for specifically?" he asked.

I was more surprised than he. I had an idea in my mind of what it should look like but wasn't sure if anything like that could be built and work. I thought about it a few seconds and then asked, "Is there anything that has an accumulator pump, a small triplex that can take the pressure up to three thousand PSI then shut off on a pressure switch, with some type of relay, kicking the air pumps in to reach five to ten thousand PSI?" I asked.

"I can build that and integrate a shut-off switch for safety reasons," he replied. "Leave that with me, and I'll take it up with our engineering department. I don't know if they were ever requested that before. It sounds like a good idea though."

I spent the better part of the day at the plant and then finally asked them if I could be taken back to the hotel room. I had a lot of phone calls to make to our office in the Middle East and to John Bull Suppliers in the UK. They wanted an update every day, I was told when I left.

I called and spoke to Mike and then called John Bull. Everyone was onboard with what I was doing. The test pump was well received by Mike, so I had to get a price on all of the equipment and relay that back to them. The next day, I got the required information and tried to phone Damascus.

My credit card wasn't being accepted to make phone calls. Somewhat bewildered, I called Visa in Vancouver and found out they had cut me off. They thought my card was stolen, as it had never been used in this manner. After assuring them it was me doing the calling, complete with name and password, they reinstated my card and I was back in business.

Barb was leaving Winnipeg that afternoon to be with me in Houston. At least I would get to see her for a day or so, so I wouldn't forget what she looked like. I had no idea when I was going to get days off. She arrived that evening, and we hugged and kissed for a good while making small conversation when coming up for air. It was good to have her there and hold her. I missed her so much. She too was working hard trying to be the general contractor for our house. I recall my dad asking me if I was going to let Barb be in charge of building the house and replied that she could handle it. He was so old school he didn't think that women were capable of handling situations like that. She sure had shown him a woman's capabilities. I was proud of her.

She took out the plans and proceeded to show me where she was having problems with the stair opening, explaining they had cut a hole in the loft floor. There was a floor joist on the outside of the opening.

"It should have been open all the way," I told her.

"That's what I thought too," she said.

"What does Keith think needs to be done?" I asked. Keith was the carpenter.

"He says it has to be done that way because there is no support for the floor or something. I wish you would come home and look at it yourself, Pat. It's hard to explain," she said.

I had an idea of what she was talking about, but the picture wasn't coming to me. I assured her I would change my flight and fly home with her even if it was for only one night. I called the airline and changed my ticket, rerouting me to Winnipeg, where I would stop over for forty-eight hours before flying back via Toronto and Heathrow and then on to Damascus.

The next morning, I got the pricing for the well control equipment and called to inform the office. Everyone agreed. I made arrangements for the equipment to leave and such. Barb and I flew to Winnipeg the next day and drove home.

We arrived home around nine in the evening, tired, but Barb wanted to show me her project right away. As we approached the lot, which had been empty when I left, I could see the project she was working on. She was smiling and assured me it was going all right. The shell of the house was completely built; the windows and doors were still being installed. No one was around at this time of night, so we could look around at our leisure. We went in through the front door, which wasn't installed yet, and looked around. The frame was up and ready for insulation. She pointed to the stair opening and said, "See there. I don't think that's what you had in mind."

"It isn't, baby," I said. "That shouldn't look like that. I'll talk to Keith in the morning."

A ladder was leaned against the loft floor so I went up to see the view from the top. I stepped out on the loft floor and looked out the windows to the west.

"Beautiful," I said looking at the lake and trees. It looked like a picture through the windows, as if it were framed. I was pleased at what she had accomplished by herself.

I called out, "Hello down there!" laughing at the echo it made. We laughed.

She was doing a good job, but I noticed a change she had made as I came down from the loft. She had installed an extra window at the entrance of the stair to the basement. She was beaming, full of confidence. It looked fine.

"I guess you don't need me here much," I said.

"I do so," she said beaming. "It's good to have you home for a couple days."

We drove back to town and home to our little trailer. It wasn't ours anymore, but we could live in it until the house was done.

The next morning, I spoke to Keith and arranged how the staircase was going to be installed. He had no problem with it if we put in some four-inch oak supports and connected the stair railing to them. It would look great.

We finished up at the site and left for the city when Tiffany got out of school, so I could catch my flight back to the Middle East. The drive back was beautiful with the sun shining and all the vegetation green. I really didn't want to go back and held reservations on what to expect when I arrived. They were still drilling the relief wells, and we were still getting the brunt of the blame for the disaster, from what Mike was telling me.

I flew to Toronto and then had a stopover in London to meet with John Bull. I had a room booked close to the airport so John came over and collected all the paperwork I had on the equipment, asking questions and chatting about many things that were going on in Syria. Everything was in order so he was going to leave and go back to his office.

"Do you want me to come to your office?" I asked.

"No. Everything looks okay. If I need anything, I'll call you," he said in his English accent.

"Okay," I said. "I'll be here until tomorrow, then, you can contact me in Damascus. You have the phone number so just call the office and Mike will get hold of me."

He left, and I lye on the bed and fell asleep. Those international flights were tiring.

I awoke around seven in the evening, had dinner, and then went back to my room. Shuffling through some paper for a while with no interest, I decided to watch television instead. I fell asleep about ten and slept through the night.

I left early the next morning for the airport. I didn't need to be there until around two in the afternoon, but I wanted to see the Concorde take off and land. I dreamed one day I would have an opportunity to have a seat on one of them. I was intrigued at their body style and how much power they had and did get an opportunity to watch one take off and land. I observed the nose cone had pointed downward for both takeoff and landing. This was weird as the commercial aircraft didn't do that. I had gotten to know quite a lot of different aircraft in my travels.

We left on time for the Middle East. I was reading a *Newsweek* magazine and enjoying the flight. I spoke to a few people and made a few more acquaintances. All the people I spoke with appeared to be good, working people. In business class, they didn't mix with us paupers. They closed the curtains so we couldn't see what they were doing, or they didn't want us to see the segregation they paid for. I was already well educated to point out the things I felt were causing some of the strife in the world. I had no qualms about them getting better service or otherwise, but I did see they were mostly corporate businesspeople in that section. A thought went through my head. *If they gave the extra they paid for their seat and service to a poor family, they would be true humanitarians.* Why was I thinking like that?

I got back to Syria and went to the staff house. Mike caught up with me later, and then we went out for dinner. We talked about the plan for the rig, and I was told things were still the same with the oil company and us. They were still trying to hang us but now at least listening to some of the information we were offering. They were cooling down some because OPEC owned the rigs we were working on with Syria being a member of OPEC. Probably some of the heavyweights from Libya and Saudi had come in and held discussions with Shell/Al Furat, showing their clout. I wasn't there but knew of a few who were oil ministers and had leadership roles in their respective countries.

We were close to establishing communication with the problem well; it was now the beginning of August. The equipment brought in to pump cement was being rigged up; everything nearly readied to kill this monster and finally have a bit of peace. I was back on the rig preparing to get back to drilling. A location had been picked, and we were to start moving soon. Our BOP equipment was being cleared at customs, but a few problems were encountered with our paperwork, which was not exactly right for Al Furat to clear. Again, I felt it was another ploy to deter us but kept my mouth shut.

On August 8, 1995, we finally made communication with the

problem well with the last rig. Preparation was now complete, and it was time to snuff this fire out and stop the flow of oil and gas. I don't remember exactly what time but it was in the early afternoon when they started pumping. The engines on the pumping units, all synchronized with the pumps connected together, roared to a start. We had begun. Many of us stood around watching the crater, hoping it would die out. Soon the flame became less and less, and then it went out. The pumpers kept pumping until they were sure enough fluid and cement was injected into the problem well to ensure it was indeed dead. Steam was bellowing from the crater now with the ground cooling down. The roaring of the engines ceased and pumping stopped. Everyone waited in anticipation, hopeful it wouldn't start up again. It was like trying to control a volcano. After a few hours of it cooling down, plans were made to go in and assess the situation.

Boots Hansen, a few others, and I went in and checked the crater. It was silent and still, eerie-like. It almost felt that something was wrong now with no hissing of gas and roaring of fire. The lion was tamed. We had red ribbon and pegs with us, so we staked out the area and didn't allow anyone in until we had finished with the removal of the human remains and the investigation was complete. We looked at that little truck again, and I said to Boots, "I think that caused the fire." He didn't answer.

We went to the passenger side of the truck and carefully looked on the ground for any sign of remains. Boots spotted a watch and ring. He picked them up and inspected them. "This is Martin. That's his watch and ring," he said.

Kneeling down now, we carefully scratched the ground looking for anything else. He was exposed to the fire longer and more closely than the others, so he was completely incinerated. It was hard to determine the fragments we gathered, but we found small fragments of bone, teeth, and a steel toe from his safety boots. In all, a small sandwich bag, about an eighth full, was all we could find, but we had something, not a lot, to lay to rest so everyone could find closure.

Inside the crane, we found the few small remains of the Arab crane operator. He too was completely incinerated, and only small fragments of bone, teeth, and fingernails were found. We also found his steel toes from his safety boots with fragments of toenails melted to the steel. It was a sad day.

I walked around the area and looked for any sign of Carlos. Peering into the crater, all I saw was water and pebble rock about three quarters of an inch in diameter piled around a crater about fifty feet wide and three to four hundred feet long now. I could not see the depth yet as the water and mud, pumped into the well from the relief wells, filled the crater. *I hope we can find him,* I thought. I looked around the wellhead; it was singed but still standing. The cross on top, blackened from the fire now, protruded from the BOP, leaning somewhat from the heat. A hole alongside the well casing was big enough to swallow up a man. I hoped he wasn't alongside of that, buried in the sand and product we so vigorously drilled for to fuel our economy. Was it worth it? I wondered, convincing myself it wasn't, but still, we needed this stuff to make the world go round.

We looked for a few hours, finding no sign of Carlos. It was getting dusk now, so we quit for the night, determined to come back in the morning to find the missing man.

The next morning, I spoke to Mike on the phone and told him we hadn't found Carlos. I inquired about a death certificate for him, if we couldn't find him. Mike didn't know what would come of it, but Carlos's wife, in her grief, had called a few days prior and wanted to know what to do. She had reported his death to the insurance company, but they wanted proof.

I went back to the site and looked for Carlos, pleading within myself to God to let us find something. A tear flowed down my cheek, as fears of not finding him haunted me. His whole family would suffer even more if they couldn't get some type of insurance claim so they could feed themselves. I was concerned for that family even though Carlos had told me he had invested in some small apartments in his city. I didn't know how well-off he was, or if he even was, for that matter. They made only six hundred dollars a month.

I stayed in Syria until September 6, 1995, helping to get things back on track. The paperwork was piled high with the problem and needed sorting out. We worked diligently trying to make heads or tails out of all this. We tried to understand what had happened. After investigating the site, the oil company declared the fire was ignited by static electricity. I begged to differ but was overruled and told to let it go. I couldn't get Carlos out of my mind and the fact I had denied him access to worshipping the Lord.

I went home for my field break, exhausted. Barb had the house ready, and we moved in. The job she did was miraculous. The color schemes were incredible. It was beautiful. *What an artist she is,* I thought. I had visions of purple, not close to the grape color she had picked for the carpet. She had assured me it looked good, and I had doubted it. The walls were off-white and very bright. Everything was clean and fresh, but I couldn't seem to get excited about it. Many things were on my mind, and maybe I was slipping into depression. I didn't know. I thought of the house as a white elephant but said nothing, because Barb was so happy. She was the rock who got it done without me being there, except for the day or so when we made a correction on the stairs. She had lived in a trailer house with dark, paneled walls and wanted something bright. With her dream fulfilled, who was I to spoil it?

I slept for the first week off and on, many times thinking about the fire and what, maybe, I could have done to prevent that accident. It shaped me in ways I never thought, making me angry at corporate business, yet I felt we were trying to do the right thing for mankind. I was helping to get a resource we so depended on for many different aspects of our lives, never thinking beyond oil and gas before. I found myself thinking of better ways to do things with the technology we had, instead of using it to destroy and instill fear into the population of the world, wasting a lot of resources to destroy willingly, rather than help the very people God created, who were supposed to be the caretakers of the lands. My spirituality was making me question myself now. I was reflecting on the world, the problems, the strife, the killing, and the greed. The power of choice, I reflected on for many days, realizing something that had eluded many for a long time: the will to use it positively for the benefit of everyone.

Was I destined to find the truth? Did I have the courage to accept the truth? I was really questioning myself now. Maybe that was a message from God? I wasn't sure what to think. I shook. I cried silently, not wanting anyone to see my emotions. I was quiet in my thoughts and jumped when nearly asleep in my bed. Was I having a breakdown, or was I just tired? I didn't think it was a breakdown, as I had full control of myself. I felt stable and sound. My inner self was telling me to move on, to move forward and not be afraid.

I went back to the Middle East and continued to work in the field drilling, but the atmosphere was very different. The oil company was giving us grief for every minute thing and was on our case because of the blowout. The company representatives were vocal at us many times, trying to intimidate us, and disrespectful. I soon became as they were and defended us as best I could. One day, I had had just about enough of that crap. The company men, as we called them, had told the hands they were going to run the rig off and they would have to find other employment. This got back to me and stirred up many problems on the rig. The hands were pouting, not wanting to work because their jobs were on the line. I called Mike and asked him if he had heard anything about this and was assured he hadn't.

"Mike, you better go to Al Furat's office and let them know this has to stop," I commanded. I was upset and didn't need this kind of strife carrying on.

"Who told the hands this?" Mike asked.

"Apparently Ian; that's what the men tell me," I said. He was the company man on tour when this broke. "I don't know for sure," I assured Mike.

"I'll straighten this out," Mike said somewhat angry and disappointed in the professionalism displayed by the company man.

He must have talked to Al Furat because it was about three in the afternoon when my door flew open. Ian, red in the face, screaming at me from the top of his lungs, angry at what had happened, came in.

"I didn't tell those guys. You're a fuckin' troublemaker," he accused. He denied being the one who told the men with many more obscenities. He was so angry, a boil on his nose had broken open and a yellowish puss ball fell onto my desk. Blood was streaming down his face as he yelled.

I sat there and listened to this for a minute or so and didn't like the personal content of his accusations. I finally stood up from my desk and calmly said, "You told me your nose was broken five times already. If you don't stop, settle down, and talk to me like a human being, it will be broken for the sixth time."

"You can clean your germs off my desk now," I said calmly but meaning every word I was saying. I didn't care if I lost my job. If he was going to make me lose my job from what he had started, I was going to take him out.

He wiped off my desk, still shouting, slowly calming down. I said, "Get the fuck out of my office and don't come back until you are ready to talk like a man, or do I throw you out?"

He went quiet and left rather hurriedly. He knew I was going to do what I said.

I sat back down and was shaking from anger but was relieved I didn't use force. I was in control the whole time but could have been pushed over the edge very easily.

When he came back, he admitted to his mistake and calmly apologized. He told me his score for performance had diminished within the company because of this. I guessed the evaluation of him had been scored by some type of numbering system from one to five. He didn't realize he was just a number in the corporation. Self-righteousness had failed him.

All went back to normal from that point, and the company man that replaced Ian was better, but still somewhat distrustful. He kept to himself most times and didn't bother us too much. Tom came by to see me and wanted to know my side of all this, so I told him the same as I had told Mike. I had not made any accusation; he was on location when it all came to a head, and I went with what the hands had told me. *Did I accuse him?* I was questioning myself.

Days off came and went quickly, and it was getting close to Christmas. I was working in the office while Mike took a few weeks off, busy trying to get Carlos's death certificate through the oil company. The government was hesitant about giving us one for some reason or another, or someone wanted a bribe. That was the way it worked, and there was nothing I could do about it.

Sometime before Christmas, we got a call that John took. Carlos's wife was distraught, crying, asking for the death certificate. She had about two weeks, and then the insurance would be null and void, she told John.

Miraculously, we received the certificate a day or so after talking with the oil company and explaining our situation, but how were we going to get it to the Philippines on time?

John suggested we send it with one of the hands working on the rig. Ding was scheduled for days off in a month, so we decided to send him early. He lived close enough to the same village as Carlos to get it there on time. Zuhair was working on securing a ticket for Ding, and I was on the phone telling Al to send Ding in immediately. We got a flight for the next morning and sent the certificate with him. I often wondered if she received this and got her payment. She should have been looked after by the oil company, I also thought. I still felt he had died for greed and economics and won't allow myself to think differently.

In 1996, we were still working under the conditions of distrust and blame. Mike and I were in disagreement on many things. He was for the oil company and I against. I didn't agree with their findings. I didn't agree with their doing the same things, as if nothing had happened. They were still doing things cheaply with the possibility of another accident. It caused many conversations and disagreements, and I didn't want any more of this, so I handed in my resignation and left. It was June. I would spend summer at home. I needed to rest and regroup. Maybe I would quit the patch and find something else less stressful. I had had just about enough of the oil patch.

Chapter Twelve

I stayed home for the summer and helped Barb landscape the yard. We built flower gardens and planted many fruit trees of various types, such as saskatoons, raspberry, chokecherry, pin cherry, currants both red and black, Evan's cherry, gooseberry, cranberry, hazelnut, strawberries, blueberries, and various ornamental trees. We installed railroad ties for barriers, outlining the driveway and surrounding flower gardens. Hedges were put in around the house and down the driveway, with old dead trees and roots used as highlights in the flower gardens and amongst the trees. We planted grass throughout the yard and covered it with a mixture of sand and horse manure and then finished off the gardens and lawns.

On many occasions, people stopped by to comment on our artwork. Some admired it, commenting on the beauty while others cringed and remarked, "That's a lot of work." They didn't see it as a form of art or pleasure and relaxation, not understanding the love and care we put into what we were creating.

We didn't think of it as work. We were proud and thankful that the good Lord had given us these talents and were happy to use them. We walked around the finished product, noticing how life and death went hand in hand, admiring the old logs and dead stumps for their beauty in the landscape. How beautiful life was and how lucky we were to be able to create small things.

We counted our blessings. Many people don't realize their potential, never counting the blessings given to them by God until they are taken away. After being able to move around freely and effortlessly, try sitting in a wheelchair, unable to do many things. When one can see, smell, touch, speak, hear, and enjoy the beauty around us, try not being able to see the beauty, to smell the flowers, hear a bird chirp, or touch anything. We will never understand until it is gone, so be positive and enjoy the little things you have and take for granted.

I was hired in the oil patch in Canada, consulting for a few different companies on smaller wells at first. Then I was asked by a consulting firm to go to Venezuela. I accepted immediately, having not been to this part of the world before.

The people were poor but happy most of the time, influenced from the Spanish Armada times, combined with some Arabic culture. The country was accepting to most cultures, and everyone mixed well. One thing I really noticed was that people could call a black man a Negro and no one took offense. Why? *Negro* meant black in Spanish. They would actually laugh and tease each other. For some reason, here, we have to be careful, correct politically, to ensure no one takes offence. Why is this?

Is it because of the history of slavery and the way people were treated in that era? Are we living in the past, not moving forward to accept people for who they are? Many times, I believe we have stalled out and are willing to stay and fight, disagreeing just because we can. I believe it is fueled by leaders of communities, governments, and parents who don't understand the cleanliness of their hearts at birth. They don't understand that it could be solved easily if all cultures quit living in the past and blaming with self-pity and self-righteousness.

I learned the language enough to communicate with the workers and had fun with them singing Christmas carols and such. They tried hard and were willing workers, but some outsiders weren't satisfied. I lost my cool too at times, mostly because of the stress of the business and the long hours, but this is no excuse for the mistreatment of people. I didn't want anyone to get hurt. I always had that concern at the back of my mind now, more so because of the blowout. It is funny how one changes from such events.

From 1997 to June of 2000, I worked at many different things in Venezuela, developing and using technology to the limits on the wells we drilled. Conoco was a good company to work with. They were not afraid to try different ideas, pushing them to limits far beyond expectations. We drilled wells with multiple legs, completing them with windows, liners, and tools that were perfected on the project, designing and modifying some equipment so it worked. The wealth of experience was incredible. Although many of us had not worked with any of this, a lot of trial and error with fresh ideas usually proved successful. We installed recorders with fiber-optic technology that was tricky, but with patience, worked excellently. The world was watching us develop this technology. It was stressful, requiring a lot of our time, and disagreements, heated from time to time, would surface, and required patience and meetings until resolved.

We had fun moving rigs in the jungle with old dilapidated trucks that did the job, even though it would take much longer than anticipated. One time, we pulled a truck apart. A Cat was tied onto it trying to get it over a small hill when the frame broke, resulting in the front end being pulled off. The radiator, front wheels, and part of the fenders were dragged about two hundred yards before the Cat operator realized what had happened. The rig rolled backward. There was no way to stop it. It came to rest against a bank three hundred feet from where it came apart. The truck push was excited at first, and then we all laughed uncontrollably, knowing no one was injured.

There were problems arising with our pay structure. The oil company wanted to lower costs and was looking for ways to do that. The consulting firm I worked for also wanted to make more money, so a plan was devised to pay the taxes on only a portion of our salaries, which wasn't the deal when we accepted the job. Taxes were included.

The consulting firm called my home when I was away, asking Barb what we paid ourselves from the money paid to my little consulting firm. I was subcontracted. Barb was unaware of what was going on, so she gave them that information, trusting them. We soon learned what it was all about, finding that was the amount they paid the taxes on. Furthermore, when I got audited, I ended up paying another twenty-nine thousand dollars because of their scheme. Again, I was frustrated with corporate business doing this to the little guy and felt the powers, the top guys, should have taken a cut. They made a hell of a lot more than we, but that's not how it works.

I stayed on disgruntled, working until they were tired of listening to me telling them the truth and how crooked they were. They hate the truth and will do whatever it takes to shut you up.

They moved me to Ecuador with the promise of a pay scale not being interfered with. There were many problems though. The Colombian guerrillas stalked the jungle, along with many little local factions. There was unrest apparently, because the Americans had set up a base in Esmeralda to combat the drug trade going on in that part of the world. The local farmers had a way to make a living by utilizing their land to grow coca; the dreaded stuff cocaine is made from when refined. It was being taken away from them, so many were disgruntled.

The coca leaves had been chewed by the tribesmen in that part of the world for many years prior to the drug trade intervention. They would get energy and stimulation from this plant, allowing them to work longer, I was told.

The extraction of and making of cocaine was founded by the outside worlds educated chemical engineers, with a lot of money being made selling this to people around the globe. Some government heads seemed to accept this and were probably enticed with the almighty dollar to go along with it. Again, this is a good example of greed and power. Many times, I wonder if our leaders are involved in some way with all this.

Its obvious drug abuse is rampant not only in the USA, but also in Canada and around the world. It's big business, causing war. They allow it until it gets out of control and then try to stop it, many times failing, so outside intervention is requested, and we, the innocent, without any knowledge of what is happening abroad, are subjected to rejection from those people. The farmers were complaining they were the victims of the intervention and couldn't make a living anymore from the drug trade. The crops were being sprayed by aircraft, trying to discourage the people from growing them. *What chemicals are being used, and what impact on people living there will we see in the future?*

Not too long before I arrived, some rig people were kidnapped and walked through the jungle for a hundred days, while negotiations were ongoing for their release. A huge sum of money was requested by the captors with negotiations underway. I don't know what happened, but I am suspicious of the deal and have a hunch that the ransom was met.

Locations were surrounded by fences with guards on towers in every corner of the location, sporting machine guns and keeping a watchful eye out for the enemy, many escorting us to and from camp. We couldn't go for a walk without a guard. It was nerve-racking at times, as gunfire would erupt mostly by accident. These guys were not trained properly on how to use a weapon safely, and sometimes, when you were talking to them, a gun would be accidentally pointed at you or in line with your body, unknowingly.

Another kidnapping occurred. A rig lost their expatriate crew to the guerrillas. They were kidnapped, and a demand was made. When the company requested proof, they found the rig manager at a specific site agreed on, shot to death, a bullet in his head.

I was given the option to quit without penalty if I felt unsafe. I accepted and went home.

For a few months, I worked out of McCallum, Texas, setting up a turnkey operation in Mexico. We set up an office and bought trucks, furniture, and everything required for starting an operation in Mexico.

Working for the local oil and gas corporation was trying. They were into our business, complaining we didn't understand Spanish well enough and our tour books weren't being filled out right.

A fellow who was working in Venezuela with us was now our drilling supervisor, and I had no respect for him. He was one of the guys in Venezuela who said he would do something about the tax situation I was forced into and didn't. To me, he was a fraud, looking after his own interest. He knew he was not going to work with Conoco in Venezuela long and had talked to the consulting firm I worked with about a job.

He would get sarcastic on the phone at times, and one morning, he did just that. I told him to get his ass out to the rig or send someone else. I quit and was leaving with no intention of changing my mind. Our rep. came to the rig and tried to downplay things, telling me when I get tired, I seem to get out of control. How the hell can you not lose control when you have to deal with these kinds of people, who sometimes think they are above the world, and corporate heads who place themselves in a position of self-righteousness with no regard for others? I'd had it with corporations wanting you to do things beyond your abilities, without support, and then complaining. It was 2001. I was going home and wasn't going to work for these types of people anymore, I thought.

I repatriated to Canada and worked at Firebag, drilling pads and installing SAG D equipment. Many times, we had four rigs on the pad, which was not what we were hired for but what was forced upon us by the company with no extra pay. Tired and sleepless nights led to conflict between some of us, cooped up in a trailer house together, with no space for self. Some of us had strong leadership personalities and couldn't get along. Some wanted to try their own ideas. Sometimes we belittled each other unknowingly, trying to get the job done.

Many times, young engineers right out of school were sent out to learn but didn't want to go on the floor to observe. They would spend most of their time on the computer, playing games, and would get upset when we forced them to learn. It wasn't a pleasant operation but it paid the bills. It was 2001, and the worst disaster in North America had just happened, 911.

Talk was negative around the rig. "Kill those bastards. Bomb them. Use nuclear warheads" and much more was being said. I was mixed in my feelings for a short while, realizing I had worked with those people and had no problem. I wasn't in agreement with war, but it was imminent. Whom did we want war with?

After finishing up the two pads we were hired for, I left and went to work to Cold Lake doing the same type of work, designing and installing equipment, trying many different ways to accomplish the company's goals. Many hands with little or no experience were sent out, causing many sleepless nights. I would tell them to get people who could handle the job so we could sleep when we were supposed to, but it's not what you know, it's who you know. They sent friends and people with little or no experience, expecting us to train on the job. I have no problem training people but not all at once, especially when expectations are high to successfully complete the wells.

Tired, I left the patch again for the summer. The long hours, with people keeping me up because they didn't know what was required and getting paid the same, were enough.

Chapter Thirteen

Nine-eleven, a major factor in everyone's life, happened with the news blaring, accusing, condemning, swaying people, hatred and self-pity rampant and exemplified. Someone was angry at us, and the hunt was on. One of the Twin Towers in New York City had been hit with an aircraft and was on fire. Then another aircraft hit the second one, and a fireball erupted, live on television, play by play. A couple hours after the aircraft hit the buildings, they collapsed into the biggest dust ball television had ever filmed. People were scrambling, running over each other through the streets, crying and screaming, trying to get out of harm's way, with many trapped inside and no way out. About three thousand people perished in that disaster, and we still don't know why. We have blamed a lot of people and different countries, but the real answer has not been exposed. No one has accepted the blame, but we know the so-called terrorists did the deed, but who is to blame?

The U.S. government headquarters, the pinnacle of power, was hit, while television crews filmed, talking about the leaders going to underground bunkers to command the troops and get order restored. Another aircraft was commandeered in Pennsylvania by people with box cutters; then passengers attempting to take control from the hijackers scuffled as the plane crashed to the ground, saving the target intended. Total chaos was observed while people were looking for answers and solutions for the problem.

The president was shown talking to children and being told of the disaster, a look of surprise, anger, and hurt on his face, as he was trying to keep his composure and stay calm until class was dismissed, and then he was blasted by the media for his slowness to respond.

When the response came, planes were instructed to land or be taken down by military aircraft, dispatched, ready to conduct whatever was required to stabilize the situation. Everything was rapidly coming together, but still, the negativity of the media, looking to sell their story, their perception to the world, was very obvious.

I looked in the mirror, and to my surprise, I saw something most people didn't get to see. I saw this figure staring back at me in bewilderment, brown eyes set deep in their sockets; a mole on the side of his face; a little round, flat nose; thin, stiff upper lip; long hair; frowning; unshaven with a puzzled look. He looked familiar, and a closer look revealed it was me! Yes, me! I had heard a lot of blame and remarks like, "Look what they've done. They hurt our feelings. We have to kill them. Blah, blah, blah."

No one seemed to recognize the problem. We were so accustomed to the fact we were right, we saw no wrong with going to war, killing innocent people. We saw no problem with the words from an educated leader telling the world, "We'll hunt them down; we'll smoke them out." We were on the bandwagon of hate, and by golly, we wanted all of them killed … no matter the cost. Most knew nothing of the people or countries they were condemning, except what the media was saying, educating them on self-righteousness. They studied too much history and were blinded by what they were taught. They were shaping up on conducting war, premeditating murder against people who did nothing, and the media was ready for the play-by-play, advertising tanks and weapons, looking for an excuse to go in and kill that group of people, accusing them of weapons of mass destruction. Not one Iraqi was involved in the 9/11 attacks was broadcasted. While these accusations were ongoing, we were polishing our own weapons, training and brainwashing our own people to kill for them. Self-righteousness was rampant.

I determined we all needed to share the blame. I did nothing to try and stop it. I supported the corporate controllers who built these weapons, the governments that used them, the oil business, taxation, and everything we stand for. We work together to build these things under the guise of protection and job creation. If we didn't pay taxes, then we could say we don't, but … everything is taxed and forced on us. Beware of the tax man. He will drag you in. The only ones who don't support this are the forgotten ones on the street with nothing to give.

Hello! George, the weapons are here. We built and sold them to the enemies. Hello, George! You also have one in your living room, don't you? You do have a television, the worst weapon of mass destruction, don't you? Are you laughing at the people you are stirring up, or are you not educated properly? George! Did you learn that in history? George! You should never use the Bible wrongly. Why didn't you say we'll leave no rock unturned, rather than we'll smoke them out, we'll hunt them down? Why did you refer to the Crusades? Why did you accuse us, Canada, of harboring terrorists? We cannot harbor what we are. We are the terrorists, George. The West is the terrorists. Remember the Cold War. Russia and you guys had us frozen in fear about the nuclear bomb. That went on for a lot of years. As a matter of fact, we are still scared to death.

We have been living in fear since the atom bomb was developed, and we used it first in Japan. We have sold weapons all over the world through corporate business and even gave some to these guys. We helped Iraq when they were fighting the Iranians. George! Stop. You're mad. Your pride has been hurt. Your power has been slapped in the face. Your self-righteousness has been challenged. George! Be a man. Pray! Ask for guidance! Read the Word! If you live by the sword, you will die by the sword! George! Please don't use the young people and have them killed so you can show power and flex your muscles! George! You made lots of money with corporate business! Ask them to fix it! George! Wait! Wait! I was talking to my television and didn't have his number. It was too late.

Damn that self-righteousness, I thought. I wish we didn't have a choice. We wouldn't have this mess. They were right in their minds, and we were right in our minds. Problem … we didn't want to talk. We did talk but demanded. We did talk but threatened. We did talk but they wouldn't listen. Why? We are good people. Why won't they listen to us?

The time had come to show them who is right. Aircraft were dispatched off aircraft carriers to bomb Baghdad with a vengeance because someone said the accused enemy was at a certain place. Streets crowded with innocent people were hit, killing many as the bombs dropped. The reality show was in full bloom all over our living rooms. The ground forces were racing in toward Baghdad, unstoppable, basically unopposed, making many miles before coming into some resistance.

They would stop, with cameras rolling, television crews making the movie. Resistance groups were decimated, because they had no defense against our corporate-sponsored weapons, and we had no remorse, no mercy. Aircraft entered unchallenged the city limits dropping payload after payload, attempting to succeed in their command of shock and awe. Men and women of every color and creed mixed together in the most powerful country's military were getting along, fighting side by side, but couldn't get along in peace. Many soldiers were brave and battle ready to inflict pain and suffering on another human, possibly to see if their blood was the same color as theirs. Bodies were lying around, being stepped over as if they weren't there, meaningless to the opposed, treated as an enemy, now silenced.

Men captured and displayed as an ace or king, like a bad poker game, waiting to be exiled to a manmade prison, tortured to speak by means acceptable in the codes of battle, the rules of engagement. Statues were being pulled down, dragged and kicked as if to hurt the plaster or bronze. People were boasting through the camera. Flags were lifted claiming success as if to say, "Look what we have done."

Doors were being kicked down on dwellings occupied by women and children, without respect, looking for the enemy, scaring those children for life, embedding more hatred, warping minds of already doubtful, suppressed people, with no shame. *We are going to win. We will not falter. We have resolve. We have courage.* The world was subjected to all the boasting broadcasted to intimidate the supposedly opposing faction.

Finding the ace of the country was a disgrace with news media explaining the situation like a rat being caught in a trap, sneering and enjoying what was happening to another human being, who thought nothing more than that he was right, as we did. We had him condemned for the exact reasons we were trying to justify: self-righteousness. We didn't only have military prisoners of war but many innocent victims, fleeing their homes to refugee camps, imprisoned to suffering because of our choice.

This was played on television all over the world. Many bought into it. I believe all the governments in the world understood what each of them was doing and played their roles to a tee. What a Hollywood play. It was the first reality show started on television. It was big bucks for the corporate world as it was sponsored and advertised by them. Through using these weapons, people were subjected to the advertising of products sold to them by corporate business and sales would probably be high. They had our full attention didn't they?

The World Bank, run by corporate business and government, loaned you money to conduct war and now are collecting interest through taxation from you, the labor force, who built the weapons they paid you so little for and sold, making huge profits. You have a huge debt to pay back now. Evil pays big dividends. The ten-billion-dollar cost of replacing those buildings lost in 9/11 is now a lot of blood, with no interest, and trillions to pay back, and you are held ransom for this through bailouts and taxation. The fuel used to do this evil could have reduced the price of the commodity but now has escalated it, nearly out of reach for the working class, who are left to foot the bill, trying to make it to work with our gas-guzzlers, because they didn't want to talk for the last number of years. Had we used our speech properly without threat, condemnation, and stipulation, we could have worked this out I'm sure.

Ever since the beginning of history, the beginning of man, we have had the urge for power and to become better than God. We want to be his equal through self-righteousness. We know we can't, but we keep trying.

The universe was created by God, and there is no man who can make a stone from nothing. We can't make a bird. We can't even make a male or female by choice, naturally. We have played with nature and genetics and are able to disrupt and destroy the natural but have created nothing but hardships and grief on ourselves. Disease, oppression, starvation, and hate are all derived by man or caused by what we have done not only to ourselves but to the environment around us.

Maybe by changing genetics, we have allowed these diseases and viruses to accumulate, compound, and become immune, because we took their natural enzymes, chromosomes, and other genetic abilities that may have helped us, away, not knowing how to replace them. Maybe we are the cause of what science classifies as evolution, through pollution of air, food, and water, causing animals and ourselves to change because of what we do.

We have done a lot of damage and very little good over the centuries. We have destroyed empires, moved mountains, defied gravity, and many other things in a quest to control and overpower others through self-righteousness. We are doing stem cell experiments, mutating bacteria, and filling our bodies with nuclear energy and other chemicals, possibly causing many to suffer the many problems we see today. We patent many things for the benefit of one over the other, rather than share freely and help man, mostly for money. Maybe we should have a thought about the greed we have, first.

We build weapons, aircraft, and warships, and sell them, making huge sums of money from others who want to have power and control at the expense of others. We then pick sides. Whoever has the same self-righteous ideals as we, we help them. Whoever derived self-righteous ideals of their own we fight, never coming to some common agreement through our power of speech.

We build all kinds of unnecessary items, creating garbage and hatred all over the world. When a starving man sees a wealthy man throw out a meal, he gets another day without the essentials. He sees the money wasted on space, war, and stupidity, while his people suffer, angry at his government. We have just created a rebel, haven't we? Now we tag him a terrorist. Then we want to kill him. Why? Is it because we are self-righteous? People should come first.

History hasn't taught us a thing. We have studied it and now try to figure better ways to fight and destroy people and cultures through the development of all types of technology and weaponry. If we are civilized, we should have learned by now protection, true protection of people comes from peace, not from more sophisticated weaponry. We should have learned to get along, becoming friends instead of foes. Friends don't hurt each other.

We have thrown God out of our lives and support systems, so we have school killings, people in parliaments bullying, some good people getting killed secretly through conspiracies, and then we try to justify our actions, blaming and tagging someone as a lunatic or terrorist. We create laws to protect the evildoers and sway the judicial system to follow the leader. We do many unnecessary, evil things and forgot we are all God's children, who are different in the way we worship. We are different in the way we look only because God was smart enough to give us a cover suitable for the climate we were born in. We use this against each other for power and self-righteousness. Shouldn't we stop? Shouldn't we look in the mirror to see where the problem lies, or are we afraid?

We have done this to ourselves. Everyone on this planet is responsible. Admit it like an alcoholic, and we will cure it. If we don't admit it, then how do you think we can fix the social problems around the world when many of the leaders, the teachers, and parents are in denial? One by one, we can stop this. Educate ourselves properly. Change the way we are. Govern ourselves.

Many people are dying and scores are kept on coalition and American troops like a board game, with no numbers shown for enemy or civilian casualties. Is this civilized? Is this who we want to be?

Chapter Fourteen

In May 2004, I picked up and read a book called *Armageddon, Crisis in the Middle East*, written sometime in the early seventies. I was amazed at what the book was about and how it secured my thoughts. It was written in such a way that it used some of the quotes from the book of Revelation and pointed out how it is playing out today in the world. It made me understand the things I saw in my travels and pointed out the fact that God and Jesus predicted the mess we would be in, if we became as we are. It predicted the condition of the Middle East and the strife it is in with all the oil they have. It talks about the Israelis and how this being the third time they have been reinstated to their homeland, they will not be moved off. The prediction in the quote says they will be forced off and return; the third time, they will stay. This book frightened me with its accuracy of prediction.

It discusses the rapture of the church, and today, we are seeing just that with all the garbage being blown out of proportion through the media, convincing people the churches are corrupt. So is everything else, but they keep moving in the direction of greed and control as predicted. There are problems in everything we do in an organized fashion, because rules and politics have to be involved. The planners can dictate self-righteousness through these means for control.

It talks about the rapture of the people, leaving only Satan's advocates here to be destroyed at the end time, along with a few witnesses, from the believers. It points out armies, complete armies disappearing, on their way to defend Satan and his followers. It also talks about the end time itself and the color of the sky being orange-red with the sun being blocked out from the dust and destruction. Did I see this in the Middle East? Was I given a premonition? Cities will be shaken to the ground like matchsticks. It talks about the Jews who study Judaism, who in the end, are saying, "Blessed is He who comes in the name of the Lord," they, finally believing in the goodness of who he sent as Savior and Messenger. Many messengers have been sent but none as remembered as he. All of what I read appears to be what the world is doing today. A chill ran down my spine as I read and reread many chapters.

Upon finishing that book, I picked up another book called *The Greatest Miracle in the World*, a great book written by Og Mandino. This book, combined with the other one, opened my eyes up immensely and has shown me who is at fault. It pointed out that we, all of us, are at fault. Why? We have a choice. We have not used the power of choice properly. We have allowed, through our education, the leaders to govern in such a way that greed and suppression are the result. We have allowed this to happen, through the power we have given and allowed a few to have. We have schooled many but educated none.

As I read this particular book, many times, I would have to reread a paragraph or chapter to see if I understood what was being said. The story was about a man who, I felt, by chance met with God or someone sent by God, because he had the ability to write. It was told by a rag picker who does the work of God, teaching one how to live and pull himself off the heap of rubbish we have today.

It told of how to do that and help others who seem to be on the wrong path of self-pity, self-destruction, and continuing to go the wrong way, because of their misuse of the power of choice. It educated me on many things and pointed out where we are going wrong and how our values have diminished.

When reading, I felt this tremendous power come within me and knew it was nothing I could control. This power guided my mind, my thoughts, and my ability to think, as if it took complete control of me. As I read chapter after chapter at the kitchen table with Barb and the company of family around me, I would stop and feel the source within me, guiding me to think. "Think deeply," it kept telling me. "How far can you really remember?"

Testing myself, I could remember things as a child, having fun, a child wanting many things, pouting if I couldn't have them. I could think of the siblings and myself playing, fighting, Mom trying to control us. I could remember back to when I was around two years old, and then it would stop. I paced the floor and tried to think more, but my thoughts were stalled. This humble voice then said, "Come on. Think! What did you learn in school? What about the conception? What about the womb? Your mind is powerful, and we don't use it all. We only use a small portion. Think!" I sat down and began to think.

I drifted off thinking about splitting the sperm from the egg, drifting off and floating into oblivion. My mind took me through the ice ages, many of them, through dinosaurs, the universe, and beyond. I sat there at the table shaking. I had no control over the power doing this to me. I was controlled by something so powerful, I didn't understand. I heard my wife ask a couple of times if I was okay, and I didn't respond. She came over and looked into my eyes puzzled. I was cold, sweating, and shaking uncontrollably at times. What was happening? Was I having a nervous breakdown? I was still in control of my mind, but I didn't have the strength to move.

I finally ended up at this gate, a huge gate with a rustic lock and bolt. I knocked and knocked at the gate until finally the bolt slid and the gate opened. A voice said, "Come in." A sense of peace came over me, and I stopped shaking.

"Thank you," I replied.

"You look a mess," the humble voice said. "What happened to you?"

"I don't know. I don't know," I cried, wiping away tears. I began to shake again.

"Calm down, my child. Let's see what we can do to help."

I felt it was the Holy Spirit talking to me and was somewhat confused. I immediately started to confess things I deemed as wrong, babbling and not listening to what he was trying to say.

"Tut, tut, tut… Listen. You come here and think I don't understand. You are living in a world that seems to teach you negative things. I know everything, and I know the wrongs man has done. All of you! I want to hear the good things. Tell me good things."

My mind was racing trying to think of the good things I had done. Many of us do good things and never think about them, which is absolutely incredible. I tried and tried to think of the good things I had done but my mind was continuously going to confess the negative. I would say one good thing and then babble on about nothing and look for justification. "Tut, tut, tut," I heard many times. "Good things. Let's start with … have you ever opened a door for an elderly person?" the voice asked.

After thinking back, I replied, "Yes! I have many times."

"There you go. If more people would do that, life would be more enjoyable. You have enjoyed that with no return. You have succeeded with small things as I have asked," the voice said.

Soon, the positive things started to come. I had done many things for different people but had not gloated on them and rarely remembered them. I had done a good number of things from bringing medicines to other countries for the men who worked with me whose wives needed garlic tablets, giving my boots to another man who wanted them, giving my jeans away, helping people to understand things from different angles, and much more. I had done many of these things, as have others and never thought about them, yet I had allowed myself to be on a pile of rubbish and couldn't figure out why.

"You have been engulfed in manly things. The way you perceive the way of life I wanted for you has become difficult for many. You are not alone, my child. Everyone is caught up in this, and many don't know it. You have been fortunate in your life and have seen many things. Use those things you learned for the benefit of man."

Sobbing, I replied, "What can I do? I don't have the power to do this."

"Everyone has the power. I have instilled this in everyone. Everyone was born with a clean heart. No more do I want to hear; you can't. You were told that once before. You could write a book. Many of you can, and many don't."

"How can I write a book? I didn't go to school long enough to learn those skills."

"Anyone can write a book. You know how to write. I have seen you write letters. I have seen you fill in forms. You have so much education from your travels. You can write."

"But I can't," I pleaded. "How can I write when I have to work many hours to survive? I am disrupted all the time and lose my train of thought. I don't have the financial means of supporting myself while I write. It will take me a lifetime."

"No one said you had to do it in one night. Just make an effort, and things will work out. Now go, and I will guide you. I will not interfere, but if you need me, just call. I am always here," the voice said. "Write to instill the positive. Tell people what you have learned."

I heard the gate close, then, I was back in my chair at the table. I wasn't shaking anymore. Calmly, I got up and poured a coffee. Barb looked at me somewhat bewildered and again asked if I was okay. Smiling now, I declared, "I need to write my book."

"You always said you wanted to do that. Why don't you?" she asked.

"I'm going to," I said. "I really am, and I don't care how long it takes."

"I'd like to read it," she said. "It will be good."

Since May of 2004, after reading those books, I have not read any more. These were the first good books I had read since leaving school when I was sixteen years old. I was now fifty-one and realized that I too had forgotten what we were supposed to be doing. I had understood for many years, since I was taught by my parents, right and wrong, to give and forgive, to share, to be honest and responsible, and to use the powers given to me wisely. Because we are so caught up in this human world trying to make a living, trying to get ahead, trying to compete for greed, we forget what is necessary. We forget what is required and important. We forget how simple it was supposed to be.

I decided I was going to change and allow myself to open up my mind and think. I wasn't going to keep myself so busy that I couldn't think properly. I wasn't going to be led around by the nose by a system that is based on self-righteousness. I was going to do something about it. I was going to utilize my education from travel and from my parents, use my own mind to the fullest, and share a different view with people who are struggling to make ends meet. I was going to help where I could and find a way to educate properly. I was going to try and point out how we are being used as pawns for the big boys, for control, power, and greed. God gave me and everyone out there a mind, a clean heart, and the will do what is right to man by his word. To do what is right by speech, to teach, to get along and cooperate without the interference of regulation and controls used for power and protection of the wrong things, is true protection. Protection will be accomplished only through peace. You can have all that is materialistic, but no air and water means you have nothing.

The summer went by quickly. It was a whirlwind that I can't find words to explain. My mind raced, and many things came to me. I spoke to people who, like me, were frustrated with all this but claimed they couldn't do anything about it. They were children of God and lost. Coffee shop patrons were discussing matters with concern but had no conclusions. Many talked of voting leaders out, which I thought was good, but who do you get? Corporate business has control of the government. The government is in bed with corporate business. How do we solve the escalating problems we have? How do we make these leaders understand what they are doing at the population's expense, for greed and power, is evil? How can we tell these guys about self-righteousness and that the values they are instilling in generations are meaningless? They are very powerful, but we really have control if we want it. Many questions went through my mind.

What could they do if we stopped working and paying taxes? What would they do if we decided to block roads, legislatures, municipal offices, airports, army barracks, police, and the works, to protest injustice? We have enough people to do this. We only need to make sure we do it peacefully, or we would be self-righteous and worse than what we were condemning. Sure, they would use force on us, try to legislate us back to work, and threaten more immigration. They may kill some of us, which would be devastating, but they would come to their senses. Gandhi did it. We would have them surrounded. We would cut off much of the communications, disallowing them to work also. We would educate, not just school people. My mind was so full I thought my head would burst. I knew what to do, and physical force was not the way. Evil spawns evil. We would have to do this peacefully. God was guiding me, I felt. My mind seemed to be controlled, and everything I had seen was coming back. Everything I had discussed was coming back. I hadn't hit the delete button.

I received a call to go to work for another oil company. A friend of mine wanted me to go and help until they could learn the SAG D operations. Since I had done quite a lot of this, I agreed to go for the winter. He was excited about doing the project.

"Pat, we need to meet in Calgary and have a meeting soon about the project. Could you make it in for a meeting on Wednesday and Thursday?" Ray asked.

"I think I can," I said.

"Good. I'll see you there," he said and hung up.

I drove to Calgary for the meeting. Trying to park my truck was a nightmare in those small downtown parking areas. I ran over a curb, got hung up, and had to use four-wheel drive to free myself. Chuckling because people were behind me honking their horns, I thought, *this is what we have become. We're in such a hurry to work ourselves to death for these people. What a bunch of puppets we are. We have to be on time, don't we?* We were regulated, even to our time, so we would give them power and don't understand.

We discussed the drilling plan and when we would go to work. The projected start time was in about two weeks, but they said they would let us know.

I had to be in Nisku to write a first-aid certification test, so I drove Thursday evening and got a room at the Royal Oak. I drove to the truck stop, had my dinner, and then visited a sister in Leduc and sat around, watching a hockey game, sipping on a couple beers. After the game, I went to my room and had a good sleep.

I awoke to the phone ringing and answered my wake-up call. I showered and got ready to go to my course. I always liked the idea of a coffeepot in the room so one could leisurely have coffee, relax, and prepare for the day ahead. I drank coffee until about eight thirty, then went to the course, which was a full day, with training on CPR and first-aid bandaging. I stayed the night; then Saturday morning, the oil company called informing me I wouldn't be going to work for a couple weeks on the project, but I could work on some small rig outside of Medicine Hat. I would be able to start on Tuesday and could either stay in Nisku or go home and come back. The distance from home to

Medicine Hat was seven and a half hours and from Nisku to Medicine Hat was six hours. I chose to go home and spend the few days with Barb.

After leaving Nisku around noon or shortly thereafter, I drove home through Lloydminister and was headed for North Battleford. I stopped at Raddison for fuel, a coffee break, and to stretch. After having a coffee and a Reuben sandwich, I walked over to the counter, paid for my meal, and then walked through the little convenience store, suddenly realizing they sold lottery tickets. I remembered I hadn't bought mine for the draw that evening. I went to the truck, found my envelope containing the cards I had played for many years, and purchased the tickets. Many times, Barb had to drop what she was doing, run to the store, and get them for me, when I would call and remind her. She told me I was wasting my money and would never win. Maybe she was right, but I had fun trying. "You never know. If you don't have a ticket, you can't win," I would remind her.

I walked around outside for about a half hour, content to stretch and relax, which is something I never do when I'm traveling. I had scored a job and things were pretty positive all summer. It was a beautiful day, sunny and warm, September 11, 2004.

I hopped in the red dually, threw my ticket envelope on the passenger seat, and headed for home. I turned the radio on, and something about the anniversary of 9/11 on the news caught my attention. I listened briefly and then tuned in to a country station and listened to some music. Aaron Tippin's song was blaring, and I started to sing, "A door ain't nothing but a way to get through a wall. A window won't work and the ladder is much too tall. Now you get a hammer and I'll get a saw, and we'll give that wall what for. Cause the only thing left to do is build a door." I thought about that for a long way listening to the hum of the diesel engine, purring along on the dually.

How true those words are went through my mind. How many scholars have tried to tell us through music and song about the things we do for the betterment of man, like John Lennon, bless his soul, gunned down by a weapon sold by corporate business, with "Give Peace a Chance." Many songs, such as "Eve of Destruction," "Life Is a Highway," and "Signs," about showing judgment on one because of the way he appeared, whether he was clean or not, tried to tell us something. Many people were treated with disrespect in this era and made to cut their hair if they wanted a job, whether educated or not. Time has corrected some of these little problems, but we still need to heed many things. We had to regulate for this, because we weren't educated enough to tolerate and accept whoever.

I motored home and arrived around eleven that evening. I was greeted by a big smile and a happy, loving hug from my darling. She was so generous with her smile and made you melt whenever she greeted someone. We talked for a while and had coffee then went to bed. I was tired and needed to sleep.

I awoke the next day, late. Rubbing my eyes, I asked Barb, "What time is it?"

"It's noon," she replied. "You must have been tired."

"Oh man, did I sleep. I have never slept that long," I said to her. I hadn't. Normally, I would be up at seven, and if I slept until eight, that was sleeping in.

"Want some coffee?" she asked.

"Yes. That sounds good. What have you been doing?" I asked. "I didn't hear anything."

"I've been doing things. And reading the paper," she added.

Sipping our coffee, I said, "Let's go outside. It looks beautiful."

"Okay," she replied.

We went out and looked around the yard. The fall colors were gorgeous with the crimson, yellow, and red leaves on the trees and hedges we had planted.

Realizing I hadn't been around at that time of year for some reason or another, I said, "I think this is the first time I've seen the yard in the fall." Maybe I hadn't taken the time to notice, but I was convinced it was the first time.

We chatted for a while and then went inside and refilled our cups with coffee.

About one in the afternoon, I went downstairs and started up the computer. I checked my e-mail and then went to the lotteries page. Upon opening the Lotto 649 page, I found that my numbers had popped up, and I thought I had made a mistake, so I closed down the page and restarted it. Barb needed to use the toilet so she went into the downstairs washroom and was sitting there when I announced, "We won the lottery."

"Yeah, right!" she said. "You're always saying that."

Laughing, I said, "No, look! We won!" I was excited, yet not overly.

She came out of the washroom still buttoning her jeans and looked at the numbers. She recognized them from having to buy my tickets all the time when I was at work. She immediately started crying and laughing and was full of excitement. She hugged me and said, "You can stay home now."

"I guess so," I said. "How come you didn't believe me?"

"You're always pulling my leg. I guess I'll buy your tickets now and never say a word," she said still excited. "What are we going to do? Don't tell anybody."

"I better go to the truck and make sure I bought the ticket and see if they are still there," I said. I had thrown them on the seat, and they could have blown out the window for all I knew. They weren't signed or anything.

I printed off the winning page and then went out to see if I indeed had the ticket. Three winners were declared on the draw, and we were supposed to be one of them. Sure enough, my tickets were there, and when we checked, they matched. "Yahoo!" was all I could say.

We hugged and kissed then calmed down and collected our thoughts as we signed the ticket.

"See! There is a God," I said. "Remember when I read that book and I said that I didn't have the financial ability to write. Well, look at this. God allowed us to have this gift so we need to do the right things with it." A flood of relief went through us, and I had never felt so relaxed. I was so thankful for all the gifts I had received. There was no other explanation.

We tried to call Tiffany, our daughter, but there was no answer. We wanted them to be part of this and come to the city to collect the rewards.

I left a message. "Tiff, this is Dad. Please call me ASAP."

"Well! We might as well go and pick up our winnings," I said.

"What are we going to pack?" Barb asked so excited she forgot we had clothes, I guess.

"Whatever you want," I said laughing. "We need some new clothes, so don't pack too much."

Once ready, we decided to go into Roblin and get a printout of the numbers from the co-op gas bar. We wanted to make sure of our good fortune and still were doubtful about winning. The computer-generated numbers could be wrong.

I walked into the store and must have had a grin on my face bigger than Dallas. My niece was working behind the counter. She looked at me and must have thought something was up when I asked her for a printout. I remained calm, so no one in the store would know, but I'm sure she knew. Smiling, she went about her work as I walked out.

As soon as I got into the truck, we checked the ticket against the printout and found it was a winner. Again, still unsure, we checked the computer printout against the store numbers, verifying we had won. Putting the truck in gear, we were on the road to collect our good fortune.

As we drove, Barb kept looking at the ticket and would remark, "I don't believe it." It was Sunday, and we would have to wait until morning to collect the prize, so we took our time and enjoyed the trip to the city. Tiffany hadn't called yet, and we were nearly in Neepawa. We were stopping for lunch, and the phone rang as we were pulling into the restaurant.

"Hello," I answered.

"Hello, Dad. What's up?" Tiffany asked. "I hate when you leave a message like that."

"Are you sitting down?" I asked.

"No, why?" she asked concern in her voice.

"I think you should sit down," I said.

"Dad, what's going on? Are you all right?" she asked.

"Yes, I'm fine," I said. "Are you sitting down?"

"Is Mom okay?" she asked.

"Yes, Mom is okay," I replied holding out on her.

"Dad, what the hell is going on?" she asked again, getting anxious.

"Are you sitting down?" I asked again.

"Yes dad. Now what's going on?" she asked.

Still holding out, I asked, "Could you and Digger make it to Winnipeg?"

"I don't know. Depends on what's happening," she said.

"Well! We won the lottery," I finally told her.

"Oh! Bullshit!" she said. "Really; Congratulations!"

"Yes, really," I said. "We're in Neepawa right now and going to have dinner."

"Dad, I don't believe you! I have to hang up, and I'll call you back. Digger wants to know what's going on," she said excitedly, crying and laughing all at the same time. "I'll call you right back."

We waited outside the restaurant for her call. She was excited and wasn't sure if I was pulling her leg. The phone rang.

"Dad, are you sure?" she asked.

"Positive," I said. "We have the print off from co-op and the computer with us, and checked numerous times."

"You're not going to believe what Digger thought. He could only hear one side of the conversation, and as soon as I hung up, he said, 'Your mom's pregnant.'" She was so happy for us she was laughing and crying while telling me this.

"Can you come to Winnipeg tonight? I want you guys to be part of this," I added.

"Yes. We'll pack up and leave right away," she said.

"Okay! We'll meet you at Auntie Adrienne's place," I said.

"We'll be there around ten tonight. Dad, are you sure?" she asked again.

"Honey, I wouldn't ask you to come if I wasn't sure. It's real," I said.

"Okay! We'll be there. Bye for now, Dad," she said. "I love you."

"Love you too, sweetheart. See you in Winnipeg," I said.

"Can I speak to Mom?" she asked.

"Sure," I said handing the phone to Barb.

They talked for a few minutes and then hung up. We had our dinner and then left for Winnipeg.

The drive the rest of the way was short. We talked of what to do with our fortune and relaxed, knowing we would be secure financially for a while. We called Adrienne on our cell just before arriving and told her we would be in and had won the lottery. As we arrived at

Adrienne's apartment, the excitement grew even more. There were hugs and kisses galore, laughter and chatter for an hour, and then we phoned my other sister, Janet. They arrived a short time later, a bottle of vodka in hand as I had requested for a celebration. We poured a drink and toasted each other and then called Diane, another sister who lived in the city. Around ten that evening, Tiffany and Digger pulled in with their girls, again setting the stage for the excitement around us. Everyone was happy for us and couldn't believe the good fortune we had come into. We decided to call my mother and Barb's parents, thinking it was better if we told them, rather than them hearing it on the television. They couldn't believe it and wished us well.

Around one in the morning, finally everyone decided to call it a night. Here we were at Adrienne's place, a one-bedroom apartment, and we all needed a place to stay. It never crossed our minds to get a hotel room so we could be comfortable. Instead, the men went to Janet's, and the girls stayed at Adrienne's. I couldn't sleep with all the excitement, so I sat up and pondered what we would do over a couple more vodkas. I finally slept on the couch for about two hours and then heard Janet and Brian get up for work. I got up, brushing the cobwebs from my eyes, a little woozy from the drinks I had had, and got ready to go pick up Barb. Janet and Brian had given us the name of a lawyer to see, so we knew what to expect when we arrived at the lotteries commission. I stopped to see him for a few minutes. He called an investor who would meet us at the lotteries office, and then I drove to Adrienne's place and picked up Barb. They were ready to go, so we all left, with us leading the way and Tiffany and Digger following.

We arrived at the lotteries office around eleven, met the investor then took the elevator to the tenth floor, I believe it was. We entered the office, and a fellow at the desk asked if he could help us. I gave him my ticket and asked if he could validate it, telling him I thought I had won part of the main prize. He validated the ticket and turned around, a grin on his face, and said, "We didn't expect anyone in today as the winning tickets were bought in Saskatchewan and Ontario."

"I bought this ticket in Raddison, Saskatchewan," I replied.

"You will have to excuse the way we are dressed, unprepared for a winner," he apologized. "Would you like to sit and have some coffee in this room while I get your ticket processed?"

"Sure," we said, moving to an office with a huge table, large enough for a board meeting.

They brought coffee, and then a fellow came in and had us sign some papers, a formality, he said, so the lotteries commission could use our pictures and story for advertising purposes. I looked at the investor and asked if this was normal.

"Yes," he replied. "I think they do that to everyone. I'm not sure if you need to though."

It did seem odd they would take our right to privacy away from us to advertise, I thought.

I read the information and signed the forms. I knew it wouldn't matter and people would find out anyway. "We might as well get this part of it out of the way," I told Barb.

We sat around for a couple hours, taking pictures. They made us pose for the cameras, holding balloons and a giant-sized check for the amount for everyone to see in the media. They handed me the check with the amount to use as I wished, telling us we had a room at the Radisson Hotel and we could stay there until the media was able to come in on Tuesday at eleven.

Calmly, we went to the bank, paid off all our loans, and deposited the rest, for three months or so, until we decided what to do. We had never had that amount of money, so it was difficult to comprehend.

We went to the room, cleaned up, and then called my sisters. We wanted to take them all out for supper at a good restaurant. We enjoyed a nice meal and a few cocktails, paid the bill, and then went back to the room. We had a date with the media and didn't want to be sick when they asked their questions.

The next morning, we met in the Radisson boardroom with the media, lights and cameras flashing all around us. Some were in our faces for a close-up, and we, never having experienced this before, were blinded by the flashes. After about a half hour of this, it was over.

Tiffany and Digger had to get home so Kennedy could rest for school the next day. When the media was finished, I threw Digger the keys for my rig truck and told him, "It's yours."

Looking at me puzzled, he said, "What?"

"I don't need it anymore. It's your truck. Do what you like with it."

"What am I going to do with a Ford?" he said jokingly.

"Do whatever you want to. Trade it in," I said, knowing he liked GM.

They left with both vehicles loaded with our belongings and theirs, while we hailed a taxi. We were going to buy a new car and travel some, so we went to the Chevrolet dealer and bought a new car.

Driving home slowly, tired and still full of excitement, we paced ourselves, so we could enjoy life and our new wheels. We arrived in Roblin around seven, after stopping briefly at Tiffany's for our luggage, and then we went to Barb's folks' place for coffee.

They were excited for us, and Dad said, "I don't know if I can take any more of this excitement."

"Yes! It's been a whirlwind for the last few days," we said.

"Don phoned. He caught us pretty good," Dad said.

Don had been a family friend for many years now. I guess with all the commotion on the news about us winning, he decided to play a prank on Dad.

When he called, masking his voice, he said, "I am a lawyer from Mason and Jar solicitors, and I'm filing a suit on behalf of a client, for damages incurred on him at your anniversary party at your daughter's place. He broke his collarbone while playing football with the children at the anniversary party we held in honor of Barb's parents."

I guess Dad stammered for a few minutes not knowing what to say. Don had him fooled, and then he started to laugh.

"Don, you bugger, you had me fooled," Dad told him, recognizing his voice. They both laughed. Mom was still laughing when we arrived.

We had coffee and then went over to my mother's, had another coffee, and then went home. That was enough excitement for one day.

The next morning, we awoke to quite a number of calls from well-wishers, happy someone in our community had won. People were excellent with their wishes.

We spent the whole day at home, planning a trip out west to visit my cousin and some of the family. My oldest sister was sick with cancer and could use some help.

We left for Calgary, stopping at my cousin's place for the night, had dinner the next day with them, and then drove to Edmonton, staying at the West Edmonton Mall. We had taken very little with us and were in need of some new duds. Because we had lived from day to day most of the time, new clothes were sometimes not affordable.

We went our separate ways and bought a new wardrobe each. It was fun, buying and not having to worry for a change whether we could afford it. We always bought only what we needed and believed we needed little to survive. There were more important things to do with the money.

We stopped to visit my sister in Vilna, Alberta, and she told us she was doing okay for now. We left, and I told them to call if they needed anything.

After going to Alberta for a few days, we stayed home for a week, and then I felt the urge to find my brother. He was desolate and living on the street, still drowning out his life in alcohol and substance abuse. He was seen drunk, picking up cigarette stubs in downtown Winnipeg, hopelessly trying to survive. Even though I vowed I wouldn't try again, because of the hopelessness of his situation, I decided it was worth one more try. I knew Mom would want us to at least find him and see if he was doing well.

Chapter Fifteen

Barb and I packed up and went into the city to stay with Adrienne for a few days. They found enough to do while I went out looking for my brother. The first day, I walked up and down Main Street for hours, looking through the crowds of people; some people were drunk and did not know what was going on. Many were busy walking to and from workplaces and shopping, appearing not to notice the mayhem on the street.

I looked in bars, asked people on the street, looked in the parks, checked the social services offices, everywhere, but could not find him. A couple times, I thought I had seen him, but when I would arrive at the spot, he would disappear or it wasn't he. I looked in soup kitchens and asked if they had seen or heard of him. Many knew he was around but would not tell me where. I found he had last stayed at the Occidental Hotel on Main Street, so I checked with the people there and was informed they had evicted him for bad behavior.

I went back to my sister's around five in the afternoon empty-handed and no closer to finding him.

We went to Janet's for supper and sat around for a while, watching television. The news was blaring about the Iraq War with gruesome video of the battle plastered on televisions throughout the country. Everyone was sitting in the living room, trying to converse, but our attention kept going to the television, which was blaring loudly. My hands were freezing, and I was tense with anger and frustration about the war. Barb grabbed my hand and asked if I was all right. I was but couldn't control my thoughts. Concerned, she asked again if I was okay. Apparently, I didn't look too good, sweating, cold, and tense.

Finally, Brian announced he was going outside for a smoke. Immediately, I jumped up and followed him, glad to be out of that room, away from the television blaring with those gruesome scenes on it. We lit up, and soon the coldness left my hands and I started to settle back down. We didn't talk much outside, I recall, just enjoyed the peace of the moment.

We went back in, and I could feel the tension again building. This time, however, I was able to control it somewhat better. Finally, Barb asked if I wanted to leave and get some sleep. Immediately, I responded by getting my jacket on and standing by the door, waiting for her to say her good nights.

Driving back to Adrienne's, she asked, "Are you all right?"

"Yes. I'm fine," I said.

"How come you were so tense and cold at Janet's?" she asked.

"Honey, you don't know how close I was to throwing the television set through the window," I replied.

"What?" she said in disbelief.

"I'm serious. You don't know how close that was."

"Why would you do that, honey?" she asked.

"That thing blaring with all the killing over the last few years is just about all I can handle. They should outlaw or make those news stations that report that pay-per-view. Goes to show you how uneducated those reporters are, showing all this negativity to make money for their corporations. They don't give a damn what they do to get ratings. They sway everybody to believe its all someone else's fault."

I was angry at the governments for allowing this and for allowing us to be subjected to this type of media, this weapon of mass destruction, in our living rooms, swaying people and warping minds all over the world, causing hatred. "Our education has failed us immensely," I said out loud.

We drove silently the rest of the way to Adrienne's. We had coffee and then went to bed. I couldn't get this out of my head. Finally calming down, I prayed silently asking God to show me to my brother. That was what I was in the city for.

I awoke the next morning ready to pound the streets, determined to find him. I drove back downtown, this time driving slowly, looking around every corner, trying to catch a glimpse of him. This man stumbled through some doors, and I thought it was him. I hurried, found a parking spot, and then ran down the street to the building I thought he went into. Throwing the doors open, I found nothing. No one was in the halls of that building. I slowly walked out and down the street. In front of the Bell Hotel, a crowd of street people were gathered around, looking down. Walking over to see what the commotion was about, I observed someone lying on the sidewalk, the medics working on him and putting him on a stretcher. I looked at the person being cared for and found it wasn't him. A feeling of relief came over me. I couldn't understand how people would let themselves be subjected to this life of misery.

As I walked away, I saw a man, who was about forty, standing just off to the side of the Bell Hotel, making faces at the crowd. He appeared to be out of it, but maybe he had incurred brain damage from his lifestyle. I walked toward city hall, and as I approached the stairs entering the building, I felt this anger building again about what I had seen on television the night before. The closer I got, the more determined I was to speak out and try to have this banned. Why don't they put the news on pay-per-view? Climbing the stairs rapidly, heading for the doors, I caught myself and stopped, dead in my tracks. I had a choice. I could watch it, or I could shut the television off. Even though it was on nearly every channel, I could shut the television off and find something else to do. Sheepishly, I turned around and walked away, a weight lifted off my shoulders. Surely, God saw what was happening and intervened. I was too angry to come to my senses alone.

As I walked the streets looking, I thought about what could have happened. They would have called the hospital, pumped me up with drugs to settle me down, labeled me schizophrenic, and locked me up. They had cause to believe I was losing my mind even though I was sane. "Thank you, God, for intervening," I prayed.

I sat on a planter and lit a smoke, taking a much-needed break. As I sat there, I observed people from many different cultures. There were Arabs, First Nations, Pakistani, East Indian, Polish, African, and all kinds, mixing and mingling. It was a reunion on earth. *This is what heaven will look like,* I thought.

The effect 9/11 had on me was immense. I had worked with many different cultures and found we could get along. I had friends around the world who were affected by all this and felt they too were immensely frustrated, and many felt they were in danger. By this time, it was obvious I was adamant about what I believed, wanting to do something, anything, to make people think. I wanted people to utilize the mind God gave them and open some eyes so we could start to see clearly what life is about. What have we learned? How stupid we really are.

I left downtown about six that evening, empty-handed. It appeared the street people were covering up for him. Many people I talked to on the street told me they knew where he was and gave me addresses, but upon checking, I would find he had either just left, or they hadn't seen him for a day or so.

Adrienne made supper and invited Jason, our nephew, over for a visit. We ate and sat around for a while, and then I said I was going downtown to see if I could spot my brother. Jason volunteered to come with me.

We drove the downtown area for about fifteen minutes, taking side streets and checking every nook and cranny, and then headed down Main toward Higgins. Driving slowly, we crossed Higgins under the Sutherland Bridge, proceeding to Inkster Boulevard, turned left, drove for about four or five blocks, and then turned around.

"I guess we aren't going to find him tonight either," I told Jason.

"Kind of looks that way, eh, Uncle Pat?" Jason replied.

We entered back onto Main Street, heading back to Adrienne's place, driving slowly, hoping we might still spot him. We went under the Sutherland Bridge and were approaching Higgins when I spotted him.

"There he is," I said to Jason excitedly, pointing to a man on the corner, weaving back and forth, wearing a thin, dirty blue jacket, oblivious to his surroundings. His hair was matted and long, sticking out about his head like an Afro. He was so skinny his clothes hung on him, baggy and too large for his structure.

"Yep, Uncle Pat, that's him," Jason said.

Slamming on the brakes, without any concern for traffic behind me, I told Jason, "Jump out and grab him. Just throw him in, and let's get out of here."

It was like a kidnapping scene on television. Jason hopped out, grabbed him, threw him in the front seat with me, and then hopped in the back closing the door as best he could. I accelerated, the doors half open and turned left, finding a factory parking lot. As I put the truck in park, I looked over at Popeye and asked, "Do you know who I am?"

"No. Am I in trouble?" he asked, not realizing what had just happened yet and not knowing if we were going to hurt him.

"I'm your brother Pat," I introduced myself, sticking out my hand. He attempted to shake my hand but his right arm was bent at the elbow and swayed back and forth as if there was no movement at the joint.

Turning toward me, he said, "Well! It is you." He didn't recognize me but said it like he did.

"Do you know who that is?" I asked, pointing to Jason.

"No. Never saw him before," he said.

"That's Jason. You remember Jason. He's Monique's son. He was pretty small when you last saw him," I said.

Slurring, he said, "I wouldn't recanize him."

Due to his lifestyle, Emile never kept in touch with the family and was oblivious to life. He wouldn't know many of his nieces and nephews and had no clue how fast the world had advanced. He was stalled out in his twenties, knowing nothing about the world today, because of alcohol and substance abuse. That was all he seemed to live for, and he blamed it on everything else. I was determined to help him no matter what.

"Are you hungry?" I asked.

"I want a steak," he said getting bolder now, realizing we weren't going to hurt him.

"Okay! You show me where to go," I said putting the truck in gear.

He was out of it, and I wanted to see if he knew the city yet. I pulled out on Main Street and then turned on Portage Avenue, going west. I tried to keep conversation going, happy to have found him, but it was difficult. He would repeat himself and ask where certain people were. I had no idea most times who he was asking about, determining some must have been his buddies. Driving slowly, we passed Polo Park, and I asked him where we were.

"I don't know," he said.

"We're in Winnipeg," I said jokingly, playing with him, trying to make him laugh. He'd had a scowl on his face and looked sad since we had picked him up.

We turned down Route 90, swinging around the traffic loop heading toward Pembina Highway. I was trying to sober him up enough to speak to him.

"Where are we going?" he asked.

"To have a steak," I replied. "Where are you taking me for a steak?"

He had forgotten about asking for a steak and answered, "What steak?"

Changing the subject, I said, "We'll go to Adrienne's for coffee and visit for a while."

"I don' know where she lives," he said.

"We're just about there," I said, approaching Pembina Highway. "About ten more minutes."

We drove quietly for the rest of the way, and as we pulled into the apartment complex parking lot, he seemed to have fear in him. "What are we doing here?" he asked.

"This is where Adrienne lives," I said reassuringly. "It's okay."

Adrienne made coffee and fed him what we had for supper that evening. He ate hungrily, like he hadn't eaten in a while. I watched him eat his meal observing his matted hair sticking outward like an afro Michael Jackson had when he was a young star but longer, and the little blue jacket, too light for the temperatures we were getting, dirty from days of wear without washing. He smelled like he hadn't had a shower in a while. He was skinny, a hundred and twenty pounds and six feet tall. His pants, baggy and filthy, hung like rags. He complained about pain in his right arm quite a lot. After complaining, he would say, "Chop it off."

"What happened to your arm?" I asked.

"Donno; Must have fell down or something," he said speaking without pronouncing some letters.

"Where did you fall?" I asked.

"Donno; Must've bin downtown," he replied.

"Can you straighten it out?" I asked.

"Nope; It's broke," he offered.

"Let me see," I said finally.

I looked at his elbow and found it was red and swollen. It had scars from an operation that seemed to still be healing. I wasn't sure what had happened, because of the way he lived.

"Where did you get operated on?" I asked.

"Seven Oaks," he replied.

"Tomorrow, we'll go there and check to make sure," I said. "I want you to come to Roblin. Come and visit Mom for a while."

We talked for a while and then asked him to clean up. At first, he didn't want to, and then sobering up, some understanding coming back, he went to the bathroom and attempted to clean himself up. We had found a razor, a washcloth, and shampoo in Adrienne's cabinet, laid them out, and told him to feel free to use it all. After taking his clothes and washing them while he showered, we found some sweats he could fit into when he was done, while his clothes dried. He was in the shower for a good three quarters of an hour, washing himself, shaving, and trying to comb his hair. When he came out, he looked somewhat better but still sickly.

We found some extra blankets and pillows, made him a bed on the floor, and asked him to stay the night. He accepted. I slept on the couch while Barb slept with Adrienne in her bed. I watched as he undressed for bed and saw how skinny his torso was. Shocked, I said to him, "You need to look after yourself better."

"I know," he said.

"Look, I won a lot of money, and I can spend some time with you and help if you like," I offered.

"Where did you win a lot of money?" he asked.

"The 649," I said. "I'm willing to help you, but you have to come to Roblin with me for a while."

"What am I going to do with my stuff?" he said.

"What stuff?" I asked.

He rattled on about furniture left at the Occidental and at Diane's and pictures he left elsewhere. His mind was all over the place as he tried to remember. He was a mess and needed to be helped or he wouldn't survive the winter, I thought. *Thank you, God, for letting me find him,* I said silently, as we turned out the lights and went to bed.

"Have a good sleep. We'll talk in the morning," I said.

"Yeah; Good night," he said.

I lay there a while and listened to his breathing while he slept. Long breaths of air rushed into his lungs and were expelled with a slight whistle. He appeared to breathe normally, I thought, but we'd have to get him checked out. I wondered if he had any liver problems or AIDS. One never knew with the lifestyle he led.

The next morning, we got up and ate breakfast. I started to make phone calls to get an appointment at the Seven Oaks Hospital and find out about his elbow. Barb went to the mall and bought Emile some new clothes, a jacket, and shoes. We had to go to emergency at the Seven Oaks and would be called in when the doctor had an opening.

Having arrived about eleven in the morning, we waited for about an hour and a half and then were called into a little room for a checkup. A nurse asked what we were there for, and I said, "Apparently, he was operated on here and his elbow isn't doing very well. Could we see a doctor?"

She asked for his medical number, but he didn't have it. "I'll check and see what I can find," she said.

We waited for another hour or so, and then a doctor came in and told us he hadn't had the operation there. It was done at the Miseracordia Hospital about six or seven months earlier.

"Why can't he move his elbow, and why is it so sore?" I asked.

"I'll take an X-ray and see," the doctor offered.

They took an X-ray and came back. The doctor hung it on the light board and announced there were a lot of pins. "What did you do?" he asked Emile.

"I don no. I never seen dose pins before," he replied.

"That's a major operation," the doctor said. "You don't remember?"

"Nope; I remember falling down, and when I woke up, I had this band-aid on," he said.

"You don't remember the hospital?" the doctor asked.

"Nope; Woke up in my own bed," he said.

Puzzled, the doctor looked at me, trying to find an answer. I shrugged my shoulders and said, "I don't know, Doc. I'm his brother and found him last night. I'm trying to take him to my place and see if I can help."

"That's very good of you," he said politely.

"Listen. Is there anything we can do to fix that elbow?" I asked.

"Medical science can do many things, but I don't think we can do anything with it now. The way it healed, the bone fused together and locked it up. Had he exercised it, he may have some movement in it, but as it stands, he will be like that forever or until the medical sciences can do something," he said.

"They do knee and hip transplants all the time now. What about Toronto?" I asked.

"I'm sorry. I don't think there is anything they can do either. It would be a waste of your money to go there," he said.

"Will he be able to stay in Roblin like that? What are the complications?" I asked.

"He can stay at your place. There is nothing we can do," he said. "Emile! Listen to your brother. He's trying to help you," he said and then left.

"Let's go," I said looking at my watch. It was three thirty. "We got to get on the road."

We picked Barb up and headed home. The drive was silent most of the way. I tried to comprehend him not knowing pins were in his elbow. What did he do? Was he beaten up again? Many questions were in my mind. It appeared his mind wasn't functioning fully, but I played it off to the abuse of alcohol and thought it would come back. *It will just take time.*

We arrived home and got him settled into a room in the basement. We had shown him the bathroom he was to use and instructed him on the use of the shower. He unpacked his bag, came upstairs, and had a sandwich and coffee. I told him to make himself at home and use whatever he needed.

"Where's the beer?" he asked.

"In the fridge," I replied. "You're not going to have one though."

"I know. Just joking," he said.

The rules were set, and booze was not in them. Even though I was inclined to hide the stuff, I wouldn't. I was going to leave it where I put it, and he would have to be strong enough to abstain from it.

"Well, you go have a shower and clean up for bed," I told him.

"Where do I shower?" he asked.

I looked at him, somehow not believing what he had said. "Downstairs," I answered.

He got up and looked around. "How do I get downstairs?" he asked.

"Just down here," I said pointing to the basement stairs.

He went down, and I assumed he was going to take a shower. I could hear him once in a while shuffling in his room, but the shower never started. I went down.

"What's happening?" I asked.

"What?" he said somewhat defensively.

"Are you going to take a shower?" I asked.

"Oh yeah, right," he said.

I went back upstairs chuckling and waited to see what he was going to do. I heard the water come on and then go off. He fumbled with something and the water came on and then went off again. Barb said, "You better go down and check."

I knocked on the bathroom door, and he told me to come in.

"How do you turn dis damn ting on?" he asked, confused.

I reached over, turned the tap on, and pulled the faucet lever down. I showed him a few times trying to make him understand. "You got it?" I said laughing.

"Yup," he said, so I left him and went upstairs.

He showered finally, cleaned himself up, and went to bed.

I took him to the doctor for a medical and was surprised he was healthy. His liver was functioning properly, and he had no disease.

This was the start of a long journey, trying to teach him all over, the little things you learn as a child. His mind was not working properly, but we didn't know how bad he was. Weeks went by with us doing things repetitiously, trying to comprehend how he had lost it all. The shower took three weeks before he finally could turn it on by himself. We asked him to get the kettle for tea, and he couldn't figure out how to bring a cordless kettle off the heat pad. He would unplug it, bringing everything, and pour the water holding the pot, warmer, and cord. He hid his jacket, shoes, and many items he thought someone might steal. He hid his wallet. It was three days before we found it, tucked in the mattress protector at the foot of the bed. Had Barb not changed his sheets at that time, Lord knows when we would have found it. We had torn the house apart three times already looking for it. "He's just withdrawing and can't think," I would say.

One night, shortly after he came to live with us, he was upstairs sitting in the recliner, and we heard a bang. I went up and found him looking all around the easy chair, trying to figure out what had happened.

"I was jus' sitting here when the chair fell," he said.

"Fell," I said looking under the chair; then I started to laugh.

Barb had had the carpets cleaned, and they had put little pieces of wood under the legs to prop up the chair until the carpet dried. I guess when he leaned back the chair fell off the little blocks and had him confused.

I went back downstairs laughing and told Barb. We both had a good chuckle. I had a bear rug on the floor and thought we would have a little fun with him. I wanted to make him laugh and feel at home. I found an old ottoman and some cans, and then propping the bear rug on top to make it look like a live animal I called him down and waited, hiding around the corner to see his reaction. He came down and froze for a second and then said, "Good thing I wasn't drinking, or I would have attacked it." We laughed.

We noticed he was lost most of the time, restless and wanting to do something. We told him to go for a walk. He was scared at first but went. He walked about a half a mile down the road around the circle from my house, through the neighborhood ending up back at the approach. Barb was outside and noticed he was standing at the approach not knowing where to go. He was lost. Barb called him, and when he realized where he was, he smiled broadly as if to say, "Thanks for finding me." It was pitiful, but I thought he would get over the hump.

About a month went by, and he wasn't changing. I would take him to town every day and ask him to show me the way back. This, he could never do. My oldest brother took him for some weekends and tried to help him but couldn't. He couldn't remember. He reminded me somewhat of the Rain Man.

We conversed about many different things, read the Bible to him, anything I could think of to stimulate his mind. I wasn't trained to do this, so I called my uncle in Calgary numerous times, as he is a councilor for ADAC, an alcohol foundation in Calgary. He would give me guidance, but Emile seemed to retain nothing in his mind. He would forget what we had talked about ten seconds after we talked. It was getting frustrating at times, but I was convinced he could be retrained, so we plugged along.

He would see a councilor in Roblin once a week and couldn't remember what they discussed. I took him to the doctor and asked if they could do a scan on his brain, but they told me it would be a few months.

One day, I took him to church. We went through the whole ceremony, and he sang, prayed, and visited with the people. We went out for lunch with Barb's mom and dad, Deb and Tony, and their girls. We came home and then went to Russell, met Tiffany and the girls for supper, and came home.

Sitting at the table, around eight o'clock that evening, I asked, "What did we do today?"

He couldn't remember anything. He guessed a lot, trying to cover up the problem, and then admitted he couldn't remember. I couldn't help him. His memory was deteriorated to the point of no return it appeared. Short term was gone. I was dumbfounded and started looking around for help.

I called the mental health institution, explained our findings, and was told there was no help for these people. They wanted me to advocate because they saw a need for this. I didn't know where to turn.

I wanted to go back on the rigs and was booked into a well-control course in Nisku. I took my brother with me and wanted him to associate with my sisters in Alberta. Maybe they would jog his memory.

I left him at Sue's place for a night, but she couldn't do anything with him. He went to Claire's, and she got frustrated with him after two days and brought him back to me. I was in a hotel room and couldn't leave him alone, so I missed the rest of the course. We went out for dinner one evening, and I introduced him to my sisters' husbands. He sat quietly and ate, not conversing much. The next morning, we drove back home.

I asked, "Where were we?"

"I don't know. Vancouver?" he guessed.

"Edmonton," I said.

"What is Sue's husband's name?" I asked.

"I don't know. Gordon," he said.

I then repeated about twenty times, "Sue and Al, Monique and Don, Donalda and Marcel, Claire and Gerard. Okay. Sue and ..." I waited. "Al!"

"Oh! Yeah! Al," he would say.

"Monique and ..." I waited. "Don!"

"Oh! Yeah! Don. That's right," he said trying to cover up his problem.

"Donalda and ..." I waited.

He guessed, "Bill?"

"Not for twenty-five years now," I said laughing. "Marcel."

"Oh, yes, right, Marcel," he said.

"Claire and ..." I waited and then said, "Gerard."

He could not remember two seconds later. As hard as I tried, from Nisku to Shoal Lake, about a nine-hour drive, I couldn't get him to remember. He was getting frustrated from time to time and told me to shut up for a while, so I did.

I had problems getting him back on social assistance, but finally, they started to give him a little money. I thought, *they are responsible for this* remembering when I tried to get them to stop in eighty-seven or eighty-eight. Now they wanted nothing to do with this.

I sent e-mails to some of the government officials explaining my problems and frustration with them only to be told he needed to fit into certain criteria. He had to have an alcohol problem, be a threat to the public, have committed a crime, or fit the criterion of possibly being a repeat offender and such. I was shocked to hear this kind of gimmick, being told to us under the guise of help. Our tax dollars could support these kinds of people. There are many out there who can't make choices because of their problem.

I was even told he had a choice. If he wanted help and assistance, he could ask himself. He could get off the street and do something if he wanted. I got angry. He couldn't remember anything short-term. As long as he was capable of saying yes and no, that's all they required to tell me he could make his own choices, even though the psychiatrists thought differently.

They wanted him to stay at the Towers hotel in Dauphin one time when I needed a break because he was getting violent. I refused to send him there knowing how much work I had done to keep him from alcohol and to send him to a hotel patronized by people with the same problems was not going to happen! This is well educated, isn't it? They waffle telling us things without listening to us and appear to have no common sense.

We placed him in Brandon for assessment and when I brought him home for Christmas, we found he was getting frustrated and wanting to go back on alcohol. He was at an alcohol and drug place where they put him through a fourteen day program. He didn't remember a thing about the program or where he had been. I talked and talked to him again and was successful in stopping the craving. He started to get violent, cussing me for knowing his problem and threatening me many times. I wanted him to sign authorization of his affairs to me, and he refused, knowing I couldn't proceed because the powers had told us this had to be done. I was hooped.

All the money they spend on war, space programs, schooling incorrectly, and animal shelters, they couldn't justify helping a derelict. *What a joke these people are! This is humans at their best,* I thought.

I called Brandon and found another place where they would keep him for a few weeks and reassess him. I would have to pay two hundred dollars a day for this if I wanted the assessment done. Even though they supplied him with social services for all those years, allowing him to do the things he did, they weren't going to look after him and find out what was wrong. There was no help.

They assessed him for six weeks and told me he had a problem with his short-term memory, something I knew already. They said he had brain damage and that it was progressive, probably from alcohol and substance abuse.

"What about the lumps on his head? He has taken a beating years ago, been hit with wine bottles, been thrown down a stair fracturing his skull, and hit by a car. No one was charged because we classify him a street derelict," I said.

"The accidents could have affected him," I was told.

I was getting frustrated with the system, designed to help with no help. Again, I found this to be absurd. *Fooled again,* I thought. *They're working under the guise of help and safety.*

I called the mental health institution again, explaining our findings, and was told again there was no help for these people.

I sent a letter by e-mail to the Manitoba health minister, telling him our problem and letting him know I wasn't going away. I explained our findings and told them they, the social system, were part of the problem for giving him money for nothing for years, because he had learned the system. I explained how government operates under the guise of help where there isn't any. I told him to look at the situation where they claim help by sending these people to dry-out centers for twelve days and turn them out on the street right in front of the hotels on Main Street. I explained they make a lot of money on the tax they collect on alcohol, giving these people four or five hundred dollars a month and then collecting the majority back on alcohol taxes, because these people have a problem.

It was about three days after I sent this letter when I got a call and help was abundant. Psychiatrists, scans, social services, and more, all found a way ironically, to find a solution. Now we had the people involved we required to assess him properly and possibly help him. It wasn't to be.

They picked him up in Brandon after six weeks of assessment and took him back to Winnipeg, telling me, "That is where we have the facilities to help him." Even though I requested they send him elsewhere, away from the crowd he knew, they wouldn't listen. They were right, and that was all there was to it. They got him an apartment, saying they would have people check on him and ensure he wasn't drinking. That lasted for a few months. He is still doing the things he did before I intervened, and the taxpayer is still supporting it. My mother cried when we told her this had happened. They need to be held responsible for him if he dies on the street.

Chapter Sixteen

After four months of helping my brother out we sat down and tried to figure out what all this meant. We hadn't had time to think yet.

We were thankful and at peace with ourselves for our accomplishments, so why were we concerned about what was going on in the world? Why were we concerned about our community? We had more than we needed. We could have put our feet up and said to heck with all this craziness and became selfish but ...

"Barb, we should do something for this community. I have been gone so long with my work, I really had no involvement with the community," I said.

"That's kind of you to think that way, honey. I agree, but it will be a lot of work," Barb said.

"You and I have never been afraid of work. I have spent my whole life working in the oil patch twelve to fourteen hours a day and you did everything at home raising Tiffany. Are you willing to do this with me?" I asked.

"Of course, honey, this would be fun with you home all the time. You will need something to do," my bride said.

"You're right," I replied. "We're too young to retire and just sit around."

We had been looking at a property for a long time and bid on it when it went into receivership, before the present owners purchased it.

We were happy and extremely comfortable with our decision. We wanted to get up and running as quickly as possible so I started to draw up plans, measure out the space we had, and price out building material.

I went to the municipal office, a preliminary plan in hand, wanting to discuss the process. The reeve and deputy reeve were at the table when I walked in and asked if I could discuss my plan. I didn't even get to sit.

"The CAO and the new development officer for our area will help you," I was told. I didn't understand why I wasn't given a few more minutes of their time and looked at the reeve in bewilderment.

I asked the EDO for some information on Crown land and contact numbers. She was newly hired and just settling in so she didn't have a lot of information or phone numbers for us. We asked another lady and got a few things to get us started. We were anxious to start.

I had plans being drafted and requested permits from the highways department, informed the environmental people, and talked to conservation requesting a culvert be put in the creek to make a road across and utilize all our property. We called the surveyors and had the property surveyed, so mistakes were minimized and all the rules and regulations followed to accomplish this without problems. We were working harder than ever, trying to get going and even called the water stewardship board to find out what we needed to do about the water.

We called Crown lands.

I dialed. "Hello, Manitoba Conservation. How may I help you?" said this female voice on the other end.

"Hello," I replied. "How are you?"

"I am fine," this voice on the other end said, seemingly taken aback by my question. "Who would you like to speak to?"

"Is Lorne in?" I replied.

"Yes. Just a minute," came the reply.

I waited a few minutes, and then this voice came back, "Hello, Lorne here. What can I do for you?" His voice was loud and authoritarian.

"It's Patrick Carriere here. I just purchased Valleyview Resort and had it surveyed. It appears that I might need to purchase 1.2 acres of

Crown land so we can fit our buildings on. How does one go about it?" I asked.

"The Crown doesn't allow anyone to purchase Crown land," he said with authority. Decision made.

"Oh!" I said quite taken aback. "I need this to develop this property properly."

"Well, you could apply for it, but it could take from six months to two years. You can get the forms off the Internet," he said softening somewhat but with the same authority. "Why would you want that property?" he said as if he didn't hear me the first time.

"Like I said, I want to put the buildings on the property I just purchased and want them to face a certain way. That is why I am requesting this," I replied. "Why would it take so long?" I questioned.

"That's just the way government works," he replied.

"But can't we do anything to speed this up? What do they require me to do?" I questioned.

Bluntly, he replied, "You will just have to wait."

I thought. *I will go above him if need be and talk to someone else who doesn't think he is God.*

I got a number and talked to another fellow, who appeared to be more accommodating, but he too never returned my calls. It was around the end of January or the beginning of February 2005, and we were planning to go to Australia.

The highways department came out and measured out our property from the road and said we needed permits to put our buildings on the property we bought. I needed permission and couldn't use all of my property freely.

We left things for a while and asked Tiffany if she could go to Winnipeg for our hearing on getting permits to put buildings on our property. A controlled area, thirty-five meters back from the edge of our property, required a permit to put any buildings on. It was a long way off the highway already. Why did we need to do this when it was ours? They didn't adjust the taxes on it because they controlled it. Why? A lot of these things we didn't understand and could not get a concrete answer on. They would tell us, "That's just the way it is." We need to do something about this and change the way they control this.

We left for Australia in mid March and enjoyed our holiday,

visiting relatives and touring around the country. We talked a lot about our venture, how we were going to create the jobs the community needed, wanting to keep the younger people from going off somewhere to work, and how the town was dying from the lack of new business. We were very aware of what we could do to help.

Our daughter went to Winnipeg for the hearing. We called her that evening and asked how things went. She told me it was worse than going to court for a criminal offense. They questioned her intensely and some were rude. *Is this is how they treated people I thought? How demeaning and cruel these supposed leaders are. I would have thought they would be accommodating when people were willing to invest in a community. They all can't be like this,* I hoped. We finished our holiday and arrived back in Canada on April 12, 2005, picked up our car, and drove home. We had had a good rest and were ready to tackle the work ahead of us.

We phoned the fellow who was drawing up our plans and found out he wasn't quite finished but had the foundations drawn up for the buildings we wanted to move. The house, store, and a building that was not complete needed to be put on a proper foundation. We had our reeve come out to look at the project we were planning. We hadn't seen a conservation officer to inspect the creek we had planned the culvert for, but we were told to just go ahead.

With our foundation plans in hand, we went into the town planning office and discussed them with the town planner. The weather was nice, and we really wanted to get started.

I asked for the permit, giving him my plans outlining the foundations for the cabins and washroom facility.

"Can I start excavating while you get the permit ready" I asked.

He told us, "If you start without a permit, I'll shut you down and fine you."

I looked at him in disbelief.

He turned and said, "I don't have time," throwing our plans on the counter.

I waited for a week and phoned him. He again told me, "I didn't have time to do them up, but I'm working on it."

We went to the hydro office and asked what it would cost to get three-phase power to the resort property.

"Two hundred and fifty thousand dollars," I was told.

We'll need to sell a lot of hamburgers to cover that cost I thought

I nearly went into shock at that price. I asked him if he could get us a quote so we could be sure. "Roughly, we would require about three thousand amps."

"We'll need a drawing with the equipment on it," I was told.

I went to the municipal office for another meeting that lasted three minutes and asked the reeve if they, hydro, and myself could cost share this amount so everyone could benefit from this rather than me footing the bill alone.

I was declined. "We don't do this kind of thing," the reeve said. *They want us to bring people into this community, and are not willing to help.* It appeared somewhat like extortion, with them not wanting to cost share the hydro. They would benefit quite substantially from it being brought out to Lost Meadows, with Cupar Creek Cottage Development and other developments requiring more power. Why wouldn't they move on this opportunity? I felt I was getting pulled into something that I didn't like.

I didn't ask for a grant because it was the taxpayers' money, and I do not want to burden anyone with my business. I don't believe in taking something from the taxpayers for my personal gain. The public gets shafted every time some business needs to be bailed out. If you have to get a grant to start a business, you are using everybody's money for personal gain; therefore, everyone should have a say in how it operates and receive a benefit check once a year.

I was taught not to do these kinds of things as a child, through the disciplinary actions of my parents. That was stealing. I would do this project myself, at my cost, paying my own way.

All I wanted was answers to my questions and explanations for rules and regulations I felt were a hindrance, and for them to return my phone calls.

I asked God for his help in guiding me as I had done so many times.

The good weather of April and May was lost. We finally got the permits to put the foundations in for the cabins and washroom at the beginning of June. There was no concern for the time frame it took.

Something didn't appear quite right with the way our reeve and town planner were acting.

We got the foundations built; the buildings moved and set up. A lot of work was needed inside to renovate and bring these buildings up to the standard we had set. We had sewer lines, water lines, and electrical to put in. The store was on hold, pending a decision on whether the cost to upgrade was more than I wanted to spend. We decided to move it back forty feet, making a shower/laundry facility out of it.

The water well needed to be sufficient to run the resort so we tried to find a different source of water. The existing well was too small and required a treatment plant. The existing water well had been used for thirty or more years and people had been hauling water from it for personal use but it was now unacceptable. We were forced to put corrosive called chlorine, into the system and be part of the problem of poisoning people.

I flew to Vancouver and dealt on log buildings for our project, putting a deposit down guaranteeing they would bring them in by the end of October. It was July already, and time was running out. I was waiting for permission to use the lagoon, a commitment from hydro and the municipality, on where I could dump the effluent from the sewage holding tanks. I had to give the log builders confirmation on dates and buildings by the end of August so I wouldn't lose my deposit.

I couldn't put a septic field in because of the location and had accepted that as part of keeping the environment clean.

I phoned the reeve, as the councilors contacted did not call us when we left messages. Did I dial the wrong numbers all the time? One had family problems he needed to take care of, and I respected that, because it was a serious problem.

I dialed. "Hello," said the reeve's wife in the sweet tone she always answered in.

"Hello. Is the reeve home?" I asked politely. It was about ten in the evening, and I had some questions to ask so I could make a decision.

"Oh! Just a minute, Pat," came her reply. "I'll call him".

I waited for about a half a minute then, "Now what do you want" came his reply? He seemed upset. I had probably disturbed him that late at night.

"Sorry to bother you, but I just need to know what is going on with hydro and the sewage issue" I said as pleasantly as I could even though I didn't like the way he had answered.

"That's got nothing to do with me," he snapped.

"Well, I think it does," I snapped right back. "Who the hell am I supposed to ask? We have a commitment to make or we lose our deposit".

"It sure the hell isn't me," he replied.

"I'm tired of all this bullshit, and I will close my wallet on this project. This is costing me a pile of money, and I'm not getting anywhere with you guys" I replied.

"I don't give a damn what you do" was his reply.

Disappointed, I hung up and sat down. Barb had a concerned look on her face.

I told her I was shutting this project down. I had enough.

I had the boys build a barricade across the property back far enough that people could still use the driveway to get their mail. I was concerned they would sue us for not going ahead with this project as per our agreement.

I went to the municipal office, frustrated with the way I had been treated and told them of my plan to stop the project. She asked me if there was any way that I would reconsider and asked if I was frustrated with the process. I looked at her and said, "You mean lack of process?" Nothing was being done.

I went home and wrote out what we required to continue. This letter was sent out to all the councilors and caused a stir in council. It needed to be stirred. We needed to change the way we are controlled. We need to have our freedom back. We need to be able to help without stipulation. The thought of governing ourselves always comes to the forefront in my mind as the bible says. I don't believe it says to allow ourselves to be governed in what we do to help. I believe in going the extra mile.

My confidence in government diminished completely. My self-esteem and confidence were dwindling. I was becoming very much aware how the government operated and decided in my own mind that the municipal body was just puppets for the big boys. They didn't appear to help the community but suppress progress through the rule books handed to them from the top. I was guessing in my thoughts.

We didn't have enough power to continue with single-phase and required three phases for the size of the project we had planned. In August, the hydro people came out and told us we may be able to get three-phase power in a year or so but not to count on it. "We can give you sixteen hundred amps for now until we upgrade the power lines from town. Any more than that, you will knock out power to other areas" I was told by these people. I required at minimum three thousand amps.

I let myself cool down for about a week or so and then requested a meeting with the council so I could explain the letter to them and was granted time at the next Monday meeting.

Barb and I went to explain ourselves and voice our concerns. We were called in and told we were on camera. The meeting was to be recorded because of the threat of litigation we were told. Politics and political science for all it is worth is nothing more than lie and deny, blame and manipulate words. Maybe this is democracy?

No sooner we sat down, the reeve went ballistic throwing a tantrum. He was yelling so loud no one could get a word in for at least five minutes, and no one could understand what he was saying. Barb attempted to intervene, raising her voice so he could hear. I tried to inform council this had to stop or we were walking out but no one made any attempt to intervene. Our councilor who was dealing with a family problem in Winnipeg, was listening to the meeting through conferencing. The deputy reeve and the rest of the councilors sat there and did nothing, letting the reeve vent. Every time he stopped for a breath, Barb or I had enough time to say things like, "You never came out to see. Did you see our plan"?

He replied, "I don't want to see your plan," then sneered. "Close your wallet," trying to belittle and intimidate me.

We accomplished nothing at this meeting except being belittled.

After he caught his breath, the reeve said he would set up an ad hoc committee to help us. I wasn't going to let myself or Barb be involved in this kind of political activity anymore, and my mind was made up.

"I am forced to retire," I told Barb on the way home chuckling.

We are trying to stop bullying in our schools, I thought. *I don't need this. This is what happens when trying to help a community. I will take a breather, get myself and Barb on track, and restart.*

A report in the paper accused us of things that were not true but politically motivated, claiming they were unaware what was required. How could they not know when it was written and handed out to them? Maybe we need change these types of activities.

Good, will come of this and we will all have to clear our conscience, when judged by the truth of our Savior. Remember, one cannot escape the day of true judgment, no matter how hard government tries to protect and save us.

Let's do what we can for this community. I thought. Let's cancel those log buildings and look around for an alternative. We drew up more plans.

It was the end of September when we approached a home builder in Yorkton, Sask. and looked at their homes, finding one that could work. We asked their salesman if they could move the house and have it ready for us to move into by the first of the year.

He told us, "There should be no problem meeting that deadline."

The house was already built but needed some minor finishing inside like installing cupboards and door trim and removing the siding they had installed. There was no flooring, so we requested slate and the hardwood we had bought for the log buildings to be used. They were to build the basement as soon as possible, recognizing the nice weather we had that fall. The attached store, complete with drywall, insulation doors, windows, and vapor barrier, was to be built on site. We agreed on a price, and the paperwork was readied while we went for lunch. Upon returning from lunch, we signed the purchase agreement, expecting it would be right, and then picked our paint colors, door handles and knobs, trim color, light fixtures, taps, and stucco. The cupboards were already agreed on and were ordered from a manufacturer. We supplied our own toilets, wanting the low-flush type, which were a little more money, but perfect for a holding tank system due to water consumption. They would get the building permit, and progress was about to begin as promised. He assured me that his word was good and I need not worry. I suggested we get a lawyer, but he said they cost a lot of money and he would honor what we had talked about and convinced me he would do the right thing. I still trusted people after what we had been through.

September went by, and then in the middle of October, I phoned and asked what was going on. I looked at their purchase offer, disappointed; he had put ASAP on the delivery and had deceived us. No one came out to build the basement. No one called. No one seemed concerned that winter was coming. I told them we had agreed to be in the house by the beginning of the year and had started to take bookings on our house for the beginning of the year for the ski season. We thought they were going to honor their agreement.

November rolled in, and still, we had no basement. I phoned and was assured the deadline would be met. I had checked on the progress of the house a few times when we went to Yorkton and nothing was being done.

On November 6, it had snowed. It melted, and it was muddy when John came to start our basement, but no one had a building permit as agreed. He caused problems with my hired workers, telling them they could not work near him. Maybe he was tired and overworked trying to catch up on some of the contracted work. I spoke to him asking why he was angry. Immediately, he wanted to get into a conflict with me, so I told him, "If you came here to cause problems, then you can leave the site at any time. There is nothing holding you here." He apologized for his behavior, realizing he had a choice, and then kept on working.

A couple days later, the town planner arrived on site to see what was going on. I questioned why a sump with the weeping tile draining into the basement and having to be pumped back out on the ground outside the house was being installed in the way it was. I could drain away from the house by connecting the weeping tile around the footing to a piece of weeping tile buried from the corner of the foundation out to the creek with a natural drain. No pump would be required. He became confrontational immediately.

His answer: "That's the code, and I won't allow you to move in. That's the law." He could have said, "I will check and see if you can do that." Self-righteousness, ignorance, intimidation, and plain arrogance were all we saw. The book he carried was a minimum standard guideline, and he used it as law, judging me immediately. Every time he came to the site, all four times, he was confrontational and dictator-like, never asking if we needed help.

I wasn't allowed to think for myself. My powers to think and my power of choice were again taken away. Sometimes people in positions of authority have narrowed their minds, allowing no common sense to prevail. Is it too hard to think for oneself, beyond the rule book? Can they not at least try to do something in a civilized way without aggression and power tripping? We must strive to change this so we can stop bullying at all levels.

John piped up and said, "That's the way it is going to be, and you can go f… yourself." He felt safe with the town planner, I guess, and thought he was going to push us around because he had heard what was said.

I immediately asked him to leave the location. He phoned the home builder and returned in about ten minutes, apologizing, saying he was out of line for that. I let him go back to work, having no more problems with him. He put the drain in the middle of the room and piped the water from outside into the basement. *I guess I have to pump it out.*

I asked the town planner if the builder had gotten the permit, and he replied that they hadn't. I had the generic unstamped plan from the builder and attempted to get a permit, but was told, "I don't have time to make it out yet but go ahead, build the house, store, and continue on Lost Meadows. I will bring the permit down. It will be okay this time."

Why did he not do that at the beginning, instead of threatening me with shutdown and fines? This is a double standard that has to be corrected. Wouldn't that have been more accommodating?

The basement walls were built, but we had to wait ten days for the cement to cure. It was covered in with electric heaters installed to help it cure. Had it been done in September or October, that cost would have been saved.

While waiting for the basement to cure, we received a call from the government auditors and were warned we were going to be audited. We had been trying for months to get our GST back, a substantial amount, and they must have felt we were cheating or lying. November 15, they would be here to go through our files and check us out. We kept good tabs on our paperwork, and Tiffany came down to do the last-minute entries so we were up-to-date. This was the day the house was arriving, and all we needed was an auditor hampering our plans, but Tiffany looked after him. I watched for a while as he asked questions and requested receipts, doing his thing at the house, but he must not have believed her, because he requested to see the premises, firsthand, to see where our money was going.

Damn! He found an error of $6.78 we made throughout the whole project. It was hardly worth his time and fuel to get here, but we were dishonest until he checked and received payment.

The house arrived at about two in the afternoon with the auditor observing. He must have been satisfied, because when I told him I was busy and had to go, he left. The movers got the house down to the foundation and were setting it down when a hydraulic hose broke, shutting us down for the night.

The next day, the movers showed up around noon and finished setting the house down. The electrician tied in the power and connected the heaters to melt the snow that had accumulated in the basement. We ran the heaters for two weeks to warm the basement enough so John could return to pour the floor.

The floor was poured and we were now ready to install the furnace and plumbing. I called the plumbers who were working with us on the other buildings and asked them when they were going to come and do the work. They informed me they hadn't been awarded the contract from the home builder and asked if I could check on it before they started work.

Another plumbing contractor showed up, asking if he could get in and get an estimate to give the home builder a quote. From September to the end of November, they hadn't even put it out for tender or awarded anyone the contract.

The electrician did not have a contract. I called the home builder again and reminded them of the time frame and was told it might be the end of January now before they could finish. They seemed unconcerned. The house sat until after January 1 with the construction heaters sucking up the power, and there was nothing I could do about it.

Just before Christmas, the plumbers were awarded the plumbing work and started installing the furnace. On or around January 5, 2006, they arrived and installed the plumbing and finished the furnace and ductwork. Another contractor had arrived earlier, built the store to lock up, but nothing was done inside—no drywall, no insulation, and no vapor barrier, as agreed on with the salesman who sold us the house. A fellow came out from the builder to install the drywall much later, but we had done it ourselves. We were way behind schedule and couldn't wait. This was supposed to be completed for us to move in by the New Year. I brought the hardwood into the house in December so they could install the floor after the wood had climatized but due to the dampness in the house, it didn't climatized properly.

We decided to take a break while the flooring was being installed so we drove to Las Vegas on January 11, 2006, to visit my sister and her husband.

We arrived back around January 25, 2006, and were surprised when we found the floors were laid but were uneven to the point we would catch our shoes on the edges of the tiles. The home builder sent out a fellow to do the floors that had laid ceramic tile before and had little or no experience laying slate he admitted to some of the workers. The hardwood was laid, without a subfloor to match the slate with a sharp edging that would cut if not careful.

We informed the manager, from the building company, requesting that he come out to look at the floor. I was not going to accept this kind of workmanship. We called a number of times then finally, they came to take a look, about a month later. The manager, the installer and a fellow from the factory where the tiles were made, came out and wanted to try to fix the floor by chipping the rough edges off the slate. A fellow I had hired to do the slate in the store was there, advising them on how it possibly could be done. He suggested it was very time-consuming and may not be accepted. He did not want the responsibility.

They decided to try and told me if I wasn't happy to call and they would stop. They sent floor installers back and made an attempt. Chips of slate were hitting the cupboards, getting stuck in the walls, and going down the furnace duct. What a mess. Barb tried to stop him, but he wouldn't listen. She called me in.

I told them it wasn't working and they had to quit, so he packed up and went back to town. I called the manager, asking him to come and look at the tile. Chisel marks were everywhere. It was quite apparent the tiles were modified, and it looked worse than it had before.

A fellow from another flooring company came out to see what

could be done, shook his head, and asked what I would like to do. He told me the manager for the home builder had come to his shop after he had looked at the tile the first time, saying it looked like the *Titanic* had hit it. I told him we wanted the tile removed and new slate installed, so he went back and convinced the manager that this was what had to be done.

The manager and floor installer came out again and discussed the other deficiencies. The cupboards were not finished on top, the drywall needed painting and repair, the baseboard had to be replaced, the ceiling had to be cleaned, and the floor had to be replaced, along with the basement windows, the door locks, and on and on. The floor layer told Barb "to fix the problem with the cupboards all she had to do was put paper towel down on top of them, and when they got dirty, she could just throw the towel away and replace it with new stuff". Tension was high, and she walked out. She was crying while sitting on the step. We wanted what we paid for, and all this time, we were paying our employees to do little jobs, because we couldn't progress. An argument ensued.

In May, we decided to move into the basement. We had finished enough to at least sleep down there. A bedroom was built but not completely finished. Our other house was booked out for the May long weekend, and we couldn't afford to lose any more on it.

We moved into the house and finished the slate floors with the fellow who did our store floors. It was tedious work and took us a month to complete properly. He laid the slate, and we did all the cleaning and sealing. About two hundred man hours of our time was spent needlessly on this floor because of the problem.

Slate and hardwood is not easy to install and takes a lot of time but it was done in about a week.

Is it possible because they moved a lot of houses that fall and were swamped, they couldn't meet the time frames? Did they deceive me on the original agreement? The salesman called me around November 1, 2006, and we talked about this problem. He said, "I know, Pat. They let me down too."

From what I have seen previously, the home builder does a good job and they do build a good home. Did our problems arise from our requests of different flooring and other requests not dealt with by this company? Did they allow themselves to get too far behind and could not accommodate our time frame?

November 6, 2006, and still no permit! Our planner came out saying I had not given him the plan, but we did drop off the generic copy a long time ago. It has been a year of trying to get this permit and still nothing.

I phoned the municipal office about the driveway and approach being slippery from the mix of rain and wet snow we had causing the approach to be extremely slippery, wanting to see if they could salt the driveway down, so we wouldn't have a collision and kill someone exiting our property. Mailboxes at the edge of the property are accessed excessively by the public, and the access, I believe, should be looked after by the government or municipality but I was willing to pay for it. I was told by one of the staff, I needed to call the highways department.

I reached him at home and was told, "We do things through the municipal office. They have to authorize this before we can do anything. If we came out for a five-minute job all the time, we would be swamped."

I said, "Well, the municipal office told me I had to call you and make my own arrangements."

He replied, "I will call them and ask."

I said, "I will call them also," and hung up.

To have someone killed at our approach because they don't want to do a five-minute job at my cost is unacceptable. The approach does belong to the municipality. The mail boxes belong to the corporate government mail system How much effort would it take to salt down the approach and possibly the hill to our restaurant, which we built for this community? The CAO has been working in the municipal office for quite a number of years and surely knows what has to be done. *If someone gets killed from their lack of concern about safety on our highways, can I be held responsible? Was she following the normal procedure?* I worried about this for a time.

My taxes are higher because of the new assessment and there was no hesitation to send me another bill for extra taxes revised for this year. How can I be taxed without a permit? We don't exist until the permits are in place. I thought; *council and planning are to help, not hinder us.*

I have to question…Is this a breach of trust? Is this a breach of power and authority? Is this a breach of honesty? Is this causing evil and resentment? My power of choice is being swayed to commit evil, possibly, through a court system or inquiry and ask for resignations of some members of council and sue for recovery of loss. I don't like these options and will not lean towards these types of measures. We need to make every attempt to resolve problems without self-righteousness and with respect no matter how demeaning it might be.

Corruption exists in many areas and most of us can't understand many things. In one meeting concerning our project, I told the government official that 90 percent of the population didn't understand all the rules and regulations that I deemed Communist. Grinning, he calmly said, "I know."

This meeting was called to get future plans for the resort going. We required Crown lands representatives at this meeting, but unfortunately, they had other things to do and did not come.

About a month later, we were denied the right to lease Crown land. I don't understand how they have the right to deny anyone the use of land. Who gave them the authority? Who gave them the land? It appeared that others, some, who were using taxpayers' money in the form of grants and government loans, had access to the lake properties, but we, who didn't believe in using tax dollars, didn't. The reasons I was given were ludicrous. "Your access to the property is dangerous. It has creeks that are used by wildlife. It was being saved for Crown cottage development though. Our access was no different than the same business across the lake or the winter ski park. When they said it was planned to be used for cottage development; that threw me. They gave me all kinds of excuses why I couldn't utilize it then, said they would. The tactics used in many instances are degrading and pull one into being someone he doesn't want to be. We begin to get angry and lose our power to think and speak properly through frustration.

I waited for three years and have not had a reply on whether I could purchase an acre for a building I had in my plan for all those years. Many of the government people were shuffled through our process and some promoted causing many delays and redundant work. This is suppression and needs to change because it takes our rights away.

Feeling we had been infringed upon and our rights abused, we attempted to have the human rights commission look into our situation but were flatly denied. They didn't advocate or weren't going to concerning our matter. They told me to go to the association of municipal government and the ombudsman. It was more political bureaucracy, and I had had enough. Every department did this, I found, and we couldn't get any answers. Progress was stalled many times, and I felt they wanted us to do things illegally. I was becoming someone I didn't want to be and felt our right to do business, right to information, and right to be treated like others, who did business, were taken away. Intimidation tactics and abuse of power seemed normal in my view. A few of the councilors approached us and offered information freely, again telling us that the problem stemmed from jealousy and all of the council needed to be changed out. One councilor even told me there was another superpower controlling us, to which, I replied, "Yeah! It's Satan through corporate business and government." He didn't elaborate on his comments. This is what we have spawned through our education system. This is what we have told our children about a good government job. Do you think we need change?

I do. We must push for legislation on business, which use our education system and young people to build anything from switches, cell phones, explosives, aircraft and parts, for war, computer systems or anything sold and used to destroy knowingly or with deception. We need a seller beware clause. Our population who works for these business's need to be informed where the product is being used so one can make a conscious decision whether to participate in the destructive way we are accustomed to by working there and allowed to make a proper choice, prior to beginning a job. We need good legislation that controls the elected leaders and ensures all populations and ethnic groups have a say and a role through referendum, on how we will conduct ourselves in tough situations and before new legislation can be passed. We the people need a vote and disallow the associations to control our legislation.

I chose to write my book and strive to change what is known as the law and see if we could change it in honesty and trust. Let us see if we can do this with respect and responsibility. We need to change the way we educate the so-called leaders, not school them, reaping what continues to be sown.

To learn and try to change things is an honor and a blessing given to us all. Sometimes frustration and anger control our thoughts and actions, and things are said that may hurt others but if you say it in truth it shows you love that person or group of people. Repentance of truth need not take place but apologies for wrong doing are a blessing we all have, to start the process of our wonderful power of forgiveness, using it wisely. Our Lord and Savior would be proud I'm sure. It must be done in love not with anger still lingering.

I have learned people can get along. Leaders of many governments and corporate business seem to create many unnecessary problems throughout the world, seemingly operating under the guise of help. Many use the system to their advantage through political manipulation and judicial systems to prove self-righteousness. Many can't get along because they know not how to repent.

Chapter Seventeen

I am one with little education, who traveled and spoke to people of many cultures and believes God follows us throughout our lives, guiding us and showing us the way. A man with an open heart and mind like God gave every one of us to use properly and wisely. The way we indulge ourselves in everyday life, sometimes self-righteously, without reflection and sometimes knowingly, is not acceptable and is something we need to change.

I must reflect on who the infidels really are and question… Are the controllers and leaders who take away our freedoms throughout the lands? Are the very ones who use our young people to do the dirty work of war? Are the ones who decide our education systems? Are the ones who pull us into the deception integrated into society through courses on marketing and sales tactics, protected by the judicial system or are we all?

Remember the words, "Thy will be done on earth as it is in heaven." I have a difficult time visualizing a heaven with this much strife. The wars, greed, and control as we see it on planet earth are unimaginable. I am sure there will not be an education system training many our children to kill or strap bombs on themselves, teaching them to build weapons and artillery. I can't imagine there would be hatred, derived from some parents or adults and governing bodies saying hateful things to hurt each other, keeping the circle of distrust and hatred going on for generation after generation. I don't believe there would be history idolizing war with heroes of killing fields marked with monuments.

I have a dream, as Martin Luther King Jr. had. I dream that all of mankind will halt what they are doing; a dream that all of mankind will understand that we were born with clean hearts; a dream that all mankind will understand that we learned what we are doing; a dream that all of mankind will not live in and destroy the history of the past centuries; a dream that all of mankind will not idolize the wrong people, people who in their self-righteous ways, condemned the population of the world through leadership roles taught to them by man for power and glory; a dream that we do not harm the people in power for what they have learned; a dream we can erect monuments for good instead of war and destruction; a dream we could all look at the positive instead of the negative through media and other teachings; a dream of building friendships instead of hatred and using our young men and women to spread love around the world instead of carrying guns. I have a dream of using our resources for the betterment of man rather than to destroy life and the environment. I dream of forgiveness rather than blame; I dream of peace, of freeing the world of disease, of clean water and air for all, and I dream of helping instead of suppressing.

I have a dream that one day, the armies of the world will drop their weapons on the ground wherever they stand, turn around, and approach their leaders and governments within their own borders and ask why? When the leadership is questioned and cannot reply with proper reason, using freedom and security as an excuse for self-righteousness, greed, and power; explain to them the way of God. If they do not heed your requests to learn, then they may be the true infidels we are warned against.

We need to clean our own doorsteps; then we can help others. If we all clean our own doorsteps, no help will be required. We need to take the log out of our eyes so the speck can be found in the other mans eye. Once all of us, every one of us, have achieved the calmness within our own hearts and borders, we then can turn around smiling and approach the bordering nations, happily, with hand outstretched in forgiveness, admitting we are all wrong. Upon our return to the neighboring borders, we pick up the weapons and tanks and destroy them for they are tools of evil. Peace at last. We are bad sheep no more.

We are people, true caretakers of the world as we were designed to be, not savages wanting to kill. We are patriotic to God now; not flags.

This is true courage. It takes courage to admit and repent. It takes courage to know the truth. It takes courage to act and learn properly. It takes courage to live and let live. We are weak when we have a weapon in our hands. We are weak when we are in denial. We are weak and it takes no courage to kill. True heroism is found not in what we have done, but in what we have accomplished. It is found in what we have left undone and corrected. Heroism is not founded in hate. It is founded in love. A true hero is one who saves a life, not takes one. A true hero needs no recognition. Our armies need to know. The brainwashing of our young people needs to stop. The commanders need to be schooled for they know not what they do.

I do not stand alone in my dreams. I dream of a heaven with all different cultures getting along peacefully. I dream of a world determined to accomplish, rather than destruct. And most of all, I dream of stillness, quiet, and people content with what was given to us freely. I dream we will educate properly, in love and kindness; I dream that we use all our powers properly. We must use the power of choice, the power of speech, the power of listening, the power to do, the power of love, the power of forgiveness, and the power to think properly, in calmness and positivity.

We would have many other powers that many of us are not aware of. The one that is most important to all the others is *the power to change*. We have the ability but do we have the power? Once we accept this, in peaceful ways, we can accomplish it. We will have our powers back that are so important to survival. We will have the powers back that are so important to remain equal, to remain at peace, and to love. We will have the power to educate properly and the power to sustain … not repeat the history we have become so accustomed to, shaping our minds and making some self-righteous.

History reminds us of the negative and honors the self-righteous, warping our minds to follow the same path. We have walked a crooked path long enough. Let's change. Change the path, and pave it with goodness. Pave it with love and happiness. Pave it with truth so generations after us will be free, fulfilled with love, peace, and joy, proud of what we've done. Let us look at the books of the words of God and learn the way. Use them for guidance. Let the Lord come back in peace, and let us make him proud.

When we change, do not fret. If done peacefully, we will have the infrastructure of buildings, bridges, churches, and schools. We will need to clean the inside of these buildings. We will need these to educate properly. We will have a lot to do. We will still have jobs. We will still have economies. We will still need food and shelters. We will need to clean up the planet. We will engineer and build on the technology in goodness, finding ways to stop the pollution and destruction of this wonderful gift called earth, given to us out of love, freely. We will do these jobs with love and understanding. We will do them in peace; willingly. It will not be work. We will not revert back to history.

It will take years. Be patient. Patience is another power we have and don't utilize very much.

If we don't act, our disgrace will be immense. We will be appalled when He has to come and show us the way. We could be put to eternal death, thrown into the fire and burned as rubbish. He will have to show the rest of man the way, staying for years, educating and babysitting.

I prefer to make him proud. I would rather die in peace for peace and at least try than live this living hell of war in my living room day in and day out. I would rather be locked up and accused for trying rather than sit back and do nothing but complain and tell people, "What can we do… or, I can't". I would rather give my life to make it better for other generations than teach them to be as we are.

Remember, God has sent us an abundance of scholars. He has sent us a great number of good people with abilities to develop ways, items, and technologies to sustain ourselves and produce many things for the betterment of man. He has sent us many messengers. He has sent us many signs, through tsunamis, hurricanes, earthquakes, and the like. He has wiped out communities of corruption, taking innocent as well, and still we don't understand.

Remember Gandhi, Martin Luther King Jr., Mother Theresa, Nelson Mandela, John Lennon, John Kennedy, Pope John Paul II, and all the other people who did good for the world. Some were jailed for what they believed. They all did it peacefully and some even lost their lives, because someone used their power of choice and a Western weapon in a wrong way. They all wore different skin colors.

Let's review some good things that mankind has done with the powers given to him. We have built hospitals, roads, and bridges. We have united people somewhat through leadership and legislation of partial equal and human rights. We have developed electricity, which gives us light and warmth. We have built schools that teach us to read and write so we can learn to read the Word, even though some of what we are taught is destructive.

We have the power of people. Yes, the power of people! Enough people have been created around the world that can stop all this.

Gandhi. What a pillar of hope. He took his country back from the enemy by walking his people in peace. Many don't know of this because it was sixty or seventy years ago and not many have been educated about his struggle. He did not use force of any kind. He was belittled, abused, and beaten, and many of his followers died an early death, at the hands of the barbarians, who controlled India at that time. He went on hunger strikes, defied governing bodies, and marched forward through barricades set up by the barbarians to make his point. He was put in jail and tormented but didn't bend on his values for peace and control of his own life. He won his country back and restored peace by talking to the people. Not once did he attempt force.

Our black children did the same so they could sit with other culture in restaurants and such. They did the world proud. They are Gods children also.

Martin Luther King Jr., because he used his power to speak, died by assassination for wanting peace and unity between blacks and whites. He wanted equality amongst people and the freedom to work alongside all of mankind. He wanted unity amongst man. His speech, "I have a dream," still sends shock waves down my spine. He was denied his freedom and goodness, by whom? Was it a conspiracy? Is it because of political science that he was stopped? He had the power of people supporting him. The power of people was growing with great intensity so life for his culture and the rest of us may have been better than we have. He died a true martyr, in peace for peace. He was well received by many, black and white, but the movement was disrupted by a single shot from a weapon made and sold by corporate business to kill or control people all over the world. Governments need to look at who are biggest abusers of this weapon and stop teaching us through wars that it is okay to kill. This is bullying at its best. It is time to act again in peace and unity to ensure we do not lose our freedoms and the powers given us to use wisely.

Many more experienced the same fate: Robert Kennedy, Anwar al-Sadat, Benazir Bhutto, Lady Diana Spencer, and others too numerous to mention. These people had the will to do well for mankind, trying to find a solution for peace but were snuffed out by forces with little explanation. Who wanted them out of the way for reasons unknown? Many people have been fooled and denied the truth of what happened to these people, a crazed lunatic being blamed most times. We will be judged harshly in the end.

Proper education is the key. Trust him. He gave us, all of us, the rules for a happy life—ten of them.

Let's start.

If the Lord came back and saw us today, he would stand on the mountain and laugh, and I'm sure he would say, with love "Come. I'll show you the way again. This time, pay attention."

That's how much he loves us, all of us.

Chapter Eighteen

God's Simple Message ...

You have not heeded my words and laws of happiness. I gave you everything you needed to survive, and you exploited it making yourselves into a den of thieves. What have you done to this earth and all who live on it? Let us review the whole scope of things and see if you can help yourselves. You poor souls, you will not find joy in turmoil but will find it in peace and forgiveness.

My laws were simple and easy to follow. I gave you the power of choice, and you were my best creation. I made you better than angels. Angels do not have the power of choice. They can only be what I gave them. Goodness!! I gave you a world to live in with everything you need from food to medicine. I gave you the will to live and produce life. I gave you everything to give you happiness. I gave you hope. I gave you the ability to share in charity, and I gave you peace. I gave you many powers and have shown you forgiveness.

You can choose from so many different avenues and do so many good works, but most times, you choose the wrong path. Why? Why? Why?

Ever since the beginning of time, you have seemed to have a need to control and overpower something or someone. I did not will this to you. I did not choose the borders for you. I did not choose to use everything developed for good to suppress or control anyone. What were the laws of happiness? What guidelines did I set out for you? Do you know?

Most people around the world believe in me. Christians believe that Jesus was sent to earth as your savior. Jews, Muslims, and others do not believe this and believe that He was a messenger, as was Mohammad, and all other messengers sent before and after him. Many are believers but worship in different ways. Whatever one wants to believe is a choice I gave you, so do not condemn each other and try to tolerate one another with more acceptance, respecting their views. Remember, respect all people and everything I gave you to sustain yourselves. There is enough for the needy. I will judge at the end time. There is no need for you to judge. What happens when you judge?

When each of you was born, I instilled within you a clean heart and soul, untouched by humans, with powers so great you could do whatever you wanted. It was so clean that you did not even know how to speak. You used crying to get what you wanted, and most times, it was for food or drink. What else did you need? It was so clean you did not know how to walk. It was so clean you did not know how to think. It was so clean you did not know how to forgive. It was so clean all you knew was peace, love, and happiness—everything I stand for. Any other beliefs will create numerous problems. Everyone has these messages, and many teach them in churches, mosques, temples, etc. All the rest you learned from each other.

I watched many of you smile at your parents when you did not understand a word they said. You only watched, wide-eyed, and smiled at the pleasant face looking at you. You smiled in your sleep at the peace and love within you, content with your tummy full and a comfortable bed to sleep in. Your parents sheltered you in their home and comforted you in sickness, giving up many nights of sleep, just for you. Why? Because of the love they shared for you.

From the time you were born, you began your journey through life and began to learn things at a very early age.

What was the first thing you learned? You learned to listen. The doctor picked you up in rather a hurry and turned you upside down and would tell you to cry. Most of you did. That is how they cleared your lungs of the fluid from inside your mother's womb. Some of you even got spanked when you were just outside the womb, if you were stubborn or needed help to cry. Time was essential for you to breathe on your own.

Soon Mom was looking at you and saying "mummy" or "daddy." You were listening intently and trying to get the word out. They were trying to teach you to speak. Communicate. Finally, you said it. You listened to the repetitions of it for days, so focused on learning soon you were able to speak. Remember, I said teach. Soon you were crawling, walking, and making sentences. You were eager to learn new things.

The power to listen, the power to learn, and the power of speech, you learned within a few short weeks of your life. I was proud of you and smiled as did your mother, father, and siblings, if you had any. "My child is blessed, and everything is working fine," I heard many parents comment. Not everyone was so lucky. Some I sent to you with handicaps so you would learn acceptance, compassion, giving, and tolerance, all with love. Not all handicapped people did I send to you. Some were made that way accidentally in pregnancy, when Mom bumped into things or fell, while others were from choices that the parents made through the use of drugs and alcohol and sometimes from chemical medicines prescribed by doctors.

I knew you wouldn't stay as pure as you were at birth, but I hoped that you would learn righteousness and the power of choice properly. This is the most complex power I have given you as it has many dimensions and faults but is limited. With this power, you will learn righteousness, honesty, responsibility, caring, compassion, giving, peace, joy, happiness, respect, and many others too extensive to mention. You will learn to live.

As a young child, you learned to share your things with others, speak politely, mind your manners, respect your elders and others, tell the truth, laugh and sing, identify colors, apologize, and listen. You learned to honor your father, mother, grandparents, and all who taught you. When you did all the right things instilled in you, you were rewarded with praise, love, happiness, peace, and sometimes with monetary things. Doesn't listening always pop up when you're being taught? You also learned to pout, cry, sadness, lie, and steal. Remember when you took your brother's or sister's toy and made him or her cry, then said you didn't do it. What happened? You were disciplined, weren't you? You were learning your power of choice and didn't even know it. You were learning righteousness.

Sometimes, you dwelled in self-pity for an hour or so then went back to playing, after you were made to say I'm sorry. You were learning another power and didn't know it. After you said you were sorry, what happened? You were told it was okay and given a hug. Sometimes you were convincing enough, you got away with it. It all didn't matter then as you were learning the powers I instilled in you. As a child, you were funny and always forgiven. You learned the power to forgive, the best power for peace.

A good example of what I asked was shown on television. A school was attacked by a man gone astray with anger. I didn't hear any war cry. I didn't see any sign they wanted protection or revenge. All I saw was the goodness in their hearts. Before the dead were buried, they had forgiven the killer. They had the wife of the killer ride with them to the grave in a show of solidarity. I watched. "Forgive them for they know not what they do." They went about their business, and after the dead were buried, they tore the monument down. The school is gone. They did not erect something to remind people how stupid that act was. In all the sorrow those people felt, the sadness they have to bear, the emptiness from their children having been savagely taken from them, they forgave and trusted in me. I know what they believed and stood for. I was proud. What good people they are. Their hearts are clean, and they learned well.

Then you were old enough to go to school. You learned to read and write properly so you could read my word. You were taught to add, divide, multiply, and subtract, which is essential to function in commerce and everyday affairs. I looked at what you were being taught, and at the beginning, you were taught about me in the Lord's Prayer. Your education was a tool to make your mind function above all and to help you learn to get along with other people, other than your siblings. You met many different kinds of people with different backgrounds than yours. Acceptance, you learned, through playing and working with other children of different colors of skin, different races, and different creeds. As a child, you knew no difference, but the adults somehow got twisted, and differences appeared everywhere. Conflicts were the result. The adults learned things from their elders and others then passed them down to you, and this is still continuing today. You were taught many things and learned self-righteousness. I warned about this many years ago, but many do not heed My warnings. I did not will this to you. You were taught at home, in schools, and everywhere you went. People liked to gossip. Distrust was rampant. You even began to distrust Me. You forgot about Me. You threw Me out of your schools.

You have allowed yourselves to be herded into bigger centers through taxation and job creation. You have been pulled into the web of deceit and all are now tax collectors by manly law. I warned about the taxman. All I asked is you toil and take care of the lands.

I gave you beautiful oceans with sandy beaches for your leisure and what has happened? Many concrete structures have been built and now you have to pay dearly for leisure. The people of some nations cannot use these beaches because of rules the leadership and companies have that prevent it. You could have had leisure holidays with the local people gladly allowing you to enjoy their cultures.

Legislation against sewer disposal is now in place and disallows you to fertilize. This happened because of the chemical you dump into your septic systems. The waste secreted from your body was supposed to fertilize the land. I was not a fool when I created you and other life. Everyone is fooled, and, now allow these chemicals into your households. Was allowing this supported by the chemical companies and leadership for monetary value? Is this good for you? Do you take away the bacterium that supports and strengthens your immune system?

I have warned you of many things and explained what will happen if you didn't follow the rules I gave you but you didn't listen and exploited everything for greed. You have penetrated the protective layer of earth and may be creating a vacuum pulling the layer apart. Have you studied that closely? You have moved mountains and put highways through that are paved in blackness. Are your highways and streets creating a problem with climate heat? You are sending explosive devices to the moon to penetrate and look for water. Will this one day take the moon out of orbit? Why are you unhappy for what I gave you? Why are you so adamant on seeing what else I created spending a lot of your resources on needless research in space instead of helping the poor and sick? Now you have starvation and turmoil greater than in the time I sent Jesus, as I predicted. Hunger will cause people to do whatever it takes to survive. Maybe your education system isn't so great.

I gave you the ability to govern yourselves; not be governed. Why have you let these abilities be stolen away? Why do you think man can save you? Why do you think leaderships can protect you? You must educate with the abilities I have bestowed upon each and every one of you. You must govern yourselves through education, proper education so you do not have to be governed by someone else. Use your powers wisely for you are my best creation.

Ah! There is no more to say. Come! Come! All you fools; Let us find a way; Why do you want exercise rooms when I give you enough to keep yourselves healthy? Why do you want to poison yourselves with chemicals? Why have you become greedy? Why have you forgotten Me? Why? Follow Me! This is the way! We need to change the status quo. You throw Me out of your lives and I still love you; all of you. Why do you blame Me? Why do you fear Me? Fear what you do with your Power of Choice.

C	hildren
H	ave
A	bilities
N	ow
G	o
E	ducate

The center of the Bible, Psalms 117, 118, and 119 warn about this, I read after completion of this book. Many young people who want to join the military should read these psalms before choosing to join. As well, many of the lieutenants and commanders should read these psalms and make a decision. If they choose to leave the military, they will do honor to the human race even if they don't get a meaningless honorable discharge from man. What an honor it would be to leave the training of killing!

> Psalm 118:8: "It is better to trust in the Lord than to trust in man."

We all need to heed this prayer. It speaks to everyone.

> Our Father Who art in heaven
> Hallowed be Thy Name
> Thy kingdom come
> **Thy will be done**
> **On earth as it is in heaven**
> Give us this day our daily bread
> And **forgive** us our trespasses
> As we **forgive** those who trespass against us
> And lead us not into temptation
> But deliver us from evil.
> For Thine is the kingdom, the power and glory,
> forever and ever. Amen.

We have our first president of a different cultural background heading the most powerful country in the world. From what he said in the beginning of his campaign about change must be supported for the value of all of mankind. We must continue to give him all the support required to accomplish his goals of speaking to troubled nations with diplomacy even if it requires massive peaceful demonstration and allow the views of all cultures to be heard and tolerated with respect to achieve the peace we all so crave. When he was elected, it was with a huge majority. We must not allow opposition to his good motives and strong abilities to try and accomplish peace. We must allow him to do well, not only for our sake but for our good neighbors at every point on the globe, but for our well being. If we all get along and he succeeds in diplomacy, we will have a good foundation on which to build ties with all nations and accomplish the peace we all crave. True protection is getting along and being friends. True friends will not hurt each other.

Remember…. In God We Trust…. We are believers.

I believe we all have a dream.

Remember CHANGE? Children Have Abilities Now Go Educate.

Ability and courage are required. We all have it. We are all children, many looking for change.

Thank you for reading. I pray that we can one day live in peace and harmony as Martin Luther King Jr. said in his speech, "I have a dream."

Pope John Paul also said, "We need to build bridges. Not destroy them." He too is so correct.

"There is no need for sacrifice. The ultimate was done"

God will allow us to destroy ourselves but not his kingdom. Many of our prayers say this... "Of His kingdom there will be no end".

Printed in the United States
by Baker & Taylor Publisher Services